Outcomes in Coding Practice:

A Roadmap from Provider to Payer

Annette Butler

Outcomes in Coding Practice:

A Roadmap from Provider to Payer

Annette Butler

Director of Medical CTE Programs
River Springs Charter School

Professor, Medical Administrative
Professional Program
MiraCosta College

Outcomes in Coding Practice:
A Roadmap from Provider to Payer
Annette Butler

Vice President, Career and Professional Editorial:
Dave Garza

Director of Learning Solutions: Matthew Kane

Senior Acquisitions Editor: Rhonda Dearborn

Managing Editor: Marah Bellegarde

Editorial Assistant: Chiara Astriab

Vice President, Career and Professional Marketing:
Jennifer McAvey

Marketing Director: Wendy Mapstone

Marketing Manager: Nancy Bradshaw

Production Director: Carolyn Miller

Content Project Manager: Thomas Heffernan

Senior Art Director: Jack Pendleton

For product information and technology assistance, contact us at
Professional & Career Group Customer Support, 1-800-648-7450

For permission to use material from this text or product,
submit all requests online at **cengage.com/permissions**
Further permissions questions can be e-mailed to
permissionrequest@cengage.com

2009 Current Procedural Terminology © 2008 American Medical Association. All rights reserved.

Library of Congress Control Number: 2009922180

ISBN-13: 978-1-4018-9898-4

ISBN-10: 1-4018-9898-X

Delmar
5 Maxwell Drive
Clifton Park, NY 12065-2919
USA

Cengage Learning products are represented in Canada by Nelson Education, Ltd.

For your lifelong learning solutions, visit **delmar.cengage.com**

Visit our corporate website at **cengage.com**

Printed in the United States.
1 2 3 4 5 XX 11 10 09

Table of Contents

Preface x

Acknowledgements xii

About the Author xiii

How to Use the Book
Features xiv

How to Use StudyWARE™ xvi

Introduction xix

Chapter 1: The Correct Coding Initiative ... 1

Chapter Objectives 1
Key Terms 1
Introduction to Correct Coding
Initiative (CCI) 2
  History of CCI 2
  Organizations Responsible for
    CCI Contents 2
Changes to the CCI. 3
  Obtaining Current Updates from
    the Internet. 3
  Code Versions and Effective
    Dates. 3
Effect of CCI on the Coding
Industry 3
  Review Organizations 4
  CCI Coding Software Used by
    Payers 4
CCI for the Coder 4
  Comprehensive Codes and
    Component Codes. 4
  CCI Manual. 5
    Mutually Exclusive Codes 5
    Method, Initial, and Subsequent
      Services 5
  Significant Information for
    Individual Codes 5
  Bundling 5
  Unbundling 6
    Practices That Lead to
      Unbundling 6
    Unintentional Unbundling. 6
    Intentional Unbundling and
      the Government 7
    Contracting for Unbundling. 7
  Other Coding Tools. 7
CCI Coding 7
  Using Modifiers and Mutually
    Exclusive Codes 8
  HCPCS Modifiers 8
  CPT Modifiers 8
Incorrect CCI Coding 8
Case Studies of Coding and
CCI—Correct and Incorrect 9

Case Study 1-1—Incorrect Coding,
  Add-on Codes 9
  CCI Edit—How the Claim
    Was Paid. 10
  More Than One Provider on
    a Claim 10
  Rebundling Lab Codes 11
Case Study 1-2—Correct
  Coding, Lab Codes 11
Case Study 1-3—Lab Test Billed
  Separately Because of Coding
  Ineligibility 12
Case Study 1-4—Incidental to
  Primary Procedures 13
Case Study 1-5—Unbundled
  Procedure Stated as Multiple
  Procedures 15
Case Study 1-6—Procedure Denied
  Due to Global Allowance 17
Case Study 1-7—Services Denied—
  Not a Covered Benefit 18
Summary 19
Web Sites 20
Fill in the Blank 20
Review Questions. 21
Critical Thinking Exercises 21
  Materials Needed 21
  Directions 21
Professional Corner—Applying
CCI to the Office Setting 22
References 23

Chapter 2: Health Maintenance Organization (HMO) Contracts ... 24

Chapter Objectives 24
Key Terms 24
Introduction to HMO Contracts 25
Capitation 25
  Payment Schedules 27
  Services Included in Capitation. ... 27
  Claims for Encounter Data 27
  Balance Billing and Capitation
    Contracts 27
  Carve-outs. 28
  Risk Pools. 28
  Referring a Patient. 29
Basic Contract Responsibilities
between Providers and HMOs 29
  Service Responsibilities. 29
  Specialty Services 30
  HMO Payment Responsibilities 32
  Physician Payment
    Responsibilities 32
  Eligibility of College Students 32

Responsibility for Payment
of Claims 32
  Continuity of Care 33
  Financial Responsibilities. 33
  Financial Records 34
  Handling Claims Adjudication 34
  Recoupment Rights 34
  Agreement Correspondence
    Address 35
  Subcap Capitation 35
Subcap Providers' Claim
Types 36
  Medical Records 36
  Confidentiality of Information 37
  Contract Amendments 37
  Governing Law. 37
  Compliance with Laws 37
  Change in the Laws 38
  Quality of Service Expectations
    and Timeliness 38
  Marketing Physicians' Services
    by the Plan 39
  Professional Review and Quality
    Assurance 39
  Credentialing Process of Physician
    and Staff 40
  Liability Insurance 40
  Patient Grievance Process 40
  Nonclaim Disputes
    Resolution 40
  Separate Operating Expenses. 40
  Coordination of Benefits 40
  Equal Opportunity 41
  HMO Risk Services 41
  Evidence of Coverage. 42
  Employer Cost for Health Care 42
  Emergency Departments 42
  Agreement Terms. 42
  Termination of an Agreement 43
  Termed and Ineligible Patients 43
Case Study—How Will Dr. Obby
Stop Losing Money on Patients
Who Are Catastrophically Ill? 44
Summary 45
Web Sites 45
Fill in the Blank 46
Review Questions. 46
Critical Thinking Exercise—
HMO Physician Contract
Negotiations 47
  Materials Needed 48
  Directions 48
Professional Corner—Finding
Carve-Outs. 48
References 49

Chapter 3: Preferred Provider Organizations 50

Chapter Objectives. 50
Key Terms 50
Introduction to Preferred Provider
Organizations 51
  Staying In-Network 51
  Self-Referring Within Network 51
  Going Out-of-Network 52
    Out-of-Network Deductibles 52
Distinct Provisions to Look for
in a PPO Contract 53
  Service Areas 53
  Patient Billed on Discounted
  Fees. 53
  Administrative Penalties. 54
  Patient's Right to Treatment 54
  Seeking Payment from the
  Patient 54
Utilization Review 54
  Payment Guidelines and
  Fee Schedules 55
  Coding Guidelines 55
  Acknowledgement of Receipt of
  the Claim 57
  Payment Dates Specified in the
  Plan Contract 57
  Audited Claim Payment 57
Claims Processing Policies. 58
  Provider Termination of the
  Contract 58
  Notifying Patients of Provider
  Nonparticipation 58
  Patient Finding a New Physician 59
  Final Claims Processing 60
Case Studies—In and Out of
Network. 60
  The Outcome of In Network 61
  The Outcome of Out-of-Network. . . . 61
Summary 62
Web Sites. 63
Fill in the Blank 63
Review Questions. 64
Critical Thinking Exercise 64
  Materials Needed 64
  Directions 65
Professional Corner 65
References 66

Chapter 4: Fee Schedules 67

Chapter Objectives. 67
Key Terms. 67
Introduction to Fee Schedules 68
Fee Schedule Types 68
  Fee Schedule Established
  by Payer 68
  Fee Schedule Established by
  Provider 69
  Fee Schedule Established by
  Payer Type 69
Negotiating the Fee Schedule 69
Using the Fee Schedule 69
Various Types of Fee Schedules. . . . 70

  Fee Schedules for Capitated Providers
  Reporting Statistical Claims. 71
  When a Referral Becomes
  an Issue 71
  When a Code Is Not on the Fee
  Schedule 72
    Noncovered Services 72
    The Patient Self-Referred Out of
    Network—When Might This
    Be Paid? 72
    Holistic Medicine Can Be
    Confusing 73
  Procedures Not Included in
  the Fee Schedule but
  Eventually Allowed into the Plan . . . 73
    Unlisted Procedures 73
  Multiple Fee Schedules 74
Reciprocity Rates and Fee
Schedules 74
Investigational Procedures. 74
Insured Patient Fee for Service 74
  Nonparticipating Providers—No Fee
  Schedules Involved 75
  Participating Providers 75
Medical Necessity 75
  Billing the Payer at the Patient's
  Request 76
Examples of Various Types of
Fee Schedules and What They
Tell Us 76
  Example of a Medicare Fee
  Schedule 76
    A Medicare Clinical Laboratory
    Fee Schedule for
    Northern California. 77
    Medicare Portable X-Ray Fee
    Schedule Used Mostly in a
    Skilled Nursing Facility 77
    Chiropractors' Fee Schedule,
    Year 2007, California 78
    Medicare Durable Medical
    Equipment Fee Schedule 78
Case Studies 79
  Case Study—Spider Veins versus
  Varicose Veins 79
    Case 4-1—When a Code Is
    Not on the Fee Schedule 79
    Case 4-2—When a Code Is
    Covered on the Fee Schedule . . . 80
Summary 80
Web Sites. 81
Fill in the Blank 81
Review Questions. 81
Critical Thinking Exercise 83
  Materials Needed 83
  Directions 83
Professional Corner 84
References 84

Chapter 5: Medicare 85

Chapter Objectives. 85
Key Terms. 85
Introduction to Medicare 86
The Role of the Social Security
Administration. 87

  Medicare's Future and
  Information to Access 87
  Participating and Nonparticipating
  Providers 90
  Nonparticipating Providers Limiting
  Charge Increases the Patient
  Level of Responsibility 91
Medicare and Other Insurances. . . . 91
  Patient Deductibles 92
Medicare's Common Working
File. 92
Local Medical Review Policies 94
  Local Coverage Determinations 95
  Carrier Advisory Committees 95
  The Need for Complete Documentation
  of the Evaluation and Management
  Level of Service Chosen by the
  Physician or Coder. 96
  Comprehensive Error Rate Testing
  Program 96
The Tracking of Codes for
Utilization. 97
  Implementation of Codes 97
Average Sales Price List for
Medicare Part B Drugs 97
  Drugs Listed Separately 98
  Drug Infusions. 98
Ambulance Providers and
Medicare 98
Benefits Improvement and
Protection Act 99
Medicare Demonstration
Projects 100
The Administrative Simplification
Compliance Act 100
Medicare Fee Schedule 101
  New Procedure Not on the
  Medicare Fee Schedule 101
Clinical Labs. 101
  A Deceased Patient 102
Case Study—A Consulting Physician
Initiates Care of a Medicare
Patient, Uses Category III Code . . 102
  Diagnosis 103
  Procedures 103
Summary 104
Web Sites. 104
Fill in the Blank 104
Review Questions 105
Critical Thinking Exercise. 106
  Materials Needed 107
  Directions 107
Professional Corner 107
References 108

Chapter 6: Medicaid 109

Chapter Objectives. 109
Key Terms. 109
Introduction to Medicaid 110
Medicaid Program Funding
Process 110
Timeliness Issues Are Handled
by Each State. 112

Clearinghouse Acceptance......112
Disclosure of Outside Billing
    Services....................112
The Payer of Last Resort.......112
Adopting National Codes.......114
Requesting New HCPCS
    Codes for a State Medicaid
    Program....................114
Pricing Criteria...............115
Conversion Tables for Changed
    ICD-9-CM Codes............115
Medicaid Case Study—How
    Rates Vary in Medicaid......117
    Basic Medicaid Rates Offering
        One Fee for a Series of Codes ... 117
    Dollar Amounts in a Coding
        Series 118
    Managed Care Fee-for-Service
        Rates Vary in Medicaid
        Contracts 118
Summary.....................119
Web Sites....................119
Fill in the Blank 119
Review Questions.............120
Critical Thinking Exercise.......121
    Materials Needed 121
    Directions 121
Professional Corner 121
References...................122

Chapter 7: CPT Modifiers   123
Chapter Objectives............123
Key Words 123
Introduction to Modifiers 124
Modifiers, Scenarios of Use,
    and Their Definitions.........124
    Modifier -21 or 09921 124
        Definition of -21 125
        Scenario 125
        Explanation of Why the Modifier
            Is Used................. 125
        Diagnosis 125
        Procedure 125
    Modifier -22 or 09922 126
        Definition of -22 126
        Scenario 126
        Explanation of Why the Modifier
            Is Used................. 126
        Diagnosis 126
        Procedure 127
    Modifier -23 or 09923 127
        Definition of -23 127
        Scenario 127
        Explanation of Why the Modifier
            Is Used................. 127
        Diagnosis 127
        Procedure 127
    Modifier -24 or 09924 128
        Definition of -24 128
        Scenario 128
        Explanation of Why the Modifier
            Is Used................. 128
        Diagnosis 128

Procedure 128
Modifier -25 or 09925 129
    Definition of -25 129
    Scenario 129
    Explanation of Why the Modifier
        Is Used................. 129
    Diagnosis 129
    Procedure 130
Modifier -26 Professional
    Component or 09926 130
    Definition of -26 130
    Scenario 130
    Explanation of Why the Modifier
        Is Used................. 130
    Diagnosis 130
    Procedure 130
Modifier -32 Mandated Services or
    09932 130
    Definition of -32 131
    Scenario 1 for -32 131
    Explanation of Why the Modifier
        Is Used................. 131
    Diagnosis 131
    Procedure 131
Scenario 2 for -32 132
    Explanation of Why the Modifier
        Is Used................. 132
    Diagnosis 132
    Procedure 133
Modifier -47 or 09947 133
    Definition of -47 133
    Scenario 133
    Explanation of Why the Modifier
        Is Used................. 133
    Diagnosis 134
    Procedure 134
Modifier -50 or 09950 134
    Definition of -50 134
    Scenario 134
    Explanation of Why the Modifier
        Is Used................. 134
    Diagnosis 134
    Procedure 134
Modifier -51 or 09951 135
    Definition of -51 135
    Scenario 135
    Explanation of Why the Modifier
        Is Used................. 135
    Diagnosis 135
    Procedures 135
Modifier -52 or 09952 136
    Definition of -52 136
    Scenario 136
    Explanation of Why the Modifier
        Is Used................. 136
    Diagnosis 136
    Procedures 136
Modifier -53 or 09953 137
    Definition of -53 137
    Scenario 137
    Explanation of Why the Modifier
        Is Used................. 137
    Diagnosis 137
    Procedure 137
Modifier -54 or 09954 138

Definition of -54 138
Scenario 138
Explanation of Why the Modifier
    Is Used................. 138
Diagnosis 138
Procedure 138
Modifier -55 or 09955 139
    Definition of -55 139
    Scenario 139
    Explanation of Why the Modifier
        Is Used................. 139
    Diagnosis 139
    Procedure 139
Modifier -56 or 09956 140
    Definition of -56 140
    Scenario 140
    Explanation of Why the Modifier
        Is Used................. 140
    Diagnosis 140
    Procedure 140
Modifier -57 or 09957 141
    Definition of -57 141
    Scenario 141
    Explanation of Why the Modifier
        Is Used................. 141
    Diagnosis 142
    Procedure 142
Modifier -58 or 09958 142
    Definition of -58 142
    Scenario 142
    Explanation of Why the Modifier
        Is Used................. 142
    Diagnosis 143
    Procedure 143
Modifier -59 or 09959 143
    Definition of -59 143
    Scenario 143
    Explanation of Why the Modifier
        Is Used................. 143
    Diagnosis 144
    Procedure 144
Modifier -62 or 09962 144
    Definition of -62 144
    Scenario 144
    Explanation of Why the Modifier
        Is Used................. 144
    Diagnosis 145
    Procedure 145
Modifier -63 or 09963 145
    Definition of -63 145
    Scenario 145
    Explanation of Why the Modifier
        Is Used................. 145
    Diagnosis 145
    Procedure 145
    Modifier -66 or 09966 146
    Definition of -66 146
    Scenario 146
    Explanation of Why the Modifier
        Is Used................. 146
    Diagnosis 146
    Procedure 146
Modifier -76 or 09976 147
    Definition of -76 147
    Scenario 147

Explanation of Why the Modifier
Is Used 147
Diagnosis 147
Procedure 147
Modifier -77 or 09977 148
Definition of -77 148
Scenario 148
Explanation of Why the Modifier
Is Used 148
Diagnosis 148
Procedure 148
Modifier -78 or 09978 149
Definition of -78 149
Scenario 149
Diagnosis 149
Procedure 149
Modifier -79 or 09979 150
Definition of -79 150
Scenario 150
Explanation of Why the Modifier
Is Used 150
Diagnosis 150
Procedure 151
Modifier -80 or 09980 151
Definition of -80 151
Scenario 151
Explanation of Why the Modifier
Is Used 151
Diagnosis 151
Procedure 152
Modifier -81 or 09981 152
Definition of -81 152
Scenario 153
Explanation of Why the Modifier
Is Used 153
Diagnosis 153
Procedure 153
Modifier -82 or 09982 153
Definition of -82 153
Scenario 154
Explanation of Why the Modifier
Is Used 154
Diagnosis 154
Procedure 154
Modifier -90 or 09990 154
Definition of -90 154
Scenario 154
Explanation of Why the Modifier
Is Used 155
Diagnosis 155
Procedure 155
Modifier -91 or 09991 155
Definition of -91 155
Scenario 156
Explanation of Why the Modifier
Is Used 156
Diagnosis 156
Procedure 156
Modifier -99 or 09999 156
Definition of -99 156
Scenario 157
Explanation of Why the Modifier
Is Used 157
Diagnosis 157
Procedure 157

Groupings of Modifiers for
CPT Sections 158
E-mail Addresses for Modifiers 158
Summary 159
Web Sites 159
Fill in the Blank 159
Review Questions 160
Critical Thinking Exercise 161
Materials Needed 161
Directions 162
Professional Corner 162
References 162

Chapter 8: Usual, Customary, and Reasonable   163

Chapter Objectives 163
Key Words 163
Introduction to Usual, Customary,
and Reasonable Rates 164
Determining a Geographic Area 166
The Patient and UCR Rates 166
The Importance of UCR Rates
by Specialty for Geographic
Area 167
Favorable Reimbursement and
Fewer Disputes with Payers 167
Managing Operation of the Office
and Understanding What Is
Expected 167
Developing a Review System
for Procedures Performed and
Reimbursed 168
Case Study 8-1—Reported
Diagnosis Justifies Reported
Services 168
Any Willing Provider Regulations
from Various States 169
Freedom of Choice Regulation 170
Point-of-Service Plans and UCR 170
Not All Is Fair 171
Case Study 8-2—Sports
Billing Scenario 171
The Plan and the IPA 173
Summary 173
Web Sites 173
Fill in the Blank 174
Review Questions 174
Critical Thinking Exercise- 175
Materials Needed 176
Directions 176
Professional Corner 176
References 177

Chapter 9: CPT Conventions to Be Considered   178

Chapter Objectives 178
Key Words 178
Introduction to CPT Conventions . .179
The Six Sections of the CPT 179
Evaluation and Management 179
Second-Opinion Claims 180
Second-Opinion Issues
Not Authorized 181

Consideration for Payment 181
Case Study 9-1—E/M Based
on Medical Necessity of Care . . . 182
Case Study 9-2—What Payers
Dislike Most about Incorrect
E/M Coding Reporting 183
Standardizing Physician Notes
in the Medial Record 185
SOAP 185
CHEDDAR 185
SNOCAMP 186
Anesthesia 186
Position of a Patient Changes
the Base Value 187
Payment and Reporting 187
A Surgeon Who Anesthetizes
His Own Patient 187
Case Study 9-3—
Anesthesiologists and RVGs . . 188
Surgery Section 189
Radiology 191
Case Study 9-4—Films Not
Coded or Billed Separately for
an E/M 191
Case Study 9-5—Billing for a
Component Separately 192
Case Study 9-6—A Radiologist
Performing Technical and
Professional Components 192
Who Reads the X-rays First? 193
Rural Hospital Scenario 193
Cosmopolitan/Big-City Scenario . . 193
Case Study 9-7—Interventional
Radiology 194
Pathology and Laboratory 195
Where Do Pathologists Work? 196
Medicine Section 196
Case Study 9-8—Immunization
Administration without Bundling . . 197
Case Study 9-9—Add-on Codes . . . 198
Case Study 9-10—Chiropractic
Modalities Not Paid 199
Summary 199
Web Sites 200
Fill in the Blank 200
Review Questions 201
Critical Thinking Exercise 202
Professional Corner 203
References 203

Chapter 10: Provider Disputes and Balance Billing   204

Chapter Objectives 204
Key Terms 204
Introduction to Provider
Disputes and Balance Billing 205
Basic Identifying Information
Needed for Both the Provider
and Payer 205
Single or Multiple Claims 205
Seeking Resolution of a Billing
Determination 206
Tracking Form 206

Internal Tracking of Disputes
  by the Provider 206
How a Payer Is Paying Claims
  and the Criteria 208
Miscellaneous Reasons for a
  Dispute 209
  A Time Limit on Claim Disputes . . . 209
Interest on Claims 210
  Is The Appeal Process
    Included in Annual Audits
    of the Health Plan? 210
  Audits of Provider Disputes 210
  Acknowledgment of Disputes 210
  Information the Adjuster Needs . . . 211
  Acknowledgement of Claims 211
A Request for Reimbursement
  of Overpayment by the
  Payer 212
When a Payer Backs Out
  Overpayment from Other
  Claims 212
Settling Claims with
  Noncontracted Providers 213
Balance Billing 213
  Contracted and Noncontracted
    Providers 213
  Rebundling Based on Claim
    Check Edit Systems 214
Case Studies—Where the Primary
  and Secondary Insurance Rates
  Are Different 214
  Regarding the Write-off 215
Medicaid. 215
  Reimbursement 216
  Cost-Effectiveness in Billing 216
Noncontracted Providers 216
Retention of Files 217
  Forwarding the Claim to
    Another Payer 217
Claim Overpayment Written
  Notice 217
Summary 218
Web Sites 218
Fill in the Blank 219
Review Questions 219
Critical Thinking Exercise 220
  Materials Needed 220
  Directions 220
Professional Corner 221
References 221

Chapter 11: Compliance
and Audits   222
  Chapter Objectives 222
  Key Terms 222
  Introduction to Compliance
    and Audits 223
    Some Considerations in an
      In-House Audit for Compliance . . . 224
  General Policy Guidelines Most
    Compliance Plans Address
    and Their Corresponding
    Policy and Procedures 224

How Might Our Practice Be
  Considered for an Audit? 225
My Practice Wants To Do
  Its Own Audit. What Should
  I Do? 226
Postaudit Findings 228
Participation in Medicare
  and Medicaid 228
  Office of the Inspector General
    Work Plan for the Year 228
  Billing Medicare or Medicaid
    Incorrectly . . . Occasionally 229
  A Government Investigator Wants
    To Search My Office 229
    The Government Investigator Wants
      To Ask Me Questions 230
The Carriers and Fiscal
  Intermediaries Are Requesting
  Records. Can They Do That? 230
  What Carriers and/or Fiscal
    Intermediaries Do When They
    Suspect Fraud 230
My Doctor Wants Me To Bill for
  the Services a Nurse, Not the
  Doctor Himself, Furnished. Is
  This Fraud? 231
  Producing a Claim from the
    Superbill but Found No
    Supporting Documentation
    in the Record 231
My Provider Ignores Compliance
  Problems 231
  In Order To Make a Billing Quota,
    I Billed Services I Knew Would
    Not Be Paid 231
What if My Employer Retaliates
  for My Being a Whistleblower
  (Qui Tam)? 232
If My Provider Is Convicted of a
  Misdemeanor, Can the Provider
  Be Forced Not To Participate or
  Excluded from Medicare? 232
My Provider Has Decided To Come
  Forward with the Compliance
  Problem 232
  Steps To Clean Up Noncompliance . . 232
The Stark Rules 233
  What Is the Antikickback
    Statute About? 233
Case Study 11-1—Claims Coded
  Incorrectly and Correctly 233
  Case Study 11-1A—Incorrect Coding
    Based on Lavage Method 234
  Case Study 11-1B—Correct Coding
    Based on Impaction 234
Summary 234
Web Sites 235
Fill in the Blank 235
Review Questions 236
Critical Thinking Exercise 237
  Materials Needed 237
  Internet Sites 237
  Directions 238
Professional Corner 238
References 238

Chapter 12: Noncontracted
Providers   240
  Chapter Objectives 240
  Key Terms 240
  Introduction to Noncontracted
    Providers 241
    Providers Who Are Unable
      To Participate 241
    The Plan Can Terminate the Provider
      Contract at Any Time 242
    Some Plans Limit Patient Options . . 242
    Employers May Limit Patient
      Options 242
  Any Willing Provider Laws and
    Closed Networks 243
  Freedom of Choice and the
    Price to the Patient 243
  Incentives for Providers To
    Participate in the Plan 243
  Reciprocity and Deciding Not
    To Participate 244
    Providers Who Choose Not
      To Participate 244
    Case Study 12-1—Payment of a
      Senior HMO Claim 245
    Case Study 12-2—Commercial
      HMO Claim 246
      Commercial HMO Claims for
        Case Study 12-2 247
      What Does EMTALA Have To
        Do with Billing Charges? 247
      When a Medical Group Is
        Involved for Case
        Study 12-2 247
      Denied Claims Sent to the
        Patient for Case
        Study 12-2 247
      Claims Not Meeting
        Medical Necessity for Case
        Study 12-2 248
    Case Study 12-3—A Preferred
      Provider Organization and How
      It Was Paid 248
      Medicare Only for Case
        Study 12-3 249
      PPO Only for Case Study 12-3 . . 249
      Both Insurances—Medicare
        and the PPO for Case
        Study 12-3 249
      Senior HMO Radiology/
        Emergency Scenario for Case
        Study 12-3 249
    Case Study 12-4—Coding of
      Multiple Procedures – Sinus . . 250
  Summary 251
  Web Sites 251
  Fill in the Blank 252
  Review Questions 252
  Critical Thinking Exercise 254
    Materials Needed 254
    Directions 254
  Professional Corner 254
  References 255
Glossary of Terms   257
Index   263

Preface

Outcomes in Coding Practice: A Roadmap from Provider to Payer was written to help students and professionals alike understand the importance of correct coding as it relates to government regulations; participating provider contracts; noncontracted providers; usual, customary, and reasonable (UCR) fees; capitation; policies; and evaluation of patients.

The purpose of this book is to help you understand how the codes are seen and interpreted by correct sequencing, geographic area, insurance program, code versions, and eligibility, and the book explains how to find applicable current information relevant to your specialty. Incorrect coding may lead to disputes, audits, and noncompliance. This book looks to explain what these are, how they may be identified for prevention purposes, and the educational tools to identify such circumstances.

This book can be used as a stand-alone guide or as a supplement in a more advanced coding class. The concepts and issues introduced are designed for those who wish to go further than basic coding theory and be introduced to the various factors beyond coding selection.

Organization of the Text

This book is organized to help you understand the journey codes take in how they are considered for payment. The first four chapters (The Correct Coding Initiative, Health Maintenance Organization [HMO] Contracts, Preferred Provider Organizations, and Fee Schedules) may be prenegotiated and are usually in place before the patient's first visit. Topics in the next five chapters (Medicare; Medicaid; CPT Modifiers; Usual, Customary, and Reasonable; and CPT Conventions To Be Considered) may be considered by the coder when choosing a coding process. Material in the next chapters (Provider Disputes and Balance Billing, and Compliance and Audits) may be considered as a result of choices made by the coder. And Noncontracted Providers, although outside of participation, may be considered for payment through state laws and choices made by the patient.

The first chapter begins with the Correct Coding Initiative. We began the book with this chapter because many payers check codes through this process, most computer automated softwares check coding rules, mandates conventions and sequencing. In Chapter 2, Health Maintenance Organization (HMO) Contracts, sometimes specific procedures are prenegotiated as included or not included in the HMO participating provider contracts. This chapter helps the reader understand how payment and reimbursement of codes are specified in the contracts and basic information to be found in them. Chapter 3, Preferred Provider Organizations, helps the reader understand various provisions in contracts and how various providers are considered in payment. Chapter 4, Fee Schedules, discusses payment rates based on various factors that deal with codes in fee schedules. Chapter 5, Medicare, discusses reporting requirements for various programs the provider may participate in. In Chapter 6, Medicaid, readers see that the program itself decides what will be covered and pricing criteria. Chapter 7, CPT Modifiers, looks at coding situations using modifiers and how reimbursement affects payment. Chapter 8, Usual, Customary, and Reasonable, shows how these rates and fees are used when negotiating reimbursement for code listings. Coding examples are used to explain this. In Chapter 9, CPT Conventions To Be Considered, payers analyze code groupings and sequencing through coding conventions, guidelines, and regulation. This chapter gives coding examples to help understand the process. Chapter 10, Provider Disputes and Balance Billing, discusses why some claims are disputed through codes given. Chapter 11, Compliance and Audits, gives in-house audit considerations including compliance issues faced by many practices. Chapter 12, Noncontracted Providers, looks at various circumstances noncontracted providers face when treating a patient with insurance. Participation incentives and reciprocity options are explored for claims not meeting medical necessity.

Features

- *Chapter Objectives and Key Words* highlight important chapter concepts.
- *Case Studies* drawn from actual reports are found throughout the book to give the reader a true experience. In the case studies, we have included how the codes were reported on the CMS-1500 claim forms. This will help the reader visualize the sequencing of the codes along with their modifiers and sometimes pricing logic.
- *Web Sites* include Internet addresses where readers can find more information or reference additional content.
- *Fill in the Blank and Review Questions* found at the end of each chapter allow readers to test their knowledge of chapter concepts.
- *Critical Thinking Exercises* allow the reader to apply various chapter concepts via an activity.
- *Professional Corner:* Students in an internship or new job setting may see information they are unfamiliar with and not know what they are looking at or its significance. The Professional Corner gives those in the business setting a chance to identify paperwork (forms, regulations, physician notes, and so on) that will help them understand the meaning and importance of what it represents.

StudyWARE™

The StudyWARE™ software found on the CD at the back of the book helps the user learn and apply the terms and concepts found in the book. StudyWARE™ is a private tutor to help the user study and review in a fun and interactive environment!

It includes:

- Review questions available in both practice and quiz modes
- 12 coding case studies that allow users to test their competence in chapter concepts
- Review in a fun environment while playing concentration, or a round of championship game, a jeopardy-style game
- Electronic flashcards that test users' understanding of key terms and codes

For the Instructor

Instructor Manual to accompany *Outcomes in Coding Practice: A Roadmap from Provider to Payer*

   Order ISBN#: 1401898998

Includes:

- Answers to Fill-in-the-Blank and Review Questions
- Sample Syllabi
- Lesson Plans and Lecture Notes
- Correlation of chapters to the RHIA/RHIT, CCS and CCS-P competencies

Acknowledgements

To my contributors Linda A. Poulos, CPC-I, CPC-H, CCP-P and Linda M. Dobbins, CPC-P thank you for your coding expertise and industry knowledge; the opinions of you both have been interesting, timely, and forthwith. I would like to acknowledge the assistance of Roberta Hartley, BS, MS whose skill in copy editing was helpful to the project. Many thanks to my parents Victor and Helga.

I would also like to thank the reviewers of my manuscript for their insightful thoughts and ideas:

John Brandebura, CPC, BSBA
Medical Office Program Extern Coordinator and Instructor
Maric College
San Diego, CA

Cindy Conley, RHIT
HIM Instructor
Ozarka College
Melbourne, AR

Michelle H. Cranney, MBA, RHIT, CCS-P, CPC
Virginia College Online
Birmingham, AL

Barbara Desch, LVN, CPH, AHI
Program Director
San Joaquin Valley College
Visalia, CA

Jane W. Dumas, MSN, RN
Allied Health Department Chairperson
Remington College—Cleveland West
North Olmsted, OH 44070

Marianne Durling, CMAS
Instructor/Coordinator Medical Coding Program
Vance-Granville Community College
Henderson, NC

Rashmi Gaonkar, MS
Instructor, Subject Specialist Insurance and Coding
ASA Institute
Brooklyn, NY

Judy Hurtt, Med
Medical Billing and Coding Instructor
East Central Community College
Decatur, MS

Pat King, MA, RHIA
Instructor
Baker College of Cass City
Cass City, MI

Linda Kuhlenbeck, CMA-AAMA
Medical Assistant Instructor
Brown Mackie College
Hopkinsville, KY

Lynn Meacham
Medical Extern Coordinator, Medical Instructor, Program Author
Institute of Technology, Inc.
Modesto, CA

Professor Eva Oltman, MEd, CPC, EMT, CMA, LMR
Division Chair of Allied Health
Jefferson Community and Technical College
Louisville, KY

Karen Reger, RHIT, CRSO
E&M Coder/Analyst
MidMichigan Physicians Group—Midland
Instructor
Mid Michigan Community College
Midland, MI

Margaret Stackhouse, CPC, RHIA
Manager of Coding and Reimbursement
University of Physicians
Children's Hospital of Pittsburgh of UPMC
Pittsburgh, PA

Janette Thomas, M.P.S., RHIA, RHIT
Director of The Learning Center
Alfred State College
Alfred, New York

Stacey Wilson, CMA (AAMA), MT/PBT (ASCP), MHA
Program Coordinator, Medical Assistant
Assistant Professor, Allied Health
Cabarrus College of Health Sciences

About the Author

Annette Butler has written curriculum for the University of California Riverside, MiraCosta College, and River Springs Charter School. In her fourteen years of teaching, she has developed eight certificate programs with classes that include Medical Office Management, Physicians Coding, Physicians Billing, Hospital Billing, Collections, the Electronic Health Record, HIPAA, Anatomy and Physiology, and Medical Terminology.

Ms. Butler's business experience includes consulting, compliance, auditing, contract negotiation, billing, coding, and periodically she testifies as an expert witness.

Dedication

This book is dedicated to my daughter, Elizabeth.

How to Use the Book Features

Chapter Objectives

The chapter objectives are a list of what to expect from the chapter. As you read the objectives, some of the entries may interest you enough to pay special attention or to go directly to the section that explains the objective. For many of you, this book will be used in a secondary or more advanced class, and certain objectives may answer some questions you had formulated or may have been curious about when on an internship or job shadowing.

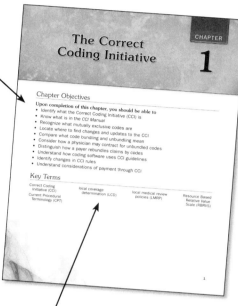

Case Studies

There are short case studies that have been drawn from actual outcomes. Some of the outcomes were correct in how they were coded and paid, and some were not. A clear effort has been made to explain why the case outcome happened as it did. This gives the instructor and you a chance to reflect upon your experiences and opinions of how the coding was perceived and paid by the payer and if the rules of the code had changed and how they are paid now. What may be correct and sound reporting of a procedure for one year can change the next. We ask that you take this into consideration and use it as a learning tool.

Key Terms

The key words feature is a vocabulary list to help you understand the meaning and concept of the chapter. You may come across these words in a professional setting, in either written or verbal form depending on your experience. They are not necessarily medical terminology but industry words and concepts to navigate your learning experience.

CMS-1500 Illustrations

In the case studies, we have included how the codes were reported on the CMS-1500 claim forms. This will help you visualize the sequencing of the codes along with their modifiers and sometimes pricing logic. This also will give you a glance into how the physician's notes or operative reports were perceived by the coder.

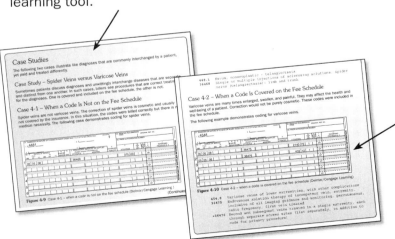

Web Sites

The Web sites should be thought of as places to explore and ways of gathering information from other entities and commentary to further your knowledge of the subject matter in the chapter. Some of the Web sites are for government entities (that is, Medicare) and offer procedure regulation and changes to billing and coding that are applied in the workplace. Learning how to navigate these Web sites can only help future need for knowledge and periodic changes in the industry.

Review Questions

The review questions look to you to give written answers, in your own words, of how you perceive the information you have read. This process will help you understand important concepts of the chapter and help the professor recognize your level of understanding. These questions can be used as a basis of discussion in any classroom setting.

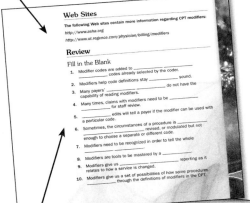

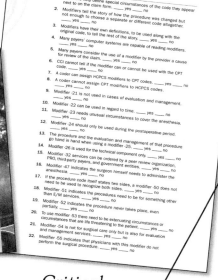

Fill in the Blank

This is an educational tool using key words in the chapter that are vital to your understanding. The words and their meanings should be remembered and reinforced in the fill-in-the-blank exercise.

Critical Thinking

The critical thinking exercise encourages you to explore the Internet to find information used in a professional setting. This will be the basis of the discussion assignment, critiques, and comparisons used in the classroom or on a narrative basis.

Professional Corner

Students in an internship or new job setting may see information they are unfamiliar with and not know what they are looking at or its significance. The Professional Corner gives those in the business setting a chance to identify paperwork (forms, regulations, physician notes, and so on) that will help them understand the meaning and importance of what it represents.

How to Use StudyWARE™

How to Use StudyWARE™ to Accompany *Outcomes in Coding Practice: A Roadmap from Provider to Payer*

The StudyWARE™ software helps you learn terms and concepts in *Outcomes in Coding Practice: A Roadmap from Provider to Payer.* As you study each chapter in the text, be sure to explore the activities in the corresponding chapter in the software. Use StudyWARE™ as your own private tutor to help you learn the material in the text.

Getting started is easy. Install the software by inserting the CD-ROM into your computer's CD-ROM drive and following the on-screen instructions. When you open the software, enter your first and last name so the software can store your quiz results. Then choose a chapter from the menu to take a quiz or explore one of the activities.

Menus

You can access the menus from wherever you are in the program. The menus include Quizzes and other Activities.

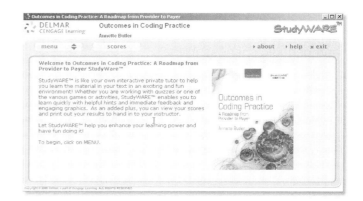

Quizzes

Quizzes include multiple-choice, fill-in-the-blank questions and case studies. You can take the quizzes in both practice mode and quiz mode. Use practice mode to improve your mastery of the material. You have multiple tries to get the answers correct. Instant feedback tells you whether you're right or wrong and helps you learn quickly by explaining why an answer was correct or incorrect. Use quiz mode when you are ready to test yourself and keep a record of your scores. In quiz mode, you have one try to get the answers right, but you can take each quiz as many times as you want.

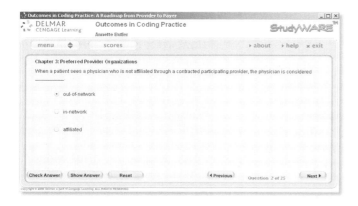

Scores

You can view your last scores for each quiz and print your results to hand in to your instructor.

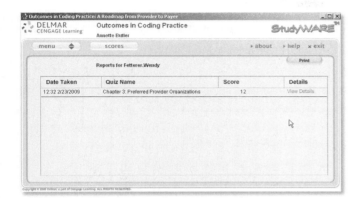
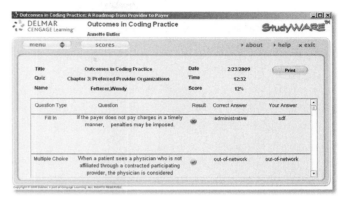

Case Studies

Two case studies per chapter allow you to apply chapter concepts.

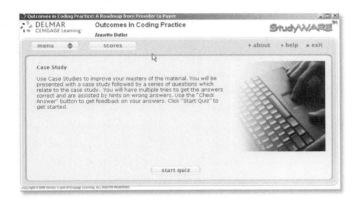

Activities

Activities include flashcards, hangman, and concentration games. Have fun while increasing your knowledge!

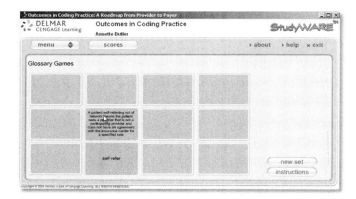

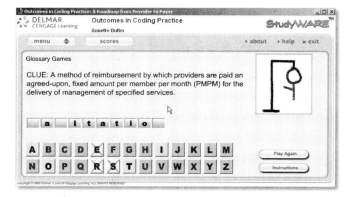

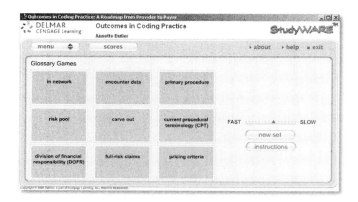

Report Templates

Templates are provided in Microsoft Word format for all report types you are learning in the textbook. You can use these templates as you work with the audio transcription exercises.

Introduction

What Are Outcomes?

The word *outcome*, according to *Webster's Dictionary*, means "something that follows as a result." In this book, we discuss outcomes of how a claim is considered for payment by a payer as a result of how it is coded. The payer takes various factors into consideration before payment is warranted. These could be federal or state regulations, coding conventions, contract agreements in force, and clean claim status. The monetary reward to the provider is payment for its services. Nevertheless, there are other factors involved in an outcome, what it means to the treatment of the disease, the patient who is ill, the way an illness is measured, and ultimately the cost of these.

As seen in UCR fees, this is measured by what a provider is actually paid in a geographic area compared to what is actually charged by the provider, and what procedures are commonly performed together for a therapeutic outcome in the treatment of a patient. Sometimes a bundling of procedures occurs in coding conventions to measure uniformity.

Statistical data is gathered by the payer to study trends and needs of the population the payer insures. When a wider range of the patient population becomes ill with a specific disease, the insurer may look to ways of handling or managing the disease through the development of better procedures, patient management, and medication.

ICD-9-CM—Outcomes

ICD-9-CM codes are available on every claim to study acute or chronic illness or multiple diseases faced by one patient or multiple claims for a group of patients. These, coupled with the procedures performed on the same claim, are a snapshot of treatment occurring at the visit, for that patient, by the provider of specialty trained to handle the patient's illness.

The study of diagnostic and procedure codes should be easily measured and information bountiful because of payment and timeliness issues for the coders and billers who must meet a reporting time line and accuracy quality. These codes for study are easily obtainable if computers are programmed to capture the data.

Measuring a disease in an outcome of a code could be tricky, since many diseases are underrepresented by "not otherwise specified" (NOS) and "not elsewhere classifiable" (NEC) designations in the ICD-9-CM. These would be seen as fourth digit _ _ _.9 and _ _ _. 8. Capturing disease specifically named but unavailable to choose by the coder, these diseases are lumped into these categories and shortchanged in their significance. It is difficult to categorize and only able to give the most general of information if measured by code only.

The introduction of the ICD-10-CM is on the horizon. This more advanced version of the ICD-9-CM uses numbers and letters to specify disease. Moreover, ICD-10-CM will eventually give all data-gathering entities the ability to capture coding information through disease, giving research, payer, facilities and government entities the ability to understand the effectiveness of procedure and claims management. If your college or university offers such a class on how to use the ICD-10-CM, taking the class would be advantageous in learning a system every other country has currently adopted.

Medical Records—Outcomes

How well is the medical record documented, and who will understand if the provider falls short of industry standard documentation? Why, a coder, of course. Coders read the chart for information they need to make an educated code choice.

The concern of medical record measurement is the care taken in recording the visit or disease process which uniformity has been attempted through methods such as SOAP, CHEDDAR, and SNOCAMP.

The coder is bound by what is written and how well the visit is documented, and decides the codes that determine payment and the measurement of outcomes from the codes.

Patient Satisfaction—Outcomes

Patient need is the very reason this industry exists. The industry measures patient outcomes in procedures and disease surveys assessing patient satisfaction and answers the question, did the patient get well? If the therapeutic procedure or approach was faster, better, and/or cheaper but did not garner the result needed, the industry may need to spend even more money on yet another procedure until the patient is satisfied. Satisfaction could be a percentage of cure (for example, Mrs. Smith's arm is functioning at 80 percent capacity). If the procedure proves to satisfy the patient or show some relief, it may be valuable enough to become an industry standard for the disease stated. Patient surveys and questionnaires will play a role in answering these questions. A physician can measure patient progress, but it is the patient who knows how she feels and how her life has been affected positively or negatively by the care she receives.

When a provider participates in these studies, the plan, the payer, or maybe the grant entity is usually willing to pay a per-patient survey fee if the provider gathers the survey or questionnaire documentation and sends the information with the claims and a report produced by the provider. Many times the payer will give one lump sum per complete submission (for example, patient survey, provider report, and claims). The focus may be a disease management or procedure. The payer may dictate a code or a range of codes the provider is to use per submission. What the payer will reimburse per procedure, patient survey, and provider report should be plainly documented, and the biller should understand what reimbursement for these individually are expected.

Coding is the final explanation of a patient visit or date of service. CPTs, ICDs, and HCPCS are noted and checked for realistic treatment of an illness or injury and what is authorized.

To the Student

Because of constant changes, it is always important to look for what is current. Publications, books, seminars, conferences, and the Internet all have their places in offering vital pieces to one's education and understanding of this industry. Many coders feel the investigative aspect of this industry is what keeps them interested and motivated. The choices a coder makes in choosing a code affect so much more than just reimbursement. It is the hope of this author that coders understand the true importance of the contributions they make to the medical field and insurance agencies respectively.

The Correct Coding Initiative

Chapter Objectives

Upon completion of this chapter, you should be able to

- Identify what the Correct Coding Initiative (CCI) is
- Know what is in the *CCI Manual*
- Recognize what mutually exclusive codes are
- Locate where to find changes and updates to the CCI
- Compare what code bundling and unbundling mean
- Consider how a physician may contract for unbundled codes
- Distinguish how a payer rebundles claims by codes
- Understand how coding software uses CCI guidelines
- Identify changes in CCI rules
- Understand considerations of payment through CCI

Key Terms

Correct Coding
  Initiative (CCI)
Current Procedural
  Terminology (CPT)

local coverage
  determination (LCD)

local medical review
  policies (LMRP)

Resource Based
  Relative Value
  Scale (RBRVS)

Introduction to Correct Coding Initiative (CCI)

Correct Coding Initiative, CCI Manual A nationally used coding reimbursement manual based on current procedural terminology codes and published by the American Medical Association. It introduces concepts and terms needed to understand claims payment as well as the tools required for success. It also describes some of the exceptions that a coder may encounter in the coding process.

The purpose of this chapter is to acquaint the coder with correct coding and billing practices as they relate to the **Correct Coding Initiative,** as described in the *CCI Manual*. This chapter introduces concepts and terms needed to understand claims payment, as well as the tools required for success, and explains some of the exceptions that a coder may encounter in the coding process.

CCI is the coding standard for Medicare, and many private commercial payers use it to determine claim payments for billed codes and their conventions, sequencing, regulations, mandates, and contracted agreements. Professional coders would do well to understand some of CCI's history; its purpose; the organization responsible for CCI contents; CCI's quarterly update schedule; and how changes, such as adding, changing, or deleting codes, are made.

History of CCI

RBRVS fees Charges are based on three key components of the Resource Based Relative Values Scale (RBRVS). Is a national value, and each procedure has value based on this system. It covers clinician's time, intensity, and technical skill required for the particular service provided. It also takes into account the practice's overhead expenses, including offices, rents, equipment, staff, supplies, and malpractice insurance.

In 1989, the Omnibus Budget Reconciliation Act amended title 18 of the Social Security Act. Replacing previous charge mechanisms such as the **Resource Based Relative Values Scale (RBRVS)** for paying claims, CCI became the new payment guidelines for physicians' services by Medicare. The resource based relative value system is a payment computation that CCI dictates to make sure that payment meets uniform standards. CCI uses national values, and each procedure has value based on this system. The system covers the clinician's time and the intensity of work and technical skill required for the particular service provided. It also takes into account the practice's overhead expenses, including offices, rents, equipment, staff, supplies, and malpractice insurance.

Medicare implemented the CCI because fee schedules and policies needed to be consistent for any carrier or fiscal intermediary, regardless of its jurisdiction. To comply with these changes, there also needed to be consistency in codes and their uses, hence the development of the CCI, as described in the *CCI Edit Manual*.

The CCI is current coding standard used by payers. Based on **CPT, Current Procedural Terminology,** it is a tool for editing claims to ensure the coding conventions, methods, and approaches are used correctly and consistently when requesting payment. The purpose of CCI is to edit improper coding practices. CPT consists of service and procedure codes and their definitions most commonly reported on claim forms, such as the CMS-1500 for professional medical procedures usually performed by a physician and ancillary staff.

Current Procedural Terminology (CPT) Consists of service and procedure codes and their definitions most commonly reported on claim forms such as the CMS-1500 for professional medical procedures usually performed by a physician and ancillary staff.

Organizations Responsible for CCI Contents

The Centers for Medicare and Medicaid Services, or CMS, are responsible for the information in the *CCI Manual*. The coding policies in CCI do not take the place of any other Medicare coding coverage or payment policies but are used in conjunction with Medicare rules and regulations. CCI edits are the coding and payment rules set forth by CMS. The edits are based on evaluations and procedures from the 1994 Healthcare Common

Procedure Coding Standards, HCPCS Level II, (pronounced "hick picks"), and the current CPT manual as of this date.

Changes to the CCI

The CMS updates the CCI quarterly, yet the information is only published in book form twice a year, in April and October. As a publication, it is available from several sources, including but not limited to the *Federal Register*, a government publication; or commercially from Ingenix or the American Medical Association (AMA). Quarterly changes are available via the CCI Web site (listed at the end of this chapter).

Obtaining Current Updates from the Internet

The practitioner is ultimately responsible for the updates, making sure they are in place and properly used. Electronic files are available on the CMS Web site, which also shows effective dates and deletion dates of all CCI edits. Most printed CCI manuals do not have the most recent CCI edits. Coders can check the Web site and download what they need regularly.

Code Versions and Effective Dates

Codes deleted from the CCI edits have specified effective dates. When CMS changes codes, there is an edit version and a date posted, which means all codes must comply with this version on and after the date specified. However, the dates before the change stay in effect for that period and are evaluated under that period's rules and edits. For example,

> **EXAMPLE:** Version B of the CCI applied and changed effective date 06/01/2008 to a certain procedure. This means that Version A is the default for 01/01/2008 to 05/31/2008 and any patients who received the procedure between those dates would have the rules of Version A apply. Procedures done after 06/01/2008 would be affected by the rules of Version B.

Effect of CCI on the Coding Industry

If uniform payment policies were not in place, many providers would have the attitude of "I bill the way I bill and expect to get paid for it." CCI protects payers and aids in fraud recognition by providing the guidelines from which to work, aiding coders and billers in distinguishing what correct coding is and is not.

Because of the CCI, all payers are able to make uniform payments for procedures based on their policies. The standard guarantees a uniform approach and a consistent methodology for billing and payment. The following example demonstrates how CCI affects "creative" billing.

> **EXAMPLE:** An oral maxiofacial surgeon may go to a workshop on billing and then become "creative" when coding. But CCI still looks at these codes based on the guidelines set forth, and, if the guidelines are not met, the codes are changed and rebundled to fit the guidelines. Hence, this practitioner may receive payment but with changes to the claims that are very different from the claims submitted.

Review Organizations

There are also national and local review organizations, such as the National Standard Medical Surgical Practices (NSMSP), and **local medical review policies (LMRP)** to ensure coding meets Medicare requirements for payment and coding policies. Local medical review policies apply to claims directly made to the local carrier that pays the claims. The carrier looks at the LMRP to make sure the claim payment meets Medicare guidelines. The LMRP will state under what circumstance the service is covered, codes that are covered and not covered, and descriptions of services. As of December 31 2005, CMS contractors were instructed to convert all existing LMRPs to **local coverage determinations (LCDs)**, which specify how a service is covered and how it is coded correctly.

CCI Coding Software Used by Payers

Most payers have claim-check systems that have the ability to correct a code to the proper level per their latest software program. Sometimes payers can be as much as six months behind in the process of reviewing claims because of the schedule for regulation updates. A code may not be incidental to another procedure but paid on its own merit.

Many payers' software programs do not let them print the explanation of why a code or procedure is not paid. The software vendor would have to give specific permission to print the explanation of edits. This usually does not happen, so the payer has to use another source to explain CCI edits and their results.

Many independent versions of CCI edit software programs only look at the codes and not at the modifiers, which may provide more information regarding a procedure. The software usually edits the codes alone.

Most claims processing systems do not look at the history of a submitted claim. Some look at procedures and date of service. In these cases, the claims could be denied as possible duplicates, also known as second-read claims. If the claim is a part of the duplicate check, it may not be caught unless the processor is researching the claim.

CCI for the Coder

When making coding choices, a professional coder should understand how the CCI works. Knowing when to use comprehensive codes, component codes, mutually exclusive codes, and modifiers and their differences is an important part of making choices and coding correctly.

Comprehensive Codes and Component Codes

A comprehensive code includes component codes that can be performed separately, but when performed together the one comprehensive code should be reported. The component codes are included in the comprehensive code because they are needed to complete the procedure. If a coder assigns a comprehensive code and a component code, the claim will either be denied or rebundled and only the comprehensive code will be paid. An example of this would be coding for local anesthesia.

LMRP 1 local medical review policies These apply to claims directly made to the local carrier who pays the claims. The carrier looks at the LMRP to make sure the claims payment meets Medicare guidelines. The LMRP will state under what circumstance the service is covered, codes that are covered and not covered, and descriptions of services.

LMRP 2 local medical review policies A tool that helps to ensure coding meets the Medicare requirements set forth by regulations of payment and coding policies.

LMRP 3 local medical review policies LMRPs are developed for specific codes for various reasons. LMRPs can be different by area/region/state, and so on. In the state of California, LMRPs are separated by northern and southern regions. For a list of these categories log on to http://www.CMS.gov/medicare/mip/index-ar.htm.

local coverage determinations (LCD) These specify how a service is covered and how it is coded correctly.

EXAMPLE: If local anesthesia is something all patients receive or is required for a particular procedure to be performed, it is probably included in the comprehensive code. A current, up-to-date, *CCI Manual* or software will help coders be aware of what can be reported separately or together during that period or time frame.

CCI Manual

A professional coder should understand the difference between comprehensive code edits and mutually exclusive edits when making a coding choice. When uncertain, a coder should use the *CCI Manual* as an aid in choosing the code suitable for reporting and billing purposes. The Centers for Medicare and Medicaid offers a Web site regarding the Correct Coding Initiative. The address is http://www.cms.hhs.gov/NationalCorrectCodInitEd.

Mutually Exclusive Codes

Mutually exclusive codes are codes that may not be coded for the same surgical session for a patient; it would be incorrect to code them together. When the physician performs a service, the coder must know how to report or code the service according to CCI guidelines. CMS identifies some of these services as the "method" and the others as "initial and subsequent" service.

Method, Initial, and Subsequent Services

A method can be how a physician repairs something, the technique or the process. In these cases, it would be realistic for the physician to use one approach but not two. The *CCI Manual* states these with each code, so when the procedure is coded, it is coded correctly the first time.

An initial service and subsequent service are services that are not performed at the same time during the same session. An *initial* service refers to the first of more than one service, and *subsequent* refers to the later service. The thought is that these are performed in different sessions at different times with the patient.

Significant Information for Individual Codes

The *CCI Manual* explains policy guidelines and payment rules through symbols and modifiers written in the manual itself. As the rules/guidelines change, so do the individual explanations of each code affected by the change. This is the benefit of having a manual/Web site as a reference for coding correctly. Figure 1-1 lists possible policies affecting an individual code, which could be defined in the manual.

Bundling

Some procedure codes are bundled together to make one comprehensive code because the services are logically related and belong together under one "umbrella" code (for example, a complete hysterectomy). CCI computer edits, in theory, catch the errors and rebundle the codes from the payer's software program. CCI edits can also indicate a claim needs manual review by payer personnel prior to payment, thus setting it aside or flagging the claim for inconsistencies.

Anesthesia included in a surgical procedure	Levels of physician supervision of diagnostic tests
Standards of medical/surgical practice	Separate procedures
HCPCS/CPT coding manual instruction/guideline	Family of codes
CPT separate procedure definition	Most extensive procedures
Designation of gender-specific procedure	Excluded services
Most extensive procedure	Unlisted services or procedures
Sequential procedures	Modified, deleted, and added code pairs
"With" versus "without" procedures	RBRVS payment computations
Laboratory panels	Relative value units
Mutually exclusive procedures	Conversion factors
Misuse of column one with column two	Related modifiers from the CPT
Surgical modifiers	Modifiers affecting code edits
Status indicators	Status indicators
Global periods	Global periods
Physician supervision levels	Physician supervision levels

Figure 1-1 Information for individual codes

Unbundling

Unbundling is a practice of billing for each portion of a complete procedure, rather than reporting all portions together under one code. When the codes are unbundled, presented as multiple procedures, and billed, typically the CCI rebundles the unbundled procedures and then pays using the rebundled code. This only happens when CCI coding edits indicate the procedure is covered by one comprehensive code. HCPCS/CPT should be reported to the payer with the most comprehensive description of the service provided, in order to eliminate the process of unbundling. Unbundling can lead to fraudulent billing.

Practices That Lead to Unbundling

Several practices can lead to unbundling a claim. Unbundling can be done unintentionally or intentionally, or a physician can contract with a specific payer for unbundling.

Unintentional Unbundling Unintentional unbundling is the result of coders or billers not understanding how to code the physician's work as it relates to the true code meanings or descriptions. The old adage "if it was not done, it is not billable" is true. Nonetheless, if the handwriting of the physician is not clear or the notes do not follow standard documentation procedures, this can innocently be misinterpreted by a coder.

> EXAMPLE: An example of unintentional unbundling is a complete hysterectomy. There is a comprehensive code covering removal of the fallopian tubes, ovaries, and uterus. Billing each one individually would be incorrect when there is a comprehensive code for all three in one procedure. This error can happen when a coder or biller does not know to properly use the CPT.

Unbundling is also known as "á la carte" billing. Take the example of a mammogram. Instead of billing for a bilateral procedure, some offices bill a unilateral, or one-sided, mammogram for both the left and right breasts and thus use two billing codes when only one is really needed or indicated in the CPT. This may not be intentional on the part of the biller/coder, but it is still incorrect coding, and the government looks at situations like these seriously.

Intentional Unbundling and the Government It can be said that the government's take on this sort of coding is "ignorance is no excuse." If an entity continues to code incorrectly after the coders learn the difference or are advised of the difference by Medicare or another payer, then they are touching on fraud. If a provider is notified a procedure submitted was unbundled and that the provider must use the bundled code, the provider should do so. If the biller/coder continues to submit the code unbundled, this can be considered intentional and may trigger an audit of claims submitted.

Contracting for Unbundling Physicians can contract for unbundling. Some services that CCI usually edits out as inclusive in a more comprehensive procedure can be contracted as separately billable whenever the physician performs the procedure(s).

Some physicians contract payment for specific codes even if they bundle into a comprehensive code, and the payer pays accordingly. A CCI edit program may rebundle the codes, but the staff of the payer must override the rebundle and pay the claim if the codes are contracted in such a way that CCI would interpret them as unbundled. The biller must watch for rebundling and ensure that it doesn't occur.

Other Coding Tools

In addition to the *CCI Manual*, a CPT coding manual is very important. There are professional, in-depth versions of these manuals with expanded code meanings and photos, and HCPCS II code books as well. The CPT and HCPCS II give complete descriptions of the codes not found in the *CCI Manual*. The CCI gives paraphrased descriptions of these codes and should not be looked at strictly from the procedural definition for nontechnical language.

CCI Coding

Frequently, many offices with coding and payment problems do not understand the significance of the CCI. It is common that many billers and coders neither know how to read the manual nor have ever seen one. However, their payers not only know what it is but many times base their payment, coding, rules, regulations, conventions, and logic on it. Therefore, it is crucial the coder understand what the CCI is; how to read it; and how it applies to coding, payment, contracts, and service agreements.

Sometimes a working knowledge of CCI is enough, and at other times, the *CCI Manual* should be referenced frequently during the coding process, to correctly code procedures and provider care from the beginning of the year or on a quarterly basis if the provider's codes are affected by change.

The CCI is an important coding tool, and having access to a manual can be crucial. Additionally, coding edits that pertain strictly to a specific office or specialty (for example, orthopedics) can be purchased. Such a purchase may be less cumbersome and more practical, since it concentrates only on procedures performed in a specific practice.

Using Modifiers and Mutually Exclusive Codes

Sometimes coders use modifiers to explain the reasons for using more than one code pair or set. Of course, if it is justified in the surgical/operative report, it may be allowed but may be edited out and denied by the payer. Usually in a mutually exclusive situation, modifiers are not allowed under any circumstances.

HCPCS Modifiers

Figure 1-2 lists HCPCS modifiers that are allowed in reports with CCI edits as of August 2003. Modifiers usually do not change very often.

CPT Modifiers

Figure 1-3 lists CPT modifiers that may be used with CCI edits successfully. They are listed numerically in ascending order.

Incorrect CCI Coding

Professional coders understand that incorrect coding is a serious problem, the dangers of which cannot be stressed strongly enough. If a pattern of incorrect coding develops, the government may audit a provider for fraud

E1 - upper left lid	LD – left artery, descending coronary artery
E2 – lower left lid	LT – left side
E3 – upper right eyelid	RC – right coronary artery
E4 – lower right eyelid	RT – right side
FA – left hand thumb	TA – left foot great toe
F1 – left hand second digit	T1 – left foot second toe
F2 – left hand third digit	T2 – left foot third toe
F3 – left hand fourth digit	T3 – left foot fourth toe
F4 – left hand fifth digit	T4 – left foot fifth toe
F5 – right hand thumb	T5 – right foot great toe
F6 – right hand second digit	T6 – right foot second digit
F7 – right hand third digit	T7 – right foot third digit
F8 – right hand fourth digit	T8 – right foot fourth digit
F9 – right hand fifth digit	T9 – right foot fifth digit
LC – left circumflex, coronary artery	

Figure 1-2 HCPC modifiers

25 – Significant Separately Identifiable Evaluation and Management Service by the same physician on the same day of the procedure or other service
58 – Staged or related procedure or service by the same physician during the postoperative period
59 – Distinct procedural service
78 – Return to the operating room for a related procedure during the postoperative period
79 – Unrelated procedure or service by the same physician during the postoperative period
91 – Repeat clinical diagnostic laboratory test

Figure 1-3 CPT modifiers

regardless of if an entity overcharges/bills or undercharges/bills in its procedures. A *Coder's Desk Reference*, published by Ingenix, can help explain, in nontechnical terms, what is included in procedures from the CPT manual.

A coder/manager may wish to be aware of the 20 most performed primary and secondary procedures by provider in her practice. In this way, the coder/manager can be watchful for edit revisions, deletions in the coding manuals, and changes in payer rules and regulations. Many billing software programs have the capability of listing performed procedures by physician.

Medical coding and billing is an important, rewarding, and ever-changing profession that can be complex. Without correct coding and billing, a provider may have payments delayed, lose money unnecessarily, be at a disadvantage during contract renegotiations, or even be audited for fraud. To avoid this, it is important to know what payers look for in a medical claim and the tools payers use to determine payment consideration.

Case Studies of Coding and CCI – Correct and Incorrect

The following examples were set aside when checked by the CCI computer system of the payer. Some were rearranged and paid; others were denied outright.

Case Study 1-1 – Incorrect Coding, Add-on Codes

This claim lists add-on codes only. This is incorrect because it reports the add-on code as a stand-alone code. Add-on codes are additional or supplemental procedures and should be listed in addition to the primary procedure. In this case, the coder may have used 17000 as the primary before 17003.

DIAGNOSIS
    702.0   Actinic keratosis

PROCEDURES
    17003   Add- on Code: Destruction of all benign or premalignant lesions for 2nd through 14th lesions, list each separately in addition to code for first lesion.

(Continued)

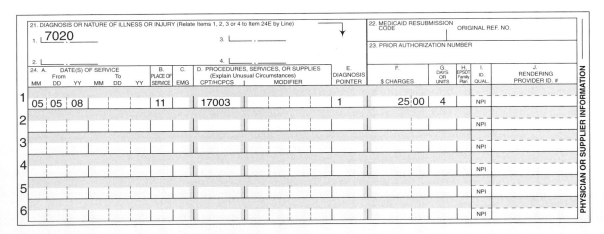

Figure 1-4 Claim form 1 – incorrect add-on codes

CCI Edit – How the Claim Was Paid

The way the claim is structured, CCI reads four of these procedures as duplicates, allowing only one primary and one add-on code. Ideally the claim should have been reported as follows:

Figure 1-5 Claim form 2 – correct add-on code

```
17000   Destruction of premalignant lesions: first lesion
17003   × 4, 2nd through 14th lesions (each listed separately)
  -51   Modifier multiple procedures
```

More Than One Provider on a Claim

There are circumstances when a payer may agree to unbundling codes. The National Correct Coding Policies and Edits (NCCPE) were developed for services billed by a single provider coding for a single patient. Sometimes, a surgeon and an assistant surgeon both bill on a single claim. Usually a claim processor separates these claims and pays the individual physicians, respectively, based on CCI guidelines.

CCI does not separate claims and pay physicians individually; the payer may do this manually or use a separate software program. Most claims are entered by one provider and many times are paid to a master vendor that then distributes payments.

Rebundling Lab Codes
Occasionally payers need to rebundle codes because a series of tests or procedures performed logically link together. Many of the CCI edits caught are for a series of lab codes billed individually when a panel, a series of lab tests necessary to diagnose the patient, would apply. Some physicians order tests on an individual basis rather than a panel. Many times physicians write down the test/services they want without checking their grouping in a panel series.

Case Study 1-2 – Correct Coding, Lab Codes
The following lab test and collection of blood are all payable because none of the codes bundle into each other.

Figure 1-6 Case study 1-2 – claim form 1 – correctly billed lab codes

DIAGNOSIS
V70.0	Routine General Medical Examination at a health care facility
600.00	Hypertrophy (benign) of prostate
780.79	Other malaise and fatigue

PROCEDURES
84153   Prostate specific antigen (PSA): total

80050   General health panel – includes comprehensive metabolic panel (80053); hemogram; automated, and manual differential WBC count (CBC) (85022); OR hemogram and platelet count, automated, and automated complete differential WBC count (CBC) (85025); thyroid stimulating hormone (TSH) (84443)

80061   Lipid panel – includes cholesterol, serum, total (82465), lipoprotein, direct measurement, high-density cholesterol (HDL cholesterol) (83718), triglycerides (84478)

36415   Routine venipuncture or finger/heel/ear stick for collection of specimen(s)

(Continued)

21. DIAGNOSIS OR NATURE OF ILLNESS OR INJURY (Relate Items 1, 2, 3 or 4 to Item 24E by Line)								22. MEDICAID RESUBMISSION CODE	ORIGINAL REF. NO.	
1. V700			3. 78079							
2. 6000			4.					23. PRIOR AUTHORIZATION NUMBER		

	24. A. DATE(S) OF SERVICE From / To MM DD YY MM DD YY	B. PLACE OF SERVICE	C. EMG	D. PROCEDURES, SERVICES, OR SUPPLIES (Explain Unusual Circumstances) CPT/HCPCS | MODIFIER	E. DIAGNOSIS POINTER	F. $ CHARGES	G. DAYS OR UNITS	H. EPSDT Family Plan	I. ID. QUAL.	J. RENDERING PROVIDER ID. #
1	05 05 08	81		84153	2	101 35	1		NPI	
2	05 05 08	81		80061	1	85 45	1		NPI	
3	05 05 08	81		80053	1	52 45	1		NPI	
4	05 05 08	81		84443	1	44 95	1		NPI	
5	05 05 08	81		85025	1	40 35	1		NPI	
6	05 05 08	81		36415	1	23 30	1		NPI	

Figure 1-7 Case study 1-3 – test billed separately

Case Study 1-3 – Lab Test Billed Separately Because of Coding Ineligibility

In this example, the lab codes are billed separately and not bundled into 80050. The insurance has decided to follow Medicare guidelines and not cover this as routine care. Instead, the tests are billed separately and will need to be medically necessary.

DIAGNOSIS (ICD)

V70.0 Routine general medical examination at a health care facility
600.00 Hypertrophy (benign) of prostate
780.79 Other malaise and fatigue

PROCEDURES

84153 Prostate specific antigen (PSA): total
80061 Lipid panel – includes cholesterol, serum, total (82465), lipoprotein, direct measurement, high-density cholesterol (HDL cholesterol) (83718), triglycerides (84478)
80053 Comprehensive metabolic panel – includes albumin (82040), bilirubin, total (82247), calcium (82310), carbon dioxide (bicarbonate) (82374), chloride (82435), creatinine (82565), glucose (82947), phosphatase, alkaline (84075), potassium (84132), protein, total (84155), sodium (84295), transferase, alanine amino (ALT) (SGPT) (84460), transferase aspartate amino (AST) (SGOT) (84450), urea nitrogen (BUN) (84520)
84443 Thyroid stimulating hormone (TSH)
85025 Blood count; complete (CBC), automated (Hgb, Hct, RBC, WBC, and platelet count), and automated differential WBC
36415 Routine venipuncture or finger/heel/ear stick for collection of specimen(s)

If you have a CPT book to reference, check to see if 80050 is a lab panel option. Sometimes, a coder can be directed by a guideline or contract rule that the coding be very specific when approaching bundled codes. Guidelines change from year to year. In this case, the codes were not bundled. Note, there are contractual adjustments throughout the Explanation of Benefits (EOB).

```
Remittance Advice
Claim # _____
Processed Voucher # _____
Vendor # _____
```

Name	HMO	MEMBER #		ACCOUNT #
Date of service	CPT code	Description		Billed
05/05/2008	36415	Collection of venous blood		$23.30
		Approved for payment		$3.00
		Contract adjustment		$20.30
05/05/2008	84153	Prostate specific antigen		$101.35
		Approved for payment		$25.70
		Contract adjustment		$75.65
05/05/2008	80061	Liquid profile		$84.45
		Approved for payment		$18.72
		Contract adjustment		$6.73
05/05/2008	80053	Comprehen metabolic panel		$52.24
		Approved for payment		$15.67
		Contract adjustment		$36.57
05/05/2008	84443	TSH lab		$44.95
		Approved for payment		$13.48
		Contract adjustment		$31.47
05/05/2008	85025	Automato hemo comp diff		$40.35
		Approved for payment		$12.10
		Contract adjustment		$28.25

Billed:	Approved:	Withhold:	Interest:
$346.64	$88.67	$0.00	$0.00

Figure 1-8 Lab code EOB

Case Study 1-4 – Incidental to Primary Procedures

In the following claim, the coder interpreted what the physician performed and made his best effort to code what was performed for the most amount of reimbursement. In this case CCI rebundled the codes and paid the comprehensive code. If the coder had a CCI manual or coding software containing CCI edits, the coder would have understood this was going to be rebundled and paid accordingly.

DIAGNOSIS
```
470      Deviated nasal septum
478.0    Hypertrophy of nasal turbinates
478.19   Other diseases of the nasal cavity and sinuses
```

PROCEDURES
```
30520    Septoplasty or submucous resection, with or without cartilage
         scoring, contouring, or replacement with graft
```

(Continued)

21. DIAGNOSIS OR NATURE OF ILLNESS OR INJURY (Relate Items 1, 2, 3 or 4 to Item 24E by Line)								22. MEDICAID RESUBMISSION CODE	ORIGINAL REF. NO.
1. 470. _____		3. 47819 _____						23. PRIOR AUTHORIZATION NUMBER	
2. 4780		4. _____ . _____							

	24. A. DATE(S) OF SERVICE From MM DD YY	To MM DD YY	B. PLACE OF SERVICE	C. EMG	D. PROCEDURES, SERVICES, OR SUPPLIES (Explain Unusual Circumstances) CPT/HCPCS	MODIFIER	E. DIAGNOSIS POINTER	F. $ CHARGES	G. DAYS OR UNITS	H. EPSDT Family Plan	I. ID. QUAL.	J. RENDERING PROVIDER ID. #
1	05 05 08	05 05 08	21		30520		1	1450 00	1		NPI	
2	05 05 08	05 05 08	21		30140	RT 51	2	900 00	1		NPI	
3	05 05 08	05 05 08	21		30140	LT 59	2	450 00	1		NPI	
4	05 05 08	05 05 08	21		30802	51	2	381 00	1		NPI	
5	05 05 08	05 05 08	21		31240	RT 51	3	750 00	1		NPI	
6	05 05 08	05 05 08	21		31240	LT 59	3	375 00	1		NPI	

Figure 1-9 Claim form – incidental to primary procedures, rebundled on the EOB

Remittance Advice

Claim # _____

Processed Voucher # _____

Vendor # _____

Name	HMO	MEMBER #	ACCOUNT #
Date of service	CPT code	Description	Billed
05/05/2008	30520	Septoplasty w or w/o cartlg scoring	$1450.00
		Approved for payment	$493.45
		Contract adjustment	$956.55
05/05/2008	30140	Exc submucous resect turbinate	$900.00
		Denied, incidental to primary procedure	$900.00
05/05/2008	30140	Exc submucous resect turbinate	$450.00
		Denied, incidental to primary procedure	$450.00
05/05/2008	30802	Cauterization turbinates, intramural	$381.00
		Denied, incidental to primary procedure	$381.00
05/05/2008	31240	Nasal endo w/concha bullosa	$750.00
		Approved for payment	$87.33
		Contract adjustment	$663.67
05/05/2008	31240	Nasal endo w/concha bullosa	$375.00
		Approved for payment	$7.33
		Contract adjustment	$287.67

Billed:	Approved:	Withhold:	Interest:
$4,306.00	$668.11	$0.00	$0.00

Figure 1-10 Lab code EOB incidental to primary procedures

30140-RT-51	Submucous resection turbinate, partial or complete, any method, right multiple procedures
30140-LT-59	Submucous resection turbinate, partial or complete, any method, left, distinct procedural service
30802-51	Cauterization and/or ablation, mucosa of turbinates, unilateral or bilateral, any method (separate procedure): intramural, multiple procedures
31240-RT-51	Nasal/sinus endoscopy, surgical; with concha bullosa resection, right, multiple procedures, distinct procedural service
31240-LT-51-59	Nasal/sinus endoscopy, surgical; with concha bullosa resection, left multiple procedures, distinct procedural service

In the EOB, codes 30140-LT, 30140-RT, and 30802 are all denied as incidental. Codes 31240-LT and 31240-RT are approved, but the contractual adjustment leaves little reimbursement.

Case Study 1-5 – Unbundled Procedure Stated as Multiple Procedures

In this case study, the physician would need to create a colostomy when performing a removal of the rectum (proctectomy). In the correct claim the colostomy is not coded separately. In the incorrect claim, the colostomy is coded separately when it is included in the partial removal of the rectum (proctectomy). The following shows correct coding of the colostomy.

In this example, the additional code is not listed with the primary procedure.

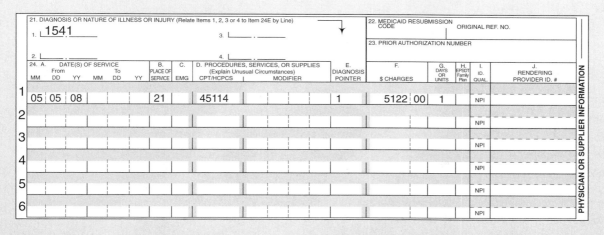

Figure 1-11 Case study 1-4 – claim form – correct procedure for the proctectomy only

DIAGNOSIS
    154.1   Malignant neoplasm of rectum, rectal ampulla
PROCEDURES
    45114   Proctectomy, partial, with anastomosis, abdominal and transsacral approach

The following is an example of how it was *incorrectly* coded and the EOB accompanying payment. In this example, the additional code is listed with the primary procedure.

(Continued)

Figure 1-12 Case study 1-4 – claim form – correct coding of stated multiple procedures (proctectomy and colostomy)

DIAGNOSIS

154.1 Malignant neoplasm of rectum, rectal ampulla

PROCEDURES

45114 Proctectomy, partial, with anastomosis, abdominal and transsacral approach

44320 Colostomy or skin level cecostomy (separate procedure)

In the Explanation of Benefits, the code 44320 is bundled into code 45114.

Remittance Advice

Claim # _____

Processed Voucher # _____

Vendor # _____

Name	HMO	MEMBER #	ACCOUNT #
Date of service	CPT code	Description	Billed
05/05/2008	45114	Partial removal of rectum	$5122.00
		Approved for payment	$1526.74
		Contract adjustment	$3595.26
05/05/2008	44320	Colostomy	$2506.00
		Denied bundled service	$0.00

Billed:	Approved:	Withhold:	Interest:
$7628.00	$1526.74	$0.00	$0.00

Figure 1-13 Case study 1-4 – EOB multiple procedures

Case Study 1-6 – Procedure Denied Due to a Global Allowance

CPT code 91056 is a breathing test a clinical assistant would usually perform. For this test, there are no global surgical allowances or follow-up days. In the procedure 91056, the coding of the 99211 indicates this procedure may be performed by an MA or a nurse and is included in a global allowance. In the EOB, the denial included in the global allowance refers to the allowance for payment of 91065, and the procedure 99211 is included in the allowance for code 91065.

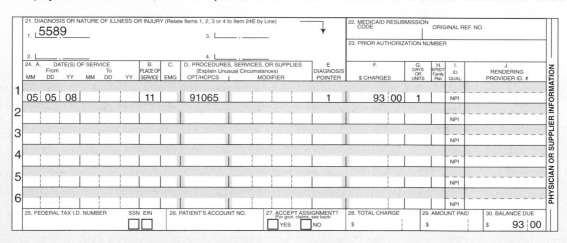

Figure 1-14 Case study 1-5 – claim form 1 – global billing

DIAGNOSIS

    558.9   Other and unspecified noninfectious gastroenteritis and colitis

PROCEDURE

    91065   Breath hydrogen test (for example, for detection of bacterial overgrowth)

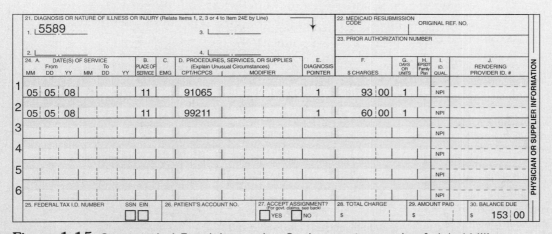

Figure 1-15 Case study 1-5 – claim number 2 – incorrect example of global billing

DIAGNOSIS

    558.9   Other and unspecified noninfectious gastroenteritis and colitis

(Continued)

PROCEDURE

91065   Breath hydrogen test (e.g., for detection bacterial overgrowth)
99211   Established Patient, Office Visit, level 1

Remittance Advice

Claim # _____

Processed Voucher # _____

Vendor # _____

Name	HMO	MEMBER #		ACCOUNT #
Date of service	CPT code	Description		Billed
05/05/2008	91065	Breath hydrogen test		$93.00
		Approved for payment		$55.80
		Contract adjustment		$37.20
05/05/2008	99211	O.V. estab PT, min		$60.00
		Denied, incl in global allowance		$60.00

Billed:	Approved:	Withhold:	Interest:
$153.00	$55.80	$0.00	$0.00

Figure 1-16 Case study 1-5 – EOB – incorrect global allowance

Case Study 1-7 – Services Denied – Not a Covered Benefit

In the following case study, J1885 and J3030 are not covered services. If this patient were a member of a traditional health insurance plan, the provider may be able to bill the patient the denied services. If this patient were a Medicare patient, the office would have needed to have the patient sign an ABN Advanced Beneficiary Notice before performing the service. If this did not happen, the physician would need to write off the services and not be able to bill the Medicare patient the difference.

Figure 1-17 Case study 1-6 – claim form, correct coding, noncovered charges

DIAGNOSIS

    346.01 Classical Migraine, with intractable pain, so stated

PROCEDURE

    99214   Established Patient, Level 4, Office Visit

    J1885   Ketorolac Trometha, 15 mg, injection

    J3030   Sumatriptan Succinate, 6 mg

Remittance Advice

Claim # _____

Processed Voucher # _____

Vendor # _____

Name	HMO	MEMBER #	ACCOUNT #
Date of service	CPT code	Description	Billed
05/05/2008	99214	OV est PT detailed moder complex	$109.30
		Approved for Payment	$109.30
05/05/2008	J1885	RX-Ketorolac Trometha, 15 mg, inj	$3.32
		Denied, not a covered benefit	$3.32
05/05/2008	J3030	RX-Sumatriptan succinate, 6 mg, inj	$63.74
		Denied, not a covered benefit	$63.74

Billed:	Approved:	Withhold:	Interest:
$176.36	$109.30	$0.00	$0.00

Figure 1-18 Case study 1-7 – EOB – correct coding, noncovered service

Summary

The CCI manual contains coding guidelines payers use in their consideration of paying claims for Medicare patients. Various other payers recognize this source and use it for payment of their claims as well. When used properly by the coding/billing office, the provider receives fewer denials due to incorrect coding. The edits make the coding payment process uniform for payers as well as providers.

Some physicians contract for services outside of the CCI coding rules, leaving the payer to consider these claims manually. Some payers have software programs that check the coding for CCI edits before considering the claim for payment. Some providers and payers base their payment agreements on CCI coding rules. Using the correct version of CCI is the key to payment and avoiding coding denials, rebundling, and fraud issues.

Web Sites

Because of its quarterly update schedule and semiannual publication schedule, coders cannot rely on printed copies of the material but will need to consult Web sites to code claims correctly. The following is a list of Web sites that contain the latest CCI information.

Centers for Medicaid and Medicare Services (CMS), *http://www.cms.hhs.gov*

CMS Training Modules and HIPAA, Health Information Portability and Accountability Act *www.cma.hhs.gov*

- Click *Partner with CMS (FIX)*
- Partnership Tools
- Training Resources
- Medicare, www.medicare.com

Review

Fill in the Blank

1. The CCI is current coding standard used by _____.

2. The CMS updates the CCI _____, yet it is only published in book form _____ a year, in _____ and October.

3. Codes _____ from the CCI edits have specified effective dates.

4. Most payers have _____ _____ systems that have the ability to correct a code to the proper level per their latest software program.

5. A comprehensive code includes _____ codes that can be performed separately, but when performed together the one _____ code should be reported.

6. Mutually _____ codes are codes that may not be coded for the same _____ session for a patient; it would be incorrect to code them together.

7. A _____ can be how a physician repairs something, the technique or the process. In these cases, it would be realistic for the physician to use one approach, but not two.

8. The CCI manual explains policy guidelines and payment rules through _____ and _____ written in the manual itself.

9. Unbundling is a practice of billing for each portion of a _____ procedure, rather than reporting all portions together under _____ code.

10. Unintentional _____ is the result of coders or billers not understanding how to code the physician's _____ as it relates to the true code _____ or descriptions.

Review Questions

Answer the following questions:

1. What is in the *CCI Edit Manual*? _____

    _____

2. What is the purpose of the *CCI Edit Manual*? _____

    _____

3. What does unbundling a claim mean? _____

    _____

4. What is the definition of NCCPE? _____

    _____

5. What is a modifier used for? _____

    _____

6. What is "á la carte" billing? _____

    _____

7. How will CCI handle more that one provider on a claim? _____

    _____

8. Are modifiers allowed under any circumstances in a mutually
    exclusive situation? _____

    _____

9. Do codes deleted from the CCI manual have effective dates? _____

    _____

10. Can the government audit a practice for undercharging as well as
    overcharging? _____

    _____

Critical Thinking Exercises

Some payers, agencies, or medical specialties help define and explain comprehensive and component codes on the Web. This exercise will give you a glance at how these codes are interpreted and explained.

Materials Needed

2 different-colored highlighters
2 printed examples of comprehensive and component code advice found on the Web

Directions

1. Use your Web browser or search engine to type in words such as
    - Correct Coding Initiative _____ (name a specialty)
    - Correct Coding Initiative changes as of _____ (type in a date)
    - Correct Coding Initiative changes in _____ (name a procedure)

- Comprehensive and component code changes
- CCI comprehensive and component code regulation

2. Find two Web sites explaining comprehensive and component code changes regarding the same codes. Print the information from both.

3. Use one color highlighter for generalized information such as the dates the information was written and the dates of when the information was to be used. Use the other color highlighter to emphasize the following:

a.   Do the two Web sites have the same explanations or interpretations of how the codes are to be used?

b.   Do any explain cases in which modifiers can be used or overrides are appropriate?

c   Does the Web information look to interpret CCI or express concerns about how CCI is using the codes?

4. Discuss the differences and similarities with your professor in class. Or, write a one-page report regarding your findings and opinion of how the Web sites are reacting to the codes and of how they give advice.

Professional Corner – Applying CCI to the Office Setting

Having access to actual outcomes of coding is important. The following outlines steps for gaining access to the outcomes and examining them.

- *Call a business associate and ask if her office uses the CCI manual.*
- *Ask the business associate how she applies the use of the manual to the practice where she works.*
  - *Is it only used in Medicare coding, or is it used for other insurances as well?*
  - *What kind of codes does the CCI effect in this associate's practice?*
- *Ask how the practice's claims denials and reimbursements have changed or varied since they began using the CCI as a reference/coding tool.*
- *Ask to see the "superbill" or face sheet the coder is coding from. Then study the reference materials used (CPT, ICD, HCPCS, and so on).*
  - *Notice if chronic illnesses were coded and included.*
  - *Notice if the medical record was perused for information.*
  - *Notice if the medical record was complete at the time of coding.*

Read any operative report, SOAP notes, and so on from which the coder took information into consideration before choosing a code, and consider if that source had an impact on the code selected.

- *Notice if the selection of the code(s) was based on or influenced by rules and regulations set forth by the government (state or federal), the contract, CCI edits, or basic coding conventions.*
- *Note if you agree with the coding selections.*
  - *Is the coding selection in depth enough? Specific enough?*
  - *Does the selection tell the complete story of that visit to justify diagnoses and procedure(s) selected?*
- *Has anything been overlooked, undercoded, overdone, not justified, or misrepresented from the documentation?*

If you feel your answers and the code selections are not the same, ask the coder who coded the claim. There should be a truthful free flow of communication, with each coder listening to the other and respecting different viewpoints and levels of experience.

- *Ask to see the Explanation of Benefits, and examine the reason(s) why the claim was paid or denied.*

- *Does the reimbursement differ from other insurance company payments?*

- *Is the payment based on a payer's fee schedule, percentage of physician fee schedule, or Medicare fee schedule?*

- *Are there codes simply not considered for payment, not included in the fee schedule, or written out of the provider contract for consideration?*

Always note the following:

- *The specialty you are studying. Realize there may be regulations and considerations that only apply to that specialty.*

- *The regulations that apply specifically to the code being considered.*

- *How the codes are used/reported in sequence. Do the codes explain what happened during this visit? Did a chronic illness need to be noted for a more in-depth procedure performed?*

- *Your business associate may wish to have you sign a confidentiality agreement that is HIPAA compliant before she shares true examples of this nature.*

References

Health and Human Services, OIG. (September, 2003). "Medicare National Correct Coding Initiative." (OEI-03-02-00770). Philadelphia, PA: Office of the Inspector General

GHI, Medicare Providers. (2005). "Bundled Codes." New York, NY: Medicare Division of Group Health, Inc.

The Medicare Learning Network, CMS. (October, 2008). "Medicare Physician Guide: A Resource for Residents Practicing Physicians and Other Health Care Professionals." Tenth Edition (ICN005933). Baltimore, MD: The Medicare Learning Network, CMS.

HCPro. (June, 2008). "Q&A Processing Outpatient Claims Against the NCCI." Marblehead, MA: HCPro, Inc.

Empire, Blue Cross Blue Shield. (2006). Correct Coding Initiatives, CCI Edits. New York, NY: Empire HealthChoice, HMO, Inc.

PMIC. (2009). National Correct Coding Manual. "Comprehensive Guide," 15.0. Los Angeles, CA: Practice Management Information Corporation.

PMIC. (2008). National Correct Coding Manual. "Unbundling Errors," 14.0, 1st Quarter. Los Angeles, CA: Practice Management Information Corporation.

Health Maintenance Organization (HMO) Contracts

Chapter Objectives

Upon completion of this chapter, you should be able to

- Identify common elements of an HMO contract
- Recognize capitation as it relates to the provider contract
- Identify claims used as encounter data
- Describe various payment methods listed in participating provider contracts
- Distinguish provider limitations
- Recognize HMO limitations
- Understand meeting patient needs in contract language
- Distinguish if a patient's needs are covered in contract stipulations

Key Terms

balance billing

capitation

carve-out

covered service

division of financial
responsibility

durable medical equipment

encounter data

evidence of
coverage

Knox-Keene Act

Medicare fee
schedule

necessary treatment
alternative

nonclaim disputes

payment schedule

primary care
physician

risk pool

surcharge

termed

Introduction to HMO Contracts

This chapter introduces HMO contracts and how such an organization works. In a contractual arrangement, an HMO and a health care provider sign a contract defining the terms and conditions of their professional and financial relationships to provide health care services for subscribers. If a dispute occurs, both the provider and the HMO abide by the terms of the contract. A coder or biller that is negotiating a debt, challenging a nonpayment, or questioning payment of a code needs ready access to the contract and a thorough understanding of the terms and conditions affecting the provider.

Usually HMOs pay general practitioners (GPs) and/or family practice physicians on a capitation basis to serve as **primary care physicians (PCPs).** These physicians provide primary care service to the plan members. They usually have a contract with an HMO plan. Sometimes a patient can name a specialist as his primary care physician of the plan. The PCP is the first physician the patient sees for medical services, and, if necessary, the patient is referred out by the PCP for specialty services.

Some specialty providers such as pediatricians, OBGYNs, or those specializing in internal medicine may also agree to see patients as a PCP, and the patients are able to choose these from the provider catalog provided by the HMO. This means these providers are the first physicians to see the patient to evaluate a problem in terms of patient Evaluation and Management. If the physician feels that the patient needs more specialized care for the presenting problem, the physician refers the patient to a specialist, such as a cardiologist, rheumatologist, or gastroenterologist. PCPs may contribute some of their capitated monies to a risk pool to pay specialists under these circumstances. The specialist usually is paid on a fee-for-service basis using a negotiated fee schedule based on CPT, HCPCS codes, and so on. The fee schedule states specific payment as it equates to a code.

primary care physician (PCP) This physician provides primary care service to plan members. He usually has a contract with an HMO plan. This physician can be a general practitioner, family practitioner, internist, and so on. Sometimes a patient can name a specialist as his primary care physician of the plan. The PCP is the first physician the patient sees for medical services. If the PCP deems specialty services necessary, he refers the patient out.

Capitation

In **capitation** an HMO pays a physician or provider a set fee per month, per patient (other terms for the patient may be *enrollee, participant,* or *insured*) whether a patient is seen or not. For the capitation fee, a physician must take care of all the patients' needs unless otherwise negotiated in the contract. In Figure 2-1 we see some of the elements in a basic contract that affect capitation, discussed in this chapter.

The paid rate per patient per month depends on the contract with the HMO, number of members in a particular plan, and other contractual factors; these factors affect the health plan and the contracted Physician's Medical Group (PMG), Independent Practice Association (IPA), or Preferred Provider Group (PPG). The following shows a simple example of a risk pool; often risk pools are more complex.

capitation A method of reimbursement by which providers are paid an agreed-upon, fixed amount per member per month (PMPM) for the delivery of management of specified services.

Payment per month per patient	$10.00
Shared risk pool monies	−2.00
Total paid to the physician per month	$8.00

Risk pool monies

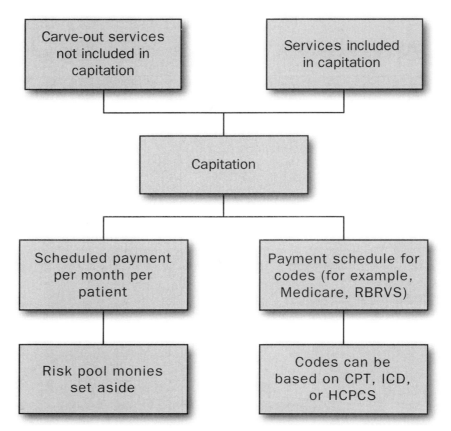

Figure 2-1 Capitation elements in a basic contract (Delmar/Cengage Learning)

The capitation contract provides the maximum number of patients allowed to choose the provider as their primary care physician. Under some contracts, the provider is paid the capitation for patients as soon as they choose the PCP; this date when the choice is made is known as the effective date. Some plans may not begin capitation payments until the patient's first visit.

Since an HMO is prepaid, the HMO distributes a list of patients participating for the monthly capitation to the physicians' group. When patients call for appointments, the appointment secretary can see who qualifies that month within the plan quickly and accurately. Most HMOs do not provide paper, or hard-copy, lists of patients participating in the plan for that month to the physicians. Instead the list is accessed electronically by computer.

Consequently, if a physician sees a patient who is not participating in the HMO capitation at the time of service, the physician may have to absorb the cost of seeing that patient because as a participating provider, he agrees not to bill HMO patients. The exception occurs when a signed release states that the patient, not the HMO, is responsible for the payment.

Payment Schedules

> **payment schedule** A list or a graph stating when payment will be made; this can be based on government regulation or agreed upon by the parties involved.

A **payment schedule** in the provider contract can be based on CPT codes, ICD-9-CM, HCPCS codes, or a combination of code types as they relate to payment schedules, such as the Medicare fee schedule (MFS), RBRVS, or a percentage of the bill. The coding system based on payment should be plainly stated and easy to read. A payment schedule is a list or a graph stating when payment will be made. This can be based on government regulation or agreed upon by the parties involved. A **Medicare fee schedule** lists fees developed by CMS and used by Medicare.

> **Medicare fee schedule** A list of fees developed by CMS and used by Medicare.

Services Included in Capitation

> **division of financial responsibility (DOFR)** In a managed care organization, a DOFR explains who is responsible for the procedure or care, the capitated provider group or the managed care organization itself. The information is usually written in a list, which clearly states specific procedures and which organization is responsible for them.

A **division of financial responsibility (DOFR)** matrix lists and defines services. A DOFR is part of the contract negotiated between a medical group, an independent practice association (IPA), a participating medical group (PMG), or a primary physicians group (PPG). It lists the services and the plan benefits for which the HMO and its providers are each financially responsible. Providers should be aware of the percentage of capitated services they perform, as defined by individual CPT code. If the services are capitated, the biller is not billing the service for payment but reporting the services performed based on real numbers. Physicians should be aware of their service percentages provided under the capitation.

The physician's office should make a list of services included in the capitation. The HMO can give the physician this information or it can be found in the HMO contract. The services should be in order of frequency performed and monitored via the CPT code numbers. Understanding what services are paid in capitation versus fee for service (FFS) is vital when submitting claims for payment or submitting claims for encounter data.

Claims for Encounter Data

> **encounter data** Examines a pattern of use for a billable encounter.

Encounter data are claims used for accounting and statistical data only. Monies are paid on these claims through capitation. Both the physician and the managed care plan benefit by knowing the true cost of treating the patients in a plan.

The dollar amount via the CPT code should be seen in the medical billing software to accurately assess what services are actually provided. The dollar amount should not be a "guesstimate" but real numbers from the practice. Not all plans include all services in the capitation, so a listing of the plan name and the services included in the capitation is needed. Figure 2-2 is an example of a DOFR, a matrix of HMO, PPG, and shared risk/hospital capitated services. Note how each item, service, or procedure is clearly indicated categorically.

Balance Billing and Capitation Contracts

> **balance billing** Charging or collecting an amount that is more than the reimbursement rate.

Balance billing is charging the patient the balance of what might normally be written off on an insurance claim.

For a physician, the contract limits his ability to balance bill the patient. If a patient sees a specialist, she may or may not need a referral. This depends on the arrangement the PMG, IPA, or PPG has with the specialist.

MATRIX EFFECTIVE DATE X1/01/2006			
	PROF CAPITATED SERVICES	HMO RISK SERVICES	SHARED RISK/ HOSPITAL CAPITATED SERVICES
AIDS – Facility component		X	
AIDS – Professional component		X	
AIDS – Drugs		X	
ALLERGY IMMUNOTHERAPHY	X		
ALLERGY TESTING	X		
ALPHA-FETOPROTEIN	X		
AMBULANCE – In area (30-mile radius) – Out of area		X	X

Figure 2-2 Example of a division of financial responsibility (DOFR) (Delmar/Cengage Learning)

However, if a specialist needs a referral and the patient does not have one, the provider may balance bill the patient if the specialist does not contract with the group. Usually the provider has the patient sign a form stating she is responsible for the bill. Once a patient does have a referral, the patient cannot be balance billed.

Some specialists may not agree with the explanation of benefits (EOB) reimbursement. These physicians need to read their contracts to verify their contracted rates for the procedure. In addition, there are certain provisions of the **Knox-Keene Act** (see Web site at the end of the chapter) that prohibit the physician from balance billing the patient. The Knox-Keene Act regulates managed care plans.

Knox-Keene Act The Knox Keene Act regulates HMO plans in the state of California. Most states have similar laws regulating HMOs.

Carve-outs

A **carve-out** is a procedure that is not included in the capitation but negotiated separately on an individual contract basis between the HMO and a provider. Carve-outs can be specialty driven based on peer norms, individually negotiated because of expertise, or negotiated based on the needs of the community.

carve-out A service not included in the capitation payment and that may be covered by a negotiated fee-for-service reimbursement. It can also apply expressly to services not covered under a particular contract.

Carve-outs can be services like mental health, chiropractic, acupuncture, or podiatry. Patients may have benefits for these based on the type of plan they have. Carve-outs may be overseen by the medical group or a different provider. These carve-outs are paid by the HMO.

Risk Pools

A **risk pool** is a fixed amount of the capitation monies set aside by the HMO until the end of the year. The PMG, IPA, or PPG physician shares the risk or cost of treating the patient. The physician has oversight management obligations for services a patient receives. Usually, risk pool monies are used to pay for services that are billed directly to the insurance, such as hospital inpatient, outpatient surgery, durable medical equipment, some infertility treatments, home health, transplants, AIDS treatment, ambulance services, and interpretations for radiology and pathology services as defined in the contract matrix.

risk pool A percentage of the capitation that is placed in a risk-sharing pool. If the cost of providing care (usually specialty and hospital services) exceeds an amount targeted by the plan, then all or a portion of the withhold is forfeited. If it is less than the targeted amount, the fees may be distributed back to the physicians.

At the end of the year, if the shared cost of the risk pool is more than the monies in it, a PMG, IPA, or PPG provider may share or split responsibility for the balance. For example, if the cost were $200,000, the provider would pay $100,000 and the HMO pays the other $100,000. Alternatively, if at the end of the year the cost of seeing patients is less and there are monies left in the risk pool, a provider would receive a distribution check from the HMO. Usually the provider must request its portion in writing. In this way, the provider shares the risk of the profit or loss of monies in treating the patient.

Referring a Patient

The following is a list of what the physician should know before referring a patient to a specialist for services. Remember, if a physician refers the patient to a specialist not contracted with the plan, the patient is not responsible for the bill. In this case, the referring physician or group would be responsible for the payment of services (risk).

For convenience, and to eliminate errors, the front office should make a ready list of the following information for referral purposes:

- Physicians by specialty
- Addresses
- Phone numbers
- Fax numbers
- What the physicians' contracts are based on, for example, RBRVS, Medicare allowable, percentage, capitation (or if not contracted, possibly obtain a letter of agreement from them)
- Anything unique in the contract, for example, carve-outs

Figure 2-3 is a basic generic referral form. On the form, there is an entry for the patient's insurance.

Each PMG, IPA, or PPG would have its own list of physicians it refers patients to. The list should be current based on its individual contracts.

Basic Contract Responsibilities between Providers and HMOs

There are some basic or standard contract responsibilities between providers and HMOs. Typically included are service responsibilities, specialty services, HMO payment responsibilities, physician payment responsibilities, and eligibility of college students. Billers, coders, and physicians should understand what these services are, as they are crucial for maintaining cost and smooth flow of patient care on a daily basis. See Figure 2-4 for basic contract responsibilities between providers.

Service Responsibilities

Service responsibilities usually state that HMO patients receive the same treatment and services as other patients not covered by the HMO, and that treatment for HMO patients also follows the same rules, regulations, and standards set forth by law. The provider may agree to coordinate the care of the patients with the HMO.

```
┌─────────────────────────────────────────────────────────────────────┐
│  Generic Referral Form                    ┌──────────────────────┐   │
│                                            │   Affix patient label │   │
│                                            │ Name: _____ │   │
│                                            │ Date: _____ DOB: ___ │   │
│  Primary Care Physician Referral           │ Provider: _____ │   │
│  & Prescription                            └──────────────────────┘   │
│                                       Date: _____   │
│    {  } Review Requested  {  } Urgent  {  } Direct Access/Auto Approval│
│    Refer to: _____                    │
│                                                                       │
│  ┌──────────────────────────────────────────────────────────────┐   │
│  │ Referring Physician:    John,        M.D.                      │   │
│  │                         Internal Medicine                      │   │
│  │ _____    Lic, #        DEA # _____  │   │
│  │                                                                │   │
│  │ Patient's Name: _____ │   │
│  │                                                                │   │
│  │ Dx: _____ ICD-9 _____ │   │
│  │                                                                │   │
│  │ Rx: _____ │   │
│  │          {  } Eval and Treatment    {  } Eval and Recommendations│ │
│  │ Clinical Information: _____ │   │
│  │ _____ │   │
│  │ _____ │   │
│  │ _____ │   │
│  │ _____ │   │
│  │ _____   _____│   │
│  │                                        Signature of Physician  │   │
│  └──────────────────────────────────────────────────────────────┘   │
│                                                                       │
│  Patient Information: DOB: _____ Phone: _____ ID # _____ │
│                                                                       │
│  Insurance: _____│
│                                                                       │
│  Information faxed: ___Labs__ X-ray Report__ EKG__ Progress Note__ Ins. Cards│
│  ____Other: _____│
│          Faxed to: _____  # of pages: _____   │
└─────────────────────────────────────────────────────────────────────┘
```

Figure 2-3 Example of a generic referral form (Delmar/Cengage Learning)

The provider may be required to adhere to the HMO's utilization review and quality of care programs. In doing so, it provides confidential patient information to the HMO in compliance with HIPAA (Health Insurance Portability and Accountability Act) laws and regulations.

The provider also agrees to accept new HMO members, up to the maximum enrollment quota, who have chosen the provider as their primary care physician.

Specialty Services

Specialist contracts are usually restricted to services authorized by the plan and a referral by the PCP. Typically, if not previously authorized, services are not paid. Most specialists refer the patient back to the PCP for follow-up after the consult or procedure is complete. Coverage is limited to what the referral authorizes.

Figure 2-4 Basic contract responsibilities between providers (Delmar/ Cengage Learning)

Additionally, there may be a mutually agreed-upon list of services or procedures restricting treatments a specialist can perform for a patient. These services are usually not research-type services but those that have a proven success rate. If a physician performs an unauthorized service, the PMG, IPA, or PPG is not responsible for payment, nor is the patient. A provider may not refuse to provide covered services to any member. A **covered service** is a service the HMO states as sufficient treatment for a disease or injury. This information is in the list of covered services supplied by the HMO.

However, if the contract states the physician may recommend a **necessary treatment alternative**, a treatment not normally covered under the plan provisions, he may ask for an authorization. Note that the plan does not guarantee coverage of those services. In this way, if the physician were motivated to give the patient a special treatment not in the plan provisions, the physician would need to complete special paperwork and/or go before a committee in the HMO for authorization.

In a contract, a physician agrees to send in the claims for a date of service by a specific time. For services billed beyond the specified time, the claim is not considered for payment. The window of time for claims submittal is specified in the contract, and the claims may be submitted

covered services These are services included in the plan and are mentioned in the booklet the patient gets from the insurance company. The patient is entitled to receive them if the patient is in need of them. The contract will identify all services covered by the capitation rate or contract and list all services not included but eligible for additional reimbursement.

necessary treatment alternative A treatment not normally covered under the plan provisions.

by paper or electronically. The physician's own contract would state claim submittal from the date of service; many times this is 365 days from the service date, but it can be as few as 30 days.

HMO Payment Responsibilities

The HMO capitation payment to the PMG, IPA, or PPG for the participating members should be made according to the time lines in the contract. Usually these payments are done by wire transfers from the HMO to the financial institution of the PMG, IPA, or PPG. These payments are made monthly by the required date set forth in the contract.

Physician Payment Responsibilities

Physicians agree to collect and/or bill patients only for co-payments. Contracts often state that a physician can give noncovered services to a patient on a fee-for-service basis if the patient agrees to the service before it is performed and understands that he, not the HMO, is responsible for payment. Most physicians do not suggest any services not covered by the HMO.

A physician may agree not to take any legal action against the patient for monies owed to the physician either by the HMO or the patient himself. This provision may be connected to state insurance laws. In the state of California, this code is California Health and Safety Code 1379(c).

A physician must report to the HMO all co-payment and deductible monies paid to him by patients. The HMO needs to know this as it considers the co-payment and deductible part of a complete payment; if not collected, then a service payment is not complete.

surcharge An additional sum usually added for a specified reason.

A provision of the Knox-Keene Act does not permit surcharges. A **surcharge** is an extra fee, sometimes considered a flat fee, for processing of the transaction. Further, if one is made, a refund must be made within a prescribed time period, per the contract.

In providing the services, a physician agrees not to discriminate or differentiate in the treatment and quality of the health services given to the patient based on race, sex, age, religion, place of residence, health status, or source of payment.

Eligibility of College Students

Some plans extend the eligibility of a college student up to the age of 23 with proof of full-time course work per semester. The patient needs to be timely and accurate in her reporting of her student status or the student may be termed from the policy.

Responsibility for Payment of Claims

The HMO contract usually specifies payment amount and always states the responsible party. For specialty claims, the payer can be the group, the IPA, PMG, or PPG. If this is the case, the IPA, PMG, or PPG may agree to pay for services the HMO does not. For the provider, this is well worth finding out in advance of billing claims.

Continuity of Care

Upon termination of the contractual agreement, a physician agrees to provide services for a specific period until the patient can choose another provider for treatment. This may take longer than the agreed-upon-time termination. The physician agrees not to abandon the patient and continues to treat the patient until he is transferred to another physician. There may be a point when the HMO chooses another primary care physician for the patient – if the patient is not timely in choosing one for himself and/or his family.

Financial Responsibilities

There is usually a provision that the HMO continues to pay the agreed-upon rates even if the plan terminates and the physician must see the patient for some reason. This would include only those services covered in the contract and can be diagnosis specific, such as gynecology, obstetrics, injury, and so on. Note these patients and the reason they are left behind by the plan. In these cases, the office may receive a contracted rate rather than the physician's regular rate. See Figure 2-5 for various factors involved in financial responsibility. These factors are discussed in the following section.

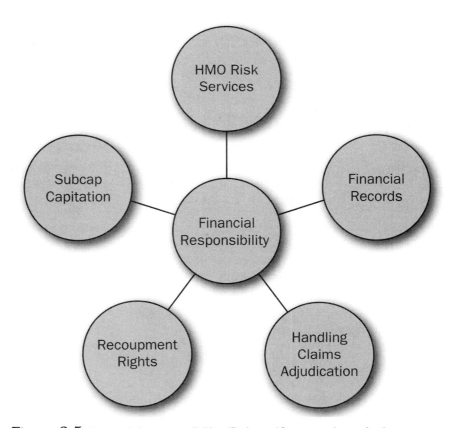

Figure 2-5 Financial responsibility (Delmar/Cengage Learning)

Financial Records

The Knox-Keene Act states the Department of Managed Care (DMC) has the right to inspect a provider's books, records, papers, and so on, on a patient's behalf. In addition, an HMO usually writes into a contract that it has access as well. An HMO usually wants to know the financial stability of its provider members. A provider's books should be open to inspection by contracting entities at all times; this is in the contract, too. In addition, there would be a listing of other agencies able to do this as well. They may be

- State department of health services
- U.S. Department of Health and Human Services
- Comptroller general of the United States
- Any authorized person stated in the contract

In these cases, there would be a specific time in which the physician must keep accessible her financial records and the dates the contract/agreement takes effect. An HMO may require an annual report of financial information.

An HMO may need certain statistical and financial data in keeping with the requirements of federal laws and regulations. The Knox-Keene Act specifies these federal laws and regulations.

Handling Claims Adjudication

Specific fee schedules and guidelines are the basis for claims processing. The contract states if it is based on CPT, MFS, durable medical equipment regional carrier (DMERC), DME, RBRVS, or an individually negotiated fee schedule. The payment process may follow

- Medicare guidelines
- Federal rules
- State rules
- Private insurance rules and regulations

Usually an HMO reserves the right to conduct postpayment review and/or auditing of paid and denied claims. An HMO may do this annually and notifies the provider in advance of such reviews.

Recoupment Rights

A payer may overpay claims and has a process to recoup the overpayment. Most identify the claims and specify how the process works for their plans. The basic information needed to identify the patient is

- Identification number
- Name
- Date of birth
- Date of services
- Amount paid
- Contracted amount that should have been paid

A payer may wish to recoup overpayment for the following reasons:

- Termination of the patient
- Student status changed
- The patient was retrotermed
- No authorization was on file for the patient

An HMO provider must give a clear explanation of its reasons as to why it overpaid the claim, the excess amount it intends to recoup, and any interest and penalties it believes are owed to it.

Contracts usually have time provisions for a provider to contest overpayment of claims in writing, for example, 90 or 180 days. Often a state law is quoted in conjunction with such a provision. Usually the parties exchange no monies during the process of contesting overpayment.

If there is no contest regarding the monies within the recoupment period, the HMO usually offsets payment of other claims with the monies owed for overpayment. There would need to be a detailed written explanation of the overpayment claims recouped and claims not paid to balance the deficit on each account.

The monies from an overpayment may be backed out of a current EOB. Many times there will be no money paid on these claims. The explanation of benefits will, however, give a reference to the backed-out claim number as the reason for nonpayment of the current claim.

Agreement Correspondence Address

Contracts have specific addresses where correspondence should be sent regarding inquiries about the agreements, and these addresses may not be the same as the addresses for claims. Usually HMOs request certified mail and a return receipt for agreement correspondence.

Parties exchange changes in address in writing, usually by mail. Correspondence regarding patient care should be kept in the patient chart. Correspondence regarding claims may be kept in the billing department.

Subcap Capitation

If a provider receives subcap capitation from a medical group, so much per member per month, the contract has the details of the covered services.

If a provider is subcapitated with a medical group, the office gets its co-pay and capitation money and no actual dollars are paid for the claim. The provider submits the claim to the PMG, IPA, or PPG, and not to the HMO, to process the claim for payment or for entry as statistical data. If a physician says she does not receive enough capitation for the services she provides, the PMG, IPA, or PPG can refer to a history of what services were provided the patients. Some uncommon services may be negotiated at a flat rate and paid outside of the capitation.

Some offices do not send in claims for subcap providers, claiming they will not send in claims they are not paid for. Yet the physician receives payment for these claims in the capitation, and when the data is not reported, it hurts the patient and the provider. The payer may believe that the patient is healthier than he really is and that the provider is performing fewer services than it really is.

Subcap Providers' Claim Types

There are two types of claims: those that are for payment and those for encounter data. The latter is statistical data used to track the services the subcap provider furnishes to the patients covered under the contract. Claims sent into the payer for statistical data should have the correct dollar amounts stated, as would a claim for payment. Providers are no longer able to send in claims for zero dollars, as the cost for the services could not be tracked.

Medical Records

An outside provider may send certain medical records to the health plan only as needed for medical review for future services, determination of coverage for an ED (emergency department), an appeal of a service, or claim denial. Providers do not usually share medical records, unless there is a "need to know" and no conflict with HIPAA guidelines.

Providers usually maintain records according to the laws of the state in which they practice. See Figure 2-6 for various medical record responsibilities stated in a contract.

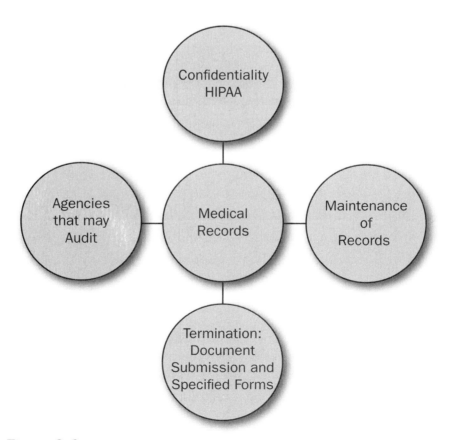

Figure 2-6 Medical records (Delmar/Cengage Learning)

Contracts typically list what agencies may audit the medical records. Some of these agencies may be

- The HMO
- The state's department of health and human services
- The state's department of managed care
- The U.S. Department of Health and Human Services

An HMO may write into the contract that upon termination of the agreement, copies of complete medical records must be given to it by a certain date or in a timely manner. The contract may even specify certain forms (for example, enrollment forms or patient information sheets, claims, and so on). Contract language is usually very plain and states that no unauthorized person shall obtain any information. Contracts always contain confidentiality of records clauses.

Confidentiality of Information

A contract may refer to HIPAA guidelines for information disclosure and its exchange. Usually contracts state that only information deemed medically necessary for treatment of a patient be exchanged, and they require written authorization from the patient in advance. The contract a provider signs with an HMO quotes specific guidelines from the office of the inspector general (OIG) or HIPAA; these guidelines are standard in the industry.

Contract Amendments

The HMO usually retains the right to change the contract to comply with changes in state or federal law, and regulations and requirements set forth by law. By signing the contract, the provider agrees to this as well.

If a contract has a waiver, it is usually defined as something specific between the two contracting parties and not a generalization for the industry. These may be carve-outs for specific services within the contract.

Governing Law

The agreement defines what laws the contract follows, such as state and county laws. These are typically jurisdictions in which a provider office is located. See Figure 2-7 for various types of laws affecting coding.

Compliance with Laws

The contract will expressly state the laws that govern the plan. Some of these may be

- State laws
- Laws of the United States of America
- Knox-Keene Health Care Services Act of 1975
- Laws of the U.S. Department of Health and Human Services

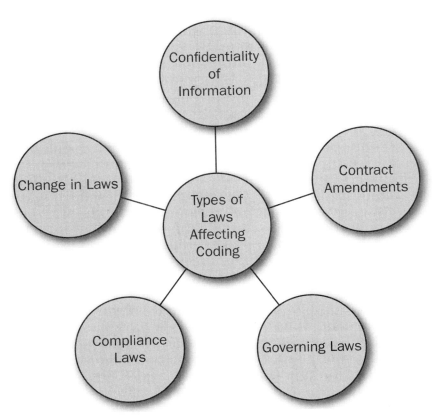

Figure 2-7 Types of laws affecting coding (Delmar/Cengage Learning)

Change in the Laws

At times during the course of an agreement between a contractor and provider, there may be changes in the law. A contract usually clarifies the handling of those changes between the two parties. Changes in the law may be due to changes in federal, state, or local rules and regulations, statutes, ordinances, guidelines, or interpretation. Usually one party notifies the other of the changes and both set the time as to when and how they are to be implemented. If the changes are not done, an agreement may terminate. Consequently, this is a very important part of the contract.

Quality of Service Expectations and Timeliness

The plan usually specifies service timeliness and quality expectations that include

- Response time to emergency referrals within 24 hours
- Routine referrals within two working days
- On-call availability for 24 hours, including evenings, weekends, and holidays
- Delivery of equipment to the patient to educate him in how to use said equipment and safety requirements

- Coordination with home care providers
- Any standards specific to the specialty

If a provider is in noncompliance due to quality-of-care issues, the contract may be terminated. Some offices have documentation issues and not quality-of-care issues. Remember, if a service is performed that is not documented, it is the same as if it never happened. See Figure 2-8 for expectations and general provisions found in most contracts.

Marketing Physicians' Services by the Plan

The plan usually reserves the right to use the physician's name, address, and specialty to market new patients. This also includes publishing the physician's information in provider booklets given to patients for choosing a PCP. Many patients have access to provider booklets on the Web.

Professional Review and Quality Assurance

These reviews evaluate the services furnished by the physician's office. If the services are not to the level of quality found in a professional review, the physician then agrees to remedial action to comply with a quality assurance program.

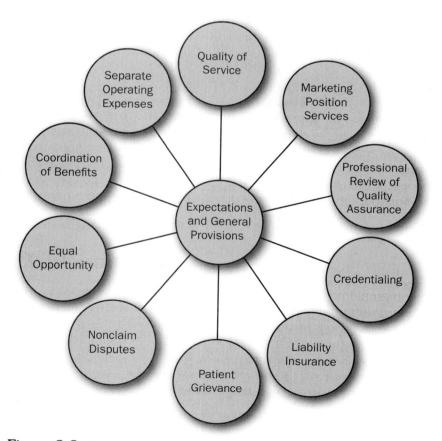

Figure 2-8 Expectations and general provisions found in most contracts (Delmar/Cengage Learning)

Credentialing Process of Physician and Staff

Physicians agree to keep their credentials and their staffs' credentials current as required by law. The HMO may require a physician to be board certified and may require completed forms to verify physician credentials according to its rules and regulations.

Liability Insurance

Plans may request physicians to carry certain amounts of liability and malpractice insurance by contract. Typically, the amounts are specific to specialty norms. If a provider's insurance lapses, usually contract termination is immediate.

Patient Grievance Process

Occasionally, a patient may file a grievance regarding a provider with an HMO. Usually HMOs have a grievance committee in place to investigate such complaints. Both patient and provider agree to arbitration. A patient agrees to arbitration as a requirement for participating in the plan, and a physician agrees to the terms of the findings as binding.

Nonclaim Disputes Resolution

nonclaim disputes These are disputes that are not about claims. Physicians and HMOs participate in mediation, and work together in a nonconfrontational or cooperative manner to resolve a nonclaim dispute.

Nonclaim disputes are physicians and HMOs participating in mediation, and working together in a nonconfrontational or cooperative manner to resolve disputes that are not about claims. Specific procedures describing how such resolutions happen are in the contract. For example, an informal discussion may take place first. If the situation is not resolved, then the parties advance to mediation. The American Arbitration Association (AAA) has mediation rules governing these situations. The fees for such arbitration are agreed upon in the contract; both parties may share them 50/50.

If arbitration fails and the case goes to court, the agreement specifies which party pays attorneys' fees, and expenses of the case in resolving the judgment.

Separate Operating Expenses

Often a plan specifies what a physician provides. This can include her own office, facilities, equipment, staff, and general items required to do business. These things are not a benefit of the plan unless negotiated specifically by the provider.

Coordination of Benefits

Coordination of benefits is how plan providers work with other insurance carriers. If another insurance company is primary, normally the contract states that insurance should be billed first.

Sometimes a patient predesignates that he wants to see his own physician in a worker's compensation case. A contract usually states that in such cases, worker's compensation pays the fees, not the HMO. A physician may agree to accept whatever the plan pays as payment in full.

The third-party beneficiary would be the patient, and the physician agrees to provide services to him as long as the agreement is in force.

Equal Opportunity

A contract usually incorporates equal employment opportunity (EEO) language that adheres to employment code developed by the United States secretary of labor. Such laws include coverage for or preclude discrimination against the following:

- Equal employment opportunity
- Employment and advancement of qualified people who are handicapped
- Disabled veterans
- Minorities and their business enterprises
- Integrated facilities

HMO Risk Services

HMO risk services are those services paid in full by the HMO. These are services for which the medical group or the provider would not have any financial risk when performed. See Figure 2-9.

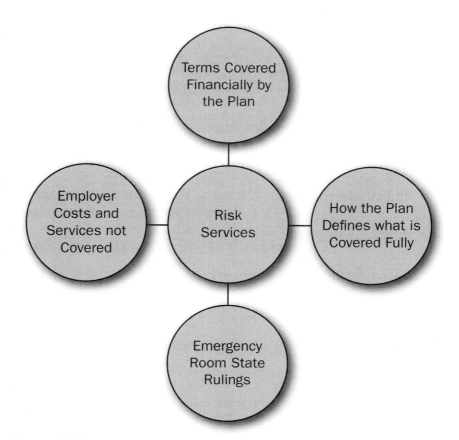

Figure 2-9 Risk services (Delmar/Cengage Learning)

Evidence of Coverage

The DOFR matrix specifies the various services covered. These are services listed under the patient **evidence of coverage** in the plan's published booklets. Evidence of coverage is a legal document that gives details about the plan. Usually this is a document given to the patient. It may describe the dates he is enrolled, first date enrolled, and/or services he is entitled to under the plan. Also, it would state any deductibles, co-pays, and coinsurances.

There are many different plans. One HMO offers more than 200 plans; it does this because many companies want contracts tailored to the needs of their employees. For example, if they have a younger population, then maternity services may be covered. Or, if there is an older population, they may omit maternity benefits and offer **durable medical equipment (DME)** instead. Insurance brokers may write contracts such as these.

Employer Cost for Health Care

Employers concerned about the cost of health insurance may split the premiums with their employees. The employer may choose a standard plan or a premium plan – one that offers more benefits. Regardless of when an employee signs up, he receives an evidence of coverage statement that explains what services are covered under his plan. The patient may want services performed that are not covered under the plan. If he elects to go ahead with a service, he would be responsible for paying the bill.

Emergency Departments

Emergency department physicians are unique. In order for a hospital to have a dedicated emergency department, it must have physicians available 24 hours a day, seven days a week. A commercial patient can be charged for after-hour, weekend, and holiday services. These codes cannot be billed for patients covered under Medicare or a Medicare HMO. Some commercial health plan insurers complain that these are unfair billing practices. If the physician is at the hospital already, why should the PPO or indemnity plan have to pay for additional hourly or holiday fees? This issue has been referred to the state's insurance commission and the Department of Managed Health Care in California, and the ruling is pending. This may also be an issue in other states.

Agreement Terms

A participating provider agreement usually has a beginning and ending date, and renews automatically if the agreement is successful. Some contracts are in place three years before renewal negotiations take place. A provider should review its agreement annually for compliance issues regardless of renewal dates. See Figure 2-10.

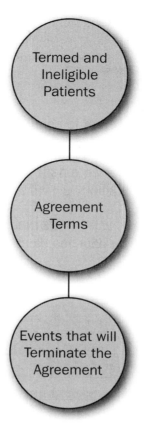

Figure 2-10 Agreement terms (Delmar/Cengage Learning)

Termination of an Agreement

An agreement may be terminated based on an event of some kind as specified in the contract. Some of those events may be as follows. A physician

- Loses her license in the state where she is practicing
- Fails to maintain adequate malpractice coverage
- Ceases to be recognized or licensed by an organization (that is, participating provider with CMS/Medicare)
- Fails to abide by quality assurance or the controls of utilization review
- Fails to correct any problems within a specific period
- Mutually agrees to termination

If the termination is not mutually agreed upon, there is usually a period of time, perhaps 90 days, that an HMO can notify its members of the termination and help patients choose another provider still participating in the plan.

Termed and Ineligible Patients

termed A patient who is no longer with the plan.

When a patient is **termed**, she is no longer covered under the insurance. Retrotermination happens when a patient changes plans or groups during the open enrollment period. For example, if the employer's open enrollment is in January and the patient chooses another insurance plan or medical group, the insurance carrier may not receive the completed information until 30 to 60 days later. The change may not be entered into the HMO's system until February or March, and the patient may be on the rolls as being with one group for that period. The patient would be retrotermed back to the effective date of the open enrollment.

If a physician is not certain a patient is with his group, or if there is no proof the patient is enrolled with the HMO, the PMG, IPA, or PPG, the physician can check for eligibility online or call the HMO's eligibility department. Also, if a patient has no proof of participating in the plan, (for example, no card or enrollment forms), the physician's group can ask the patient to pay in advance. When a coder or biller speaks to an HMO regarding patient eligibility, it is important to ask for and document the name of the HMO employee giving the information.

Case Study – How Will Dr. Obby Stop Losing Money on Patients Who Are Catastrophically Ill?

When Dr. Obby, a gynecologist, began negotiating her contract with the local in-area HMO, she read that the contract would include a set "per-month, per-patient" capitation payment wherein she would have to take care of all the patient's needs for that fee.

Also, Dr. Obby began to look at disease codes that were at a high cost for her to treat. She listed AIDS patients, certain types of high-risk cases, and so on. It would be unrealistic for her to never see patients who were this sick. Eventually, she would begin to lose money treating such patients. But how was she going to stop the loss?

The HMO explained that it could provide her stop-loss insurance for the contract. It would cost her 2 percent of her total capitation. Here's how it would work:

If the cost to treat any one patient exceeded $5,000, she would begin to be paid on a fee-for-service basis for that patient. The insurance would pay 85 percent of the bills accrued by that one patient after the initial $5,000. This sounded like a pretty good deal, but not many of her patients ran up a bill of $5,000 in one year. And, she would have to pay 2 percent of her yearly capitation to have the insurance contract.

From her biller, Dr. Obby requested a list of what procedures were performed each month for 12 months. She requested that the per-unit cost and total for each unit also be listed. The following shows an average of the 12 months.

CPT code	Units	Average payment per unit	Total
99211	5	$ 25.00	$ 125
99212	25	55.00	5,775
99213	76	80.00	6,080
99214	46	100.00	4,600
99215	3	200.00	600
All other CPTs for that month			**$3,395**

Figure 2-11 Case study 2-1 sample CPT survey for one month (Delmar/Cengage Learning)

(Continued)

The average Dr. Obby would expect to receive per month was $20,575 on a fee-for-service basis.

Then Dr. Obby looked at how much it would cost to care for patients, on a monthly basis, in a capitated setting with the catastrophic risk insurance included in the plan.

Enrollees in the plan	8,500
Capitation per month per patient	$2.50
Total per month capitation	$21,250.00
Minus the 2 percent insurance	−425.00
Total capitation per month	**$20,825**

Figure 2-12 Case study 2-2 Monthly capitation fees minus 2 percent insurance (Delmar/Cengage Learning)

In this example, Dr. Obby could afford signing up for capitation and paying for the catastrophic care insurance from the insurance company.

Summary

When a provider participates in an HMO, he may choose to negotiate his contract according to his needs, specialty, group, patient base, CPT codes, patient treatment options, carve-outs, risk pools, operating expenses, and so on. When negotiating a debt, the HMO will abide by the contract agreement. The contract will show the coder what coding system is used: CPT, ICD, HCPCS, RBRVS, Medicare fee schedules, carve-outs, services specifically not included in the contract, and so on. The biller will understand if the HMO expects encounter claims, capitation, risk pool monies, subcap provider claims, and so on.

Some billers/coders do not have access to the contracts signed by the provider, nor do they understand the provider may have a provision unique in his contract which will affect reimbursement or statistical data kept by the HMO. Sometimes responsibilities for payment are divided between the HMO, IPA, PMG, and PPG. If this is not understood by the biller, monies can go uncollected or partially collected as a result of not seeking reimbursement from the correct payer.

This chapter was written to help the biller/coder understand how a contract can play a vital role in the process of coding and reimbursement.

Web Sites

Additional information about the Knox-Keene Act is available at its official Web site. The address is http://www.harp.org/kk.htm.

Review

Fill in the Blank

1. In _____, an HMO pays a physician or provider a set _____ per month, per patient (other terms for the patient may be *enrollee*, *participant*, or *insured*) whether a patient is seen or not.

2. Since an HMO is _____, it distributes a list of patients participating for the monthly capitation to the physicians' group.

3. A _____ in the provider contract can be based on CPT codes, ICD-9-CM, HCPCS codes, or a combination of code types as they relate to payment schedules, such as MFS, _____, RBRVS, or a percentage of the bill.

4. A **DOFR**, _____ matrix, lists and defines services. A DOFR is part of the contract negotiated between a _____, an independent practice association (IPA), a participating medical group (PMG), or a primary physicians group (PPG). The DOFR lists the _____ and the plan benefits for which the HMO and its providers are _____ responsible.

5. **Encounter** _____ are claims used for accounting and statistical data only.

6. **Balance** _____ is charging the patient the balance of what might normally be written off on an insurance claim.

7. A _____ is a procedure that is not included in the capitation but negotiated _____ on an individual contract basis between the HMO and a provider.

8. A _____ is a fixed amount of the capitation monies set aside by the HMO until the end of the year. The PMG, IPA, or PPG physician shares the risk or cost of _____ the patient.

9. _____ responsibilities usually state that HMO patients receive the same treatment and services as other patients not _____ by the HMO, and that treatment for these patients also follows the same rules, regulations, and standards set forth by law.

10. A _____ is a service the HMO states as sufficient treatment for a disease or injury. This information is in the list of covered services supplied by the HMO.

11. The HMO _____ payment to the PMG, IPA, or PPG for the participating members should be made according to the _____ in the contract.

Review Questions

1. In capitation, how does the physician/provider get paid, and how do risk pool funds figure into the payment? _____

_____

2. What are encounter data claims? _____

_____

3. Name examples of service that may be considered in a carve-out.

_____

_____

4. When referring a patient to a specialist, name three pieces of information the front office should have for referral purposes on a ready list. _____

_____

5. Why is continuity of care important to the patient? What might the physician agree to do upon termination of a contractual agreement?

_____

_____

6. Name three reasons why a payer may wish to recoup overpayments.

_____

_____

7. What are the two claim types for subcap providers? _____

_____

8. An HMO contract will state the laws that govern the plan. Please write three examples. _____

_____

_____

_____

9. What does a provider/physician agree to in the patient grievance process? _____

_____

_____

10. When the patient predesignates his own physician in a worker's comp case, and the physician and patient belong to the HMO, how is this handled in coordination of benefits? _____

_____

_____

11. Name three reasons why an agreement may be terminated.

_____

_____

_____

Critical Thinking Exercise—HMO Physician Contract Negotiations

Some HMOs post their physician contract negotiations on the Web. In performing this exercise, you will see that many of the provider contracts are specific to the group the provider participates in as well as specific to the services written into and out of these contracts. Sometimes the negotiations can be controversial, finding their way into Web sites, newspaper articles, and medical journals.

This exercise will help the reader understand what is considered normal, or boilerplate, and what the negotiators consider abnormal, or unique, in their consideration for contract approval.

Materials Needed

2 different-colored highlighters
1 blue pen
2 HMO contracts found on the Web

Directions

1. Use your Web browser and search engine to type in phrases such as:
   - HMO physician provider negotiations
   - Medical HMO contract negotiations
   - HMO contracts
   - Union HMO contract negotiations
   - Municipality HMO contract negotiations

2. Print the contracts/negotiation

3. Use one color highlighter for generalized information; use the other for specified information, that is, agreed-upon and disagreed-upon terms of the contracts. Highlight answers to the following questions, if the information is stated in the contract:
   - Are specific procedures not covered in the new contract?
   - Does this contract apply to the group or the specialty?
   - Is a CPT-coded fee schedule attached?
   - Are basic contract responsibilities different or the same as those described in this text?

4. Discuss the differences and similarities in the contracts with your professor.

Professional Corner – Finding Carve-outs

What has your physician/group negotiated in carve-outs? Carve-outs are services the physician/group will be paid on a fee-for-service basis from the HMO even though a capitated contract is in effect.

- *Is there a list of carve-outs per HMO contract?*
- *Are the carve-outs listed per CPT code?*
- *Are the carve-outs for each signed contract standard, or do they vary from contract to contract?*
- *Are the carve-outs something your physician performs on a daily/weekly/ monthly basis?*

If you have access, from the billing office request a list of services from each HMO and compare what services are carve-outs. You may notice some HMO-capitated contracts are more lucrative than others regarding the categories of carve-outs negotiated/stated in the contracts. These services can be profitable if they are services performed on a routine basis.

Some physicians belonging to a group or IPA have these services negotiated for them. Many feel this is a much safer option when they are involved in capitation contracts.

References

PayScale. (Feb 9, 2009). Salary Survey Report for People with Jobs as a Physician/Doctor. Seattle, WA: PayScale, Inc.

The State of Health Care Quality 2007, National Committee for Quality Assurance, Washington D.C., National Committee for Quality Assurance.

Certa, Tracy. (2001). Incentive Effects on HMO Contracts. Cambridge, MA: National Bureau of Economic Research.

HMO Regulatory Requirements, (2007). Trenton, NJ: State of New Jersey, Department of Banking and Insurance.

Texas Department of Insurance, Subchapter J. (2008). "Physician and Provider Contract and Arrangements." (20 TAC, 11.901). Austin, TX: Texas Department of Insurance.

Texas Health and Human Services Commission, CHIP Health Insurance Services (HMO), Request for Proposal, Austin, TX, Draft 11/19/99.

Drug, Medi-Cal Direct Contract Boilerplate, Direct Provider Contract, 2006-2007. Sacramento, CA: Medi-Cal.

Preferred Provider Organizations

Chapter Objectives

Upon completion of the chapter, you should be able to

- Recognize what a preferred provider organization (PPO) is
- Understand a patient's choice of staying in network
- Classify a patient's choice of self-referral within network
- Understand a patient's choice of going out of network
- Distinguish how a PPO differs from an HMO
- Identify distinct provisions in the PPO contract
- Identify what claims processing policies are
- Understand audited claims payment
- Understand provider termination of the PPO contract
- Understand utilization review through postpayment claims

Key Terms

clean claim	in network	preferred provider	utilization review
deductible	out-of-pocket maximum	self-refer	

Introduction to Preferred Provider Organizations

This chapter introduces PPO contracts and identifies how they work through the patient's choice. We will explore what happens when a patient chooses to go out of network or to self-refer to a physician, how deductibles are handled, what service areas are, a patient's right to treatment, what happens in utilization review, payment guidelines, and various claims processing scenarios. PPOs can have a hybrid of features, from deductibles to balance billing, fee schedules and payment guidelines. This chapter explores those subjects and more.

PPOs give the patient the choice of staying **in network**, self-referring to a contracted specialist, or going out of network completely. In all three cases, the patient would receive services ordered by the provider. How the claim is paid changes depending upon where the provider sits in the three choices given the patient. In-network providers who are within the network of approved physicians and/or hospitals to provide medical services to a patient who is assigned to the PMG/IPA/PPG (Physician's Medical Group/Independent Practice Association/Preferred Provider Group) are contracted with the health plan.

Staying In-Network

Some PPOs require the patient to choose a primary care physician (PCP). Doing so will help navigate the patient through the network to receive services quickly and more efficiently. Not all PPOs require this of their patients.

When the patient visits the primary care physician, she is charged a co-pay and the provider, in turn, bills the PPO directly. The provider is usually contracted with the PPO at preferred rates. The patient is expected to pay the co-pay at the time of service. The patient receives services, and if a specialist is needed, the patient is referred through the PCP. The patient pays a co-pay to the specialist for her services as well.

Self-Referring Within Network

In a **preferred provider** organization, the patient has the right to **self-refer**. This means the patient does not need the PCP's permission to see a specialist, and a referral from the PCP is not required. To self-refer within the plan, the PPO provides a catalog or list of physicians by specialty. The PPO has contracts with these specialty providers to furnish services for a co-payment. The PPO entices the patient to stay in-network by promising a richer benefit and more services covered for the co-pay than would be available outside the network. The PPO wants the patient to self-refer to the contracted specialists to control costs and manage the plan more effectively. Even though the patient has self-referred, the contracted physicians have participating provider agreements that may suggest cost-effective, statistically viable procedures that the physicians use for treating certain diseases in the specialty. The contracted specialist works under the rules of the plan and cost containment is reached.

in network Providers who are within the network of approved physicians and/or hospitals to provide medical services to a patient who is assigned to the Physician's Medical Group, Independant Practice Association, Preferred Physician's Group and contracted with the health plan.

preferred provider A preferred provider contracts with an insurer to provide its services of expertise for an agreed-upon payment type (percentage, capitation, flat fees, fee schedule, and so on). A preferred provider can be a physician, group, facility, or practitioners.

self-refer A patient self-referring out of network means the patient sees a provider that is not a participating provider and does not have an agreement with the insurance carrier for a specified rate.

In this way, the PPO knows what to expect and effectively manages the plan.

Going Out-of-Network

The patient can self-refer completely out of network. This means the patient sees a physician who is in no way affiliated through a contracted participating provider situation. In these cases, the patient pays a percentage of what is billed. Here are two scenarios of how this can be handled by the provider's office.

Under the first scenario, the patient manages the billing process without involving the provider's billing office.

- Usually the patient is required to pay the out-of-network provider the full amount of the bill at the time of service.

- The patient is responsible for sending the bill to the insurance plan.

- The patient is reimbursed by the plan at out-of-network rates.

Under the second scenario, the provider's office handles the billing.

- The physician's office, as a courtesy, may bill the patient's insurance, with the patient assigning benefits to the physician in box 13 of the CMS-1500 form.

- The physician's office bills the patient the difference after receiving payment from the PPO.

- The patient will receive an explanation of benefits explaining his payment responsibility.

In these cases, the rates are not contracted; therefore, the patient may be paying the full fee of the physician, which can be considerably higher than what the patient would pay if he had stayed in the network. Many times, seeing an out-of-network provider requires that the patient pay a deductible as well. In these cases, the patient may pay 50 percent more for the service than he would pay if he stayed in the network. A **deductible** is a set amount the patient must pay before his insurance pays anything for the calendar year. Usually, the full amount of the deductible needs to be met once a year, during the calendar year. Most deductibles are met within the first three months of the calendar year.

A physician practicing in an affluent area will find patients more able and willing to see physicians who are not contracted with their plan. Usually, there is a reason the patient wants to go out-of-network, maybe for newer or unique procedures or because of the reputation of a physician.

Out-of-Network Deductibles

The deductibles can vary based on a maximum per year, either per individual or per family. Deductibles are usually paid up front for office visits or after other services. Some plans use deductibles to entice the patient to stay in network. Usually there is an **out-of-pocket maximum** for inpatient hospital stays or outpatient surgeries. This is a maximum dollar amount payable by the member based on the health plan contract. The amount can vary from one plan to another.

deductible A set amount the patient must pay before her insurance pays anything for the calendar year. Usually, the full amount of the deductible needs to be met once a year, at the beginning of the calendar year.

out-of-pocket maximum Maximum dollar amount payable by the member based on the health plan contract. This can vary from one plan to another.

Distinct Provisions to Look for in a PPO Contract

The following provisions may or may not be in the physician's participating provider contract. These affect the administration of the plan. Figure 3-1 shows general contract provisions.

Service Areas

If the services a patient needs are not provided or not available in a service area, the patient may need to see a provider not contracted with the plan. For such cases, most states have provisions that explain the provider will be paid up to the level of reimbursement of a participating provider in that area. But these provisions may not apply if a patient specifically goes out of area for his own convenience when the service area does provide competent licensed practitioners for the patient.

Patient Billed on Discounted Fees

Many plans have the provider agree to be compensated at rates that are less than the provider's regular fees. The patient will not be billed any more than his portion of the discounted fee. In other words, the patient will not be billed for the full regular fee or balance billed for the difference between the regular fee and the contracted rate.

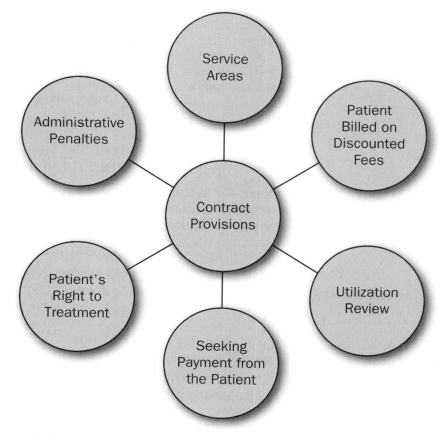

Figure 3-1 General contract provisions

Administrative Penalties

In many states, if the payer does not pay charges in a timely manner, there can be a penalty imposed against the payer. Such a penalty can take the form of a percentage of the claim. For example

> **EXAMPLE:** 4 percent of the payment amount of the claim; some commercial HMOs pay 10 percent per annum. Most PPO contracts quote a formula based on a per-annum rate.

A maximum dollar amount per day can limit the penalty per claim. For example

> **EXAMPLE:** Penalty not to exceed $XX per day if the claim is unpaid past the contracted time and/or per day the claim remains unpaid.

Each state's laws may vary; the contract should coincide with the laws in the state the provider practices in. The contract should state the penalty and any percentage per annum.

Patient's Right to Treatment

Many states have provisions in favor of the patient, stating that if the provider orders care and it is covered under the plan, the patient has the right to the treatment. In other words, the plan cannot deny the treatment if the physician ordered the treatment and it is a covered benefit. This is usually written into insurance code provisions by the state in which the physician practices.

Sometimes PPO utilization management teams disagree with a physician's diagnosis and claim or decide treatment is medically unnecessary. Nonetheless, the physician's opinion usually prevails, and the patient may have the treatment if the documentation, usually from the chart, justifies the physician's request for treatment. This information is available in the insurance code in the state in which a physician practices. Clear documentation by the physician is crucial when treatment is challenged by utilization review.

Seeking Payment from the Patient

Many contracts and state laws prohibit the physician from seeking payment from a patient who would not owe payment while participating in the plan. In other words, if the physician is not happy with his reimbursement from the payer and wants to bill the patient the difference between what the plan paid and what the bill was, he could not do this by law. The provider would be in violation of his contract, and the state law would protect the patient under the preferred provider insurance code of the state.

Utilization Review

utilization review Committee of doctors and nurses that reviews requests for medical necessity (for example, for elective surgery procedures).

Utilization Review, or UR, screens patient diagnosis and procedures to assure the patient receives services medically necessary at the time of the visit. Usually services are reviewed through postpayment claims.

The claims can be reviewed for some or all of the following reasons:

- Services billed are not a covered benefit to the patient
- Provider's practice patterns

- Unusual patterns of utilization
- Unusual charges or payments
- Number of services performed
- Sites where services performed
- Cost effectiveness and quality of health care
- Long-term tracking of services rendered by a provider
- Payments consistent with medical policies
- Underutilization, incorrect utilization, and overutilization
- Suspected fraud
- Inconsistent following of provider contract

Some URs verify their claims through on-site record reviews, interviewing patients, postpayment utilization review specialists, review by professional consultants, and provider contact.

UR will contact the provider for any disputes, needed changes in reporting practices, and refunds of overpayments. These are usually discussed and resolved at the time of audit or investigation.

If utilization review, working with the provider, cannot resolve a dispute, most have a medical review committee to hear and consider the matter. Usually the provider has the right to be present at all hearings or represented by legal counsel.

Most medical review committees reserve the right to share information or refer the matter to the following entities:

- State professional societies
- Local professional societies
- Law enforcement
- State professional license committee

Most provider contracts define the role of utilization review and their dispute resolution process. Claims are used as a checkpoint for statistical data, decision for audit, refund request, and provider performance. Figure 3-2 shows contract provisions regarding claims.

Payment Guidelines and Fee Schedules

The provider has a right to ask the payer for payment guidelines, coding guidelines, fee schedules and code procedures used in payment, and any formulas that make up the payment equation (for example, RBRVS [Resource Based Relative Value Scale], Medicare fees, UCR [Usual Customary and Reasonable], geographic limits, and so on). These may vary per plan. Many offices keep binders of payment schedules separated by plan.

Coding Guidelines

If there are changes in the coding guidelines, the payer is not allowed to retroactively apply the coding changes to a time before the provision became law and/or a regulation. The payer needs to notify the provider

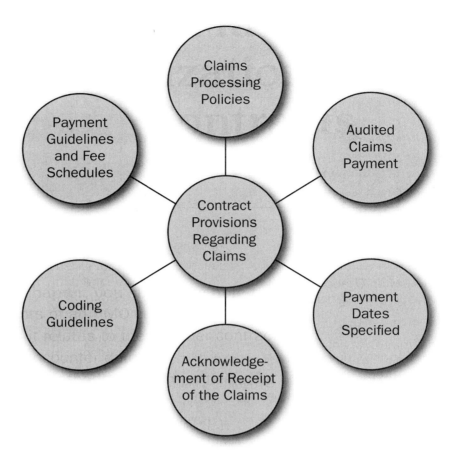

Figure 3-2 Contract provisions regarding claims

of any applicable changes and dates. Additionally, the PPO needs to notify the provider in writing of any changes in its determination of payable codes or code sets and the effective dates of change. Provider offices should keep binders with these documents for reference and appeal support.

Changes may include

- Codes deleted from one calendar year to the next
- Codes accepted into the plan
- Language/description/definition of a code changed
- Some specialties allowed by law to perform and get paid for extra services needed in the care of the patient (provided the service is in the scope of the certification/licensure or the person certified is an employee of the provider, for example a podiatrist performing X-rays)

Many billing and coding software systems accommodate changes. Updates also can be downloaded from the Internet or obtained from consulting firms or from the software companies themselves. These processes are critical to those in the office needing to implement change but who are not versed in all update changes.

Acknowledgement of Receipt of the Claim

Some state laws require a PPO acknowledge receipt of claims within a certain time period. Yet, other states may require an insurance carrier/PPO plan administrator to acknowledge claims electronically and do not require acknowledgement of claims received in writing or vice versa. The following shows how acknowledgement times differ depending on if the claim is paper or electronic.

> **EXAMPLE:** Time-frame requirements may differ for electronic claims and paper claims.

- Electronic receipt – 5 working days
- Paper receipt – 15 working days

Payment Dates Specified in the Plan Contract

Some contracts state a PPO must pay a provider no later than 30 to 45 working days from receipt of a **clean claim**, a claim that has all the necessary information needed by the payer for payment consideration. Each state has laws governing time lines. Note that if the contract stipulates working days, then holidays and weekends do not figure into the time frame.

The PPO reimburses the provider for the contracted amount and specifies on an explanation of benefits, or EOB, why any remainder is being denied. Some of the reasons may be

- A procedure or item may not be billable
- A contract adjustment
- The patient's co-pay is deducted

The EOB accompanies the check for payment in the mail, or the information can be sent electronically to the provider and the payment directly to the provider's bank account. Unlike patients in HMOs, most patients participating in a PPO receive EOBs as well.

The PPO will consider payment of the procedures on a line-item basis. The PPO may need to pay a portion of the claim that is not in dispute and notify the provider why it has not paid other line items of the claim. Disputed claims may also have time limits for review and reimbursement. Some contracts stipulate that if disputed amounts are payable, the PPO must pay interest on the amount not paid. Interest percentages are sometimes regulated by a state agency.

> **clean claim** A claim that has all the information needed to pay it.

Audited Claim Payment

If a payer intends to audit a claim, the payer will usually have to pay the claims at a set percentage of contracted rates and within a specified number of days. This can be a provision of the contract or may be written into insurance law from the state in which the physician practices. The times and percentage of claim paid varies from state to state. For example a contract could state

> **EXAMPLE:** 60 percent to 80 percent of contracted rate within 40 days of receipt of the claim

If after an audit additional monies are owed the provider or there is a need to refund the payer monies, there is a time frame for that, too. In most states, this is 30 days. Interest may also be due if the balance is not paid within the contractual or state-required time frame.

Claims Processing Policies

The insurer through the contract must supply copies of policies for processing a claim.

These are utilization review policies and claims processing procedures of how the contract will be administered. These policies specify what will need to be included in the data submitted and the format in which claims can be submitted. The insurer has elements in the contract that state its ability to change the data needed on claims and also that state how soon such changes will need to take place. When the changes are announced, an implementation date should be given or the insurer should specify that implementation begins a set number of days after the notice or announcement. The contract may also require any changes to have a 30- to 60-day notification period. The change requested must be in writing, abide by any waiting period, and usually is not retroactive. For example

> **EXAMPLE:** The following changes will take place January 1, 2009.
> All changes will take place 60 days after notification of said change.

Of course all such notifications from the payer should be timely. If not, the provider will need to notify the payer proof of when the notification was sent and the time needed to implement the changes. Figure 3-1 is a demonstration of general contract provisions.

Provider Termination of the Contract

In every contract, there is a provision for its termination. If the provider wishes to terminate the contract, it needs to notify the PPO in writing and receive an acknowledgement from the PPO in return.

There is usually a period between notification and actual termination of the contract when both the provider and the PPO need to document and complete certain administrative procedures. Basic responsibilities of the provider include:

- Notify patients a physician/provider will not be participating in the plan; specify termination date
- Assist patients in finding new physicians/providers
- Provide copies of medical records
- Perform final bill processing

Notifying Patients of Provider Nonparticipation

What is interesting about a PPO is the patient still has the option to continue to see the physician even if the physician does not participate in the plan. Once the physician is no longer participating, however, he is not an in-network provider and the patient will be paying for physician services outside of the network. If the patient does not understand this, he may

Dear Mrs. Smith:

I am writing to inform you that ABC Medical Care will, within 30 days, discontinue being a participating provider of XYZ Plan. We encourage you to seek a new participating provider in your plan within the next 30 days.

Please contact your plan for a list of participating providers. If after the above-mentioned time period, you do not choose a participating provider physician, your plan may choose one for you.

Enclosed is a medical record release authorization form. We will be happy to release your medical records to the physician/group of your choice listed on the authorization.

If you should have any questions, please call our offices at 555-555-5555.

Sincerely,
Suzie Jones
Office Manager

Figure 3-3 Patient notification of provider termination with the plan

become upset and blame the physician's billing office for the higher cost of treatment, may see the physician less often than needed for his illness, or because of the higher cost may fall behind in his payments to the practice.

The patient needs to understand, if he opts to continue treatment from the physician, the cost will change from that point forward. The cost has nothing to do with the physician, the patient's illness, or the provider billing department.

Some contracts state who will notify the patient of the termination, the provider or the PPO; how the patient will be notified, by letter, phone, and so on; and how soon the patient will be notified, within the 60 days between notification and complete termination. The PPO will explain its process and provider responsibilities in the process if this is requested. Figure 3-3 shows a basic letter stating the termination process and steps to be taken in the process.

Patient Finding a New Physician

A patient cannot be abandoned. Some patients, especially seniors, misunderstand how the system works and may think that if the physician leaves the PPO, they do, too.

PPOs encourage patients to choose other contracted physicians, so patients maintain established relationships with the PPO. Some PPOs include contact information for the customer service department, or may list other physicians in the patient's geographic area who also participate in the plan. If the provider's office decides to send letters to PPO patients, these are kept with patients' charts as proof of a physician's efforts not to abandon the patients. Some plans have one physician transfer all their patients to another physician automatically until the patients can choose other physicians for themselves.

Some providers may wish to terminate a patient relationship while continuing to participate in the plan. Figure 3-4 shows reasons a provider may decide to terminate a patient. Check with the participating provider contract or the PPO for the physician responsibilities in discontinuing care of a patient.

Reasons a physician may wish to terminate a patient:

- Not taking care of himself/not following medical advice
- Nonpayment of medical bills
- Threatening behavior
- No-show appointments
- Refusing to consent to needed medical surgery
- Inappropriate advances made to the physician or staff
- Forged medical documentation/prescription slips

Figure 3-4 Reasons a provider may wish to terminate a patient

Final Claims Processing

When a provider's office discontinues an agreement with a PPO, the billing office should take inventory of outstanding visits; accounts receivable; and aging receivables at 30-, 60-, and 90-day intervals. The billing office may need to interface with the discontinued PPO plan regarding payment of claims long after the contract has been terminated.

Case Studies – In and Out of Network

In these cases, the patient, the payer, and the codes remain the same. With a PPO, the patient can choose a physician in or out of network. Let us look at the two potential outcomes of payment for the same claim.

A 42-year-old female presents with fibroids and menorrhagia. A total abdominal hysterectomy is recommended. The patient is upset because the only physicians in network are males and she is not comfortable with male physicians, nor does she feel the physicians will have the same compassion or understanding a female physician would.

21. DIAGNOSIS OR NATURE OF ILLNESS OR INJURY (Relate Items 1, 2, 3 or 4 to Item 24E by Line)

1. 2189   3. ___ . ___

2. 6262   4. ___ . ___

22. MEDICAID RESUBMISSION CODE   ORIGINAL REF. NO.

23. PRIOR AUTHORIZATION NUMBER

	24. A. DATE(S) OF SERVICE From MM DD YY	To MM DD YY	B. PLACE OF SERVICE	C. EMG	D. PROCEDURES, SERVICES, OR SUPPLIES (Explain Unusual Circumstances) CPT/HCPCS	MODIFIER	E. DIAGNOSIS POINTER	F. $ CHARGES	G. DAYS OR UNITS	H. EPSDT Family Plan	I. ID. QUAL.	J. RENDERING PROVIDER ID. #
1	05 05 08		21		58150			3200 00	1		NPI	
2											NPI	
3											NPI	
4											NPI	
5											NPI	
6											NPI	

PHYSICIAN OR SUPPLIER INFORMATION

Figure 3-5 Case 3-1 and 3-2 claim form

The patient looks at the cost of going out of network and how much money will be saved by staying in network. The surgeon's fee is $3,200. The following two examples show the difference between staying in and going out of network.

The Outcome of In Network

The in-network physician's contracted rate is $1,800; this includes a $1,400 discount considered a PPO adjustment.

The PPO will pay 80 percent of its contracted rate. In network the patient will have no deductible and a 20 percent coinsurance fee to the surgeon of $360. With both paying their portions, the physician will receive $1,800, his contracted rate, and will need to adjust or write off the difference.

Fee	$3,200	
Contracted Rate	$1,800	
PPO Adjustment	$1,400	written off
Insurance Paid	$1,440	80 percent of contracted rate
Patient Paid	$ 360	20 percent of contracted rate

Remittance Advice

Claim # _____

Processed Voucher # _____

Vendor # _____

Name	ABC-PPO	MEMBER #		ACCOUNT #
Date of service	CPT code	Description		Billed
05/05/2008	58150	Total abdominal hysterectomy		$3200.00
		Insurance payment		$1442.00
		Negotiated adjustment		$640.00

Billed:	Approved:	Patient responsibility:
$3200.00	$2560.00	$1118.00

Figure 3-6 Case 3–1 in-network explanation of benefits

The Outcome of Out-of-Network

Many times, when the patient decides to go out of network, a deductible applies in addition to coinsurance. In this case, the female physician will give a 20 percent discount. The payer negotiated a 20 percent discount on behalf of the patient.

(Continued)

Fee	$3,200	
Discount 20 percent	$640	
Negotiated Rate	$2,560	
Deductible	$500	Patient pays
Balance Considered	$2,060	Patient pays 30 percent coinsurance; insurance pays 70 percent
Insurance Paid	$1,442	70 percent of balance
Patient Paid	$618	30 percent, coinsurance of $2,060

Remittance Advice

Claim # _____

Processed Voucher # _____

Vendor # _____

Name	ABC-PPO	MEMBER #	ACCOUNT #
Date of service	CPT code	Description	Billed
05/05/2008	58150	Total abdominal hysterectomy	$3200.00
		Insurance payment	$1442.00
		Negotiated adjustment	$640.00

Billed:	Approved:	Patient responsibility:
$3200.00	$2560.00	$1118.00

Figure 3-7 Case 3-2 out-of-network explanation of benefits

It is a good idea to give priority to the last visits billed on the contract, so that if a patient decides to stay, there is little confusion about collecting payment, changes in rates, and so on. Claims also need to be submitted within the contractual time lines, as do appeals and any other items of business between the provider's office and the PPO.

Summary

In PPO contracts, patients may choose from three ways to receive services: in-network physician referral, in-network self-referral, and out of network. Although the providers of service may have the patients receive services differently, there are commonalities that relate to payment, such as service areas, reduced fees, payment schedules, coding guidelines, claims acknowledgement, and payment dates. If a PPO claim is audited, timely payment practice must be adhered to or interest may be due on the balance not paid the provider.

Many states have provisions for the patient's right to treatment. Additionally, they prohibit physicians from suggesting that a patient have more treatment than what his plan requires. Also, providers have administrative procedures that must be completed when a contract is terminated; most of these deal with helping the patient find a participating provider in the plan.

Utilization review committees screen postpayment claims for medical necessity. Claims can be reviewed on a routine basis or for specific inconsistencies noticed in the evaluation process. The provider contract will state the role of UR, how it will report inconsistencies, and the process of resolving disputes.

Web Sites

The American Medical Association's Web site (www.ama-assn.org) is worth checking out when it comes to preferred provider organizations. Type in a search for PPOs, or preferred provider organizations. There is a wealth of knowledge and articles that link to similar subject matter.

Review

Fill in the Blank

1. What three network choices do patients have when they participate in a PPO? _____, _____, _____.

2. Claims processing policies need to include _____ and the _____ in which claims can be submitted.

3. Claims processing policy changes must be in _____ and abide by any _____ _____.

4. When a payer does not pay charges in a timely manner, there can be a _____ imposed against the payer.

5. For administrative penalties regarding payment, the contract should follow the code of the _____ the provider practices in.

6. The patient has a right to treatment if the _____ orders the treatment and the treatment is covered under the _____.

7. When PPO utilization management disagrees with the physician's opinion, the patient may have the treatment if the _____ justifies the physician's request for _____.

8. If a participating provider is not happy with its reimbursement from the payer and bills the patient the difference, the provider is in violation of its _____, and _____ _____ would protect the patient under PPO insurance code.

9. A provider wanting to terminate its PPO contract must notify the PPO in _____.

10. In a PPO contract, the patient still has the option to _____ to see the physician, even if the physician does not _____ in the plan.

11. Some providers may wish to terminate a patient relationship while continuing to _____ in the plan.

12. When a provider's office discontinues an agreement with the PPO, the billing office should take inventory of _____ _____; _____ _____; and _____ receivables at 30-, 60-, and 90-day intervals.

Review Questions

1. When a patient chooses to stay in network, what is the provider contracted to do? _____

2. If a patient decides to self-refer, why does the preferred provider want the patient to stay within the network? _____

3. Explain the commonalities between a contracted and noncontracted provider as they relate to a PPO. _____

4. If a patient self-refers out of network, what are two scenarios of how the provider's office may handle the billing? _____

5. How may a PPO use a financial argument to encourage a patient to stay in network? _____

6. How may a patient go out of her service area to see a noncontracted provider and the service still be eligible for payment? _____

7. What would a patient not be billed for if he chooses a participating provider who agrees to discounted rates? _____

8. What kinds of changes in coding guidelines need to be given in writing to the provider along with effective dates? _____

9. What are three reasons stated in an explanation of benefits of why a PPO may not pay a portion of a claim? _____

10. If a payer intends to audit a claim, what are two provisions to consider in paying this claim? _____

Critical Thinking Exercise

Many employers, unions, and municipalities post their preferred provider contracts on the Internet.

For this lesson find two examples on the Internet. Compare and highlight what is the same or similar about both contracts regarding payment (for example, both may have a defined service area mentioned).

Materials Needed

2 different-colored highlighters
1 blue pen
2 PPO contracts found on the Web

Directions

1. Use your Web browser or search engine to type in items such as
   - Preferred provider contract
   - Medical PPO contract
   - Participating provider contracts PPO
   - Union PPO contract
   - Municipality PPO contract

2. Print the contracts.

3. Use one color highlighter for generalized information; use the other for specified information (that is, dates, lists, schedules, and so on).

   Highlight the following information, if found in the contract:
   - Service areas
   - Discounted fees
   - Payment schedules
   - Coding guidelines
   - Acknowledgement of receipt of claim
   - Payment dates
   - Audited claim payment
   - Administrative penalties
   - Patient's right to treatment

4. Discuss the differences and similarities in the contracts with your professor.

Professional Corner

For this segment, biller and coders were asked if they were aware of which payers paid more for certain individual codes and which did not. Those who answered "yes" provided an explanation of how they came to this conclusion. Here are some of the answers.

In some cases, a payer would contract for a higher percentage of reimbursement for a procedure, yet in the end, a higher percentage would be written off or absorbed. The average may be as much as 35 percent. While other payers may begin at a lower rate and negotiate a 10 percent to 20 percent discount or write-off, the difference in reimbursement may be similar.

Another important factor was which contracts expected the provider to accept assignment and which, on average, expected the patient to pay coinsurance. Some professionals felt this was a huge feature of the contracts that affected their bottom lines. And while on the surface some codes were billed at a higher dollar amount, the ability to recoup a higher percentage was not there. Others felt volume performance, codes, preauthorization, or timely reimbursement was just as important as the initial contracted percentage or fee schedule.

Participating in a good plan that is profitable is every provider's goal. Many physicians belong to a group of providers who negotiate their participating provider contracts on their behalf. Some specialties are forced to join large groups in order to negotiate their contracts because some payers will not sign with an individual provider. Other providers negotiate their own agreements and are still able to make a profit.

Coders and billers are aware of the types of procedures the providers perform and the illnesses associated with those procedures. Some felt the providers had to see a higher volume of patients to make the same profit they would make if outside the plan.

What do the codes in your office tell you?

References

Welter, Terri L. (2004). Maximizing Managed Care Contract Performance. Arlington, VA: ECG Management Consultants.

State of New York. (n.d.) Provider Contract Guidelines for MCO and IPAs, Requirements to obtain contract approval. Retrieved 2007 from http://www.health.state.ny.us/health_care/managed_care/hmoipa/guidelines.htm.

American Colleges of Foot Surgeons. (2008). The Lowdown on Silent PPOs. Chicago, IL: ACFAS.

Self-Funded Preferred Provider Organization, City of San Antonio, Human Resources Department, RFP. (January, 2007). San Antonio, TX: United Healthcare

Hanon, Catherine I. (January, 2008). Paper presented at the 2008 State Legislative Strategy Conference. Managed Care Reform. New York, NY: AMA.

Fallon Community Health Plans. (2008). Physician and Provider FAQ. Worcester, MA: Fallon Community Health Plan.

BCBSGa Rico Contract Addendum, Physician Contract Templates, Wellpoint Physician Settlement Agreement (7/11/2005).

Fee Schedules

Chapter Objectives

Upon completion of this chapter, you should be able to

- Identify types of fee schedules
- Recognize fee schedule negotiation
- Know about using fee schedules
- Identify services not covered in a fee schedule
- Interpret fee schedules for capitated providers reporting statistical claims
- Understand when a referral becomes an issue
- Identify procedures eventually allowed into the plan
- Use multiple fee schedules
- Compare reciprocity rates
- Understand investigational rates

Key Terms

| beneficiaries | contracted rate | fee schedules | Medicare fee schedule |

Introduction to Fee Schedules

In this chapter, we will see examples of various types of fee schedules and learn how to use a fee schedule, who establishes fee schedules, and what to do when using multiple fee schedules. We will compare reciprocity rates, identify procedures that eventually will be allowed into the plan, report statistical claims, and learn why it is important to always be familiar with the plan's fee schedule (in the provider's contract and noncontracted rules).

fee schedule A list of all services and procedures coded using the notation of CPT, HCPCS, or ICD-9-CM, and so on. Most fee schedules have a procedure code and an agreed-upon rate or fee for that specific procedure. Fee schedules are common for participating providers that contract with HMOs and PPOs.

A **fee schedule** is a list of all services and procedures coded using the notation of CPT, HCPCS, or ICD-9, and so on. A plan pays for covered services on its list; services not on the list are theoretically not covered. Most fee schedules have a procedure code and an agreed-upon rate or fee for that specific procedure. Fee schedules are common for participating providers who contract with HMOs and PPOs. The payment rate of a fee schedule can be based on a number of factors, such as

- Usual and customary fees
- Medicare fee schedules
- Resource Based Relative Value Scale (RBRVS)
- HCPCS fee schedule
- Fees negotiated based on an established fee schedule rate between the payer and the provider
- Fees negotiated above or below an established fee schedule (that is, 5 percent above Medicare rates or 85 percent of Medicare rates)

A provider of service may wish to negotiate a fee schedule, take the fee schedule the payer offers, or may have no choice in the matter, as this may be a prerequisite for participating in the plan.

Fee Schedule Types

There are three types of fee schedules: payer, provider, and payer type. All are valid and have their place in contract negotiation for agreed-upon fee schedules between a payer and a provider.

Fee Schedule Established by Payer

Medicare fee schedule A list of fees developed by CMS and used by Medicare.

Many payers base their rates on geographic area rates, allowed amounts, RBRVS, **Medicare fee schedules**, and so on. A Medicare fee schedule lists fees developed by CMS and used by Medicare.

A payer may establish fees using data from its own information or use other known fee schedules as a baseline to begin negotiations as they agree upon individual procedure rates.

Some payers pay above established rates if they need a specialist in a particular area to serve patients in that specialty.

Other payers may have a need for providers in a specialty but not enough of a need to consider rates higher than an established fee schedule. Still other payers may not offer any contracts because they have

beneficiaries People or entities who receive benefits.

enough providers in their plan to service their population of **beneficiaries**. A beneficiary is a person or entity who receives a benefit(s).

Fee Schedule Established by Provider

Physicians have various commercial manuals or publications from which they can base their rates on specific procedures of their specialties. These may be called a physician's regular rates. In addition, specialty associations may have services available to their members to help negotiate the best fee possible for the practice and the provider in their geographic area.

Fee Schedule Established by Payer Type

Some rate amounts can be established by the payer. Medicare rates are determined nationally, whereas worker's compensation rates are used statewide. These are usually fixed rates set or attached to a government program regulated and funded by a national, state, county, or local payer. Rates and policies are tracked and/or utilized. They may be based on Medicare research and determination.

Negotiating the Fee Schedule

Some commercial payers use established fee schedules as a base to negotiate fees. One example is the Medicare fee schedule. The final agreement between the commercial payer and the provider may be a fee schedule based on 120 percent of Medicare rates or 110 percent of RBRVS, and so on.

Many commercial payers begin their fee schedule negotiation at Medicare rates. A provider may begin its negotiation slightly higher than its regular rates, and the provider and payer meet and/or agree to fees somewhere in between. In the end, not all payers, commercial insurance, groups, and so on, negotiate their rates. Commercial payers and providers may use the formula in Figure 4-1 for determining rates. Also, geographic area may be a cost factor for determining rates.

Using the Fee Schedule

The biller should have access to the agreed-upon fee schedule of the provider to understand the amount expected from the payer. This allows the biller to anticipate expected write-offs, and the accounts receivable reports will be more accurate.

Unfortunately, billers do not always have this information. Some physicians are not familiar with the rates they have contracted for and therefore do not share these with their in-house billers or billing services.

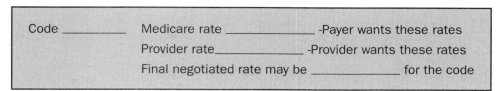

Code _____   Medicare rate _____ -Payer wants these rates

Provider rate_____ -Provider wants these rates

Final negotiated rate may be _____ for the code

Figure 4-1 Formula in determining rates (Delmar/Cengage Learning)

Not all fee schedules will have the same rates; they may vary from commercial insurance to government programs. Some billing software systems are able to list all fee schedules per payer; this helps the biller to know what payment to expect and will help the collection department recognize a mistake in payment and determine what is not collectable.

Various Types of Fee Schedules

Fee schedules may be specific in the types of services they cover. These types of services may be defined by effective dates of when those fees are in force and dates of when the schedule ends. Fee schedules will state a procedure and the amount payable. In using any fee schedule, all information should be noted before adopting those fees as expected payment from the provider. Figure 4-2 shows what a fee schedule may specify.

When fee schedules change, the billing department and those who need to monitor provider payments should be informed as soon as possible. Effective dates and time periods the fee schedule is in effect should be emphasized to those responsible for monitoring such information. Some billing software systems have the capability to recognize various fee schedules and revision dates. Figure 4-3 gives an example of fee recognition payment periods.

A fee schedule may specify

- Geographic area, for example, Oklahoma, Massachusetts
- Type of work, for example, lab, DME, X-ray
- Codes with and without modifiers
- Participating and nonparticipating fees
- Procedures performed in an office (outpatient or inpatient facility)
- Fiscal intermediary or carrier by name
- Allowed rate on a per-month basis

Figure 4-2 What a fee schedule may specify (Delmar/Cengage Learning)

The software should be able to recognize old claims for payment from previous periods and what rates were in effect for that time.
ABC Insurance Company

Fee schedule X effective January 1 through December 31, 2007

Fee schedule Y effective January 1 through December 31, 2008

Fee schedule Z effective January 1 through December 31, 2009

Figure 4-3 Fee recognition payment periods (Delmar/Cengage Learning)

Fee Schedules for Capitated Providers Reporting Statistical Claims

contracted rate The rate agreed upon by all parties through a contract.

Many times capitated providers report claims at a **contracted rate**, the rates stated in a fee schedule, even though the provider will not get paid from the claim but instead is paid the capitation monthly rates, per member, per month. Sometimes, since providers do not expect to be paid from statistical claims, the provider reports patient diagnosis and procedures on the claim but not an amount due. This is a zero-dollar claim. Payers are not encouraging providers to report zero-dollar claims as much as they have in the past. This is because the payer needs to know the actual billed charges. If the provider changes its payment structure and decides it wishes to be paid on a percentage of billed rates and charges RBRVS or Medicare rates, the payer will not have provider information as to the true cost of the service. A provider is at a distinct disadvantage when negotiating rates on a charge for fee for service and percentage of billed payment.

Reporting a dollar amount on a statistical claim helps the payer to realize the true cost of seeing/treating the individual patient. Sometimes a provider may choose to bill its regular rates on statistical claims. The provider should be consistent in its choice of reporting prices, contracted rates, regular rates, or zero balance.

When a Referral Becomes an Issue

In a consultation, the patient is referred by the primary care physician (PCP) or general practitioner (GP) to a specialist. Usually the patient returns to her PCP for care after the consultation with the specialist. However, treatment may be initiated by the consultant.

To begin the process, a referral becomes authorized for specific services by the plan.

In this scenario, the consulting physician sees other/contributing problems and wants to perform additional diagnostic or therapeutic services. In performing the services, there are three potential outcomes:

- If the consulting physician orders services that are not justified or specifically authorized, these can be denied if the diagnosis codes do not warrant the procedures performed or the medical records do not justify treatment.

- If the consulting physician wants to do additional tests or services for a diagnosis not recognized by the referral authorization, the consultant would need to justify the procedure through the newly found diagnosis. These can be confirmatory diagnoses or findings.

- If the consulting provider does not wish to wait for the new referral, supporting or confirmatory documentation with the diagnosis codes needs to be sent with the claim for review before payment is made.

In this case, the consultant does not need to make sure his procedures are included in the fee schedule, even if he currently does not have a referral. The referrals are not tied to fee schedules. Payments for the referral services are paid at the contracted fee schedules/rates.

When a Code Is Not on the Fee Schedule

Sometimes providers perform services needed by the patient that are not on the fee schedule. The payer considers these claims differently depending on the circumstances involved.

Noncovered Services

Some fee-for-service plans state they will pay only covered services. If the physician or facility performs a service which is not covered under the plan, the payer is not obligated to pay anything for this. The patient/physician/facility may appeal to the health plan for medical necessity. If this is a service denial, most of the time it is the patient who must appeal. In this case, the patient may receive a bill for noncovered services.

If the provider performed services not covered by the plan, the patient should not be surprised to receive a bill. The provider should explain to the patient, in advance and in writing, why he feels the patient needs the service and

- Offer to help the patient file an appeal to get the services paid by the payer
- Suggest a payment plan to the patient for noncovered services
- Suggest like/alternate covered services

Many physicians will not take the time to offer services not covered under the plan, believing that the patient cannot afford them. Some participating provider agreements prohibit the physician from offering or considering procedures or treatments not covered under the plan.

The patient needs to be aware of what services are covered under the plan. Providers also need to check benefits before services are performed. The fee schedule can be used as a quick listing of services covered under the plan.

The Patient Self-Referred Out of Network – When Might This Be Paid?

A patient self-referring out of network means the patient sees a provider that is not a participating provider and that does not have an agreement with the insurance carrier for a specified rate. (Medicare views such a situation a little differently; see Chapter 5.)

If a patient self-refers out of network, the provider bills the patient directly. If the patient wants the insurance to pay for the treatment, the patient needs to file an appeal with the insurance carrier itself.

The insurance might consider paying or might pay for the service if

- No physician participating in its plan could have provided the same service
- The patient reports that she requested a referral to a participating provider, in writing, and no one referred the patient. In this case, the patient had no choice but to seek care out of the plan network.

Holistic Medicine Can Be Confusing

Holistic medicine, yoga, acupuncture, essential oils, and some chiropractic care may not be covered by the plan. A payer may find such treatments help their patients and pay on a limited basis to include such treatments in their plans. The consumer may be confused by a limited benefit that is not as fully covered as other benefits.

In these situations, the responsibility falls back onto the patient. If the patient is not referred by her physician for such treatments, or the patient has not taken the time to find out what services are covered by the plan and how they would qualify, the patient may be responsible for the entire bill.

Procedures Not Included in the Fee Schedule but Eventually Allowed into the Plan

If a provider performs a procedure not included in the provider's fee schedule or an unlisted procedure, the coder would still code the correct procedure that was done. If there is no contracted rate for the procedure, then the provider may be asked to submit EOBs to the payer from other insurances or Medicare. Medicare will research unlisted codes, compare documentation, and set the value for the code to prove reimbursement determination.

> **EXAMPLE:** PET Scans
>
> At the time PET scans were introduced as emerging technology, they were not included in the original Medicare fee schedule, but eventually Medicare did assign an allowable amount, which is now included in the Medicare fee schedule.

If there is not a like code in Medicare, the payer will find a code with like components and submit this to its contracting department to negotiate a rate with the provider. After the rate is negotiated with the provider, sometimes the rate is included in the participating provider rates and is included in the provider's specific contract. If this is a new procedure not given a code by the AMA, the provider can bill an unlisted procedure code and submit the supporting medical records with the claim.

When a rate is assigned to an unlisted procedure, that procedure and that rate become a part of the contract if there is one. The payer may also write a letter of agreement for that rate and procedure specific to the patient. Most payers do this because if they were to write an addendum to the contract, this could open negotiations with the provider to change the entire contract.

Unlisted Procedures

When a provider performs a procedure that does not fit any of the descriptions listed in the section of the CPT book, the provider assigns an unlisted procedure, and the provider bills what it thinks the procedure is worth. The claim must include justification from the patient's medical record.

If the patient is a Medicare patient, Medicare will assign an amount it deems appropriate from what it reads in the medical documentation.

A commercial payer will pay what it deems as fair also, but if the provider does not feel it has received enough reimbursement, the provider can appeal the payment. The appeal may include industry research, downloads, and so on.

Multiple Fee Schedules

In a contract, there can be two, sometimes more, fee schedules built into the contract based on what the provider and the payer negotiate into the contract. Common multiple fee schedules within one office can include

- Usual, customary, and reasonable for commercial patients
- Medicare for seniors
- Type of coding system used, CPT, HCPCS and DMRC

A fee schedule may be based on specific groups of procedures, E/M, surgical, lab, X-ray, medicine, and so on. These groups may be based on sections of the CPT, HCPCS, and so on. In the example, the E/M section of the CPT manual is paid under a different fee schedule than the surgical section.

EXAMPLE: Professional Evaluations and Management codes may be based on RBRVS or Medicare allowable. Surgical procedures may be based on Medicare fee schedules and allowable rates.

Many times the contract locks the provider into these rates for senior and commercial patients or is negotiated at a percentage of the allowable amount.

Reciprocity Rates and Fee Schedules

If a patient sees a provider not contracted with the plan, the payer may use reciprocity rates instead of noncontracted rates to pay the claim. The payer may have various rates and fee schedules in use. The payer must be consistent and use the same contract or reciprocity rates for payment. The payer cannot use the lowest fee schedule or choose one fee schedule over another because it offers a procedure the other does not. One fee schedule must be chosen and used consistently; there is no cherry-picking.

Investigational Procedures

Health plans do not always pay for investigational procedures (clinical trials). Hospitals may pay for these procedures out of a special fund from other sources that are used or dedicated to these clinical trials. This kind of payment may be continued until the procedure is paid by Medicare, assigned a payment/procedure code, and/or introduced as an accepted treatment/standard of care. Pharmaceutical companies will also sponsor clinical trials.

Insured Patient Fee for Service

When a physician/facility performs a procedure or service, the service is billed to the payer on a claim form, a CMS-1500 for physician services or a

UB-04 for facilities. The insurance company pays a percentage of covered services frequently based on the allowed or usual and customary rates of the area. These are called 80-20 plans because the insurance company pays 80 percent of the bill based on its allowed charges. The patient pays 20 percent of the allowed charges, and not necessarily what was billed. The patient's benefits summary will specify what the rate is, what charges were allowed, what was paid by the payer, and what the patient needs to pay.

Nonparticipating Providers – No Fee Schedules Involved

If the payer does not have a participating provider agreement with the physician, the patient may have to pay the difference between the usual and customary rate and the physician's regular fees. This can be confusing for the patient who sees the bill and may be required to pay more than the highest percentage to a participating provider.

On the provider side, the patient usually pays a deductible and coinsurance. Facilities usually have an agreed-upon rate. The following example shows payment of a nonparticipating provider.

> **EXAMPLE:** Payment for a nonparticipating provider
>
> | | |
> |---|---|
> | The nonparticipating provider may charge | $200 |
> | The insurance paid | $ 75 |
> | The patient will pay | $125 |

In this way, the nonparticipating physician receives 100 percent of her billed rate.

Participating Providers

When the provider of service is a participating provider, it has a contractual agreement with the payer. Written into most HMO contracts are stipulations that the provider will not bill the patient the difference between what is paid and the usual and customary fee. The provider agrees to not perform services not covered under the plan. This can be confirmed through a preauthorization and/or predetermination of benefits for the individual patient.

In a PPO situation, the provider could still bill the 20 percent. If the provider is a participating provider, it will be limited in what it can bill. In a noncontracted provider situation, the patient may be required to pay the difference between what is contracted and what is billed.

The Knox-Keene Act explains a provider cannot balance bill a patient that belongs to an HMO. The act also quotes the language to be written into all managed care contracts. Although the Knox-Keene Act is California based, most states have similar laws regulating HMOs.

Medical Necessity

Some plans have various definitions of what medical necessity is. Medical necessity could be the basis of an appeal for prior authorization of services denied. The appeal would be submitted by the provider of service or the patient. An appeal may be accepted if it involves

- A comprehensive treatment under the plan
- Management of an illness
- A treatment ordered by a licensed provider
- A procedure that meets accepted standards of a disease
- A therapeutic procedure

Billing the Payer at the Patient's Request

From a payer's viewpoint, if the provider and the patient know the procedure is not a covered benefit, the patient should be billed directly. Some providers bill the payer anyway, in hopes of getting paid for something that is not covered. But if the patient requests the provider bill the payer for proof of nonpayment, the provider is obligated to bill a claim. The provider may also state it is only billing for a denial.

Note that some providers perform services that are not covered and code "like" services just to get paid. This is unethical and fraudulent. A coder should code only services performed and code as specifically and truthfully as possible.

Examples of Various Types of Fee Schedules and What They Tell Us

Fee schedules give more information than just a coding number. Many explain how they are to be applied and where they are applicable, by specialty, geographic area, modifiers, amount, and so on. The following fee schedule examples can be found at the Medicare, NHIC Corp. Web site (see http://www.medicarenhic.com/cal_prov/fee_sched.shtml).

Example of a Medicare Fee Schedule

This fee schedule is specific to a geographic area, California area 99. Sometimes payers divide their fees per geographic area if their plans cross state boundaries, county boundaries, or regional boundaries, and so on. The payer needs to divide payment through the various areas because the cost of doing business in those areas is different. In this case, the fiscal intermediary, which produced the schedule, divides fee schedules by area and pays specified rates stated in the fee schedule.

This fee schedule conveys a variety of information:

- The year it is effective
- Procedure codes with modifiers that apply
- Participating and nonparticipating charge limits specific to CPT codes/modifiers/HCPCS
- Deleted codes
- Services performed in a facility, defined by a symbol next to the CPT procedure code

Figure 4-4 shows a Medicare fee schedule.

```
AREA 99

                                        PAR        NON-PAR      LIMITING
   NOTE     PROCEDURE      MOD         AMOUNT       AMOUNT        CHARGE
----------  ----------   --------     --------     --------     --------
             G9041                      27.12        25.76        29.62
             G9042                      15.29        14.53        16.71
             G9043                      15.29        14.53        16.71
             G9044                      12.90        12.26        14.10
             33208                     512.22       486.61       559.60
             77422                     107.81       102.42       117.78
             77423                     146.15       138.84       159.67
             # - THESE AMOUNTS APPLY WHEN SERVICE IS PERFORMED IN A FACILITY
SETTING.
               LIMITING CHARGE APPLIES TO UNASSIGNED CLAIMS BY NON-
PARTICIPATING PROVIDERS.
               CPT CODES, DESCRIPTIONS AND TWO-DIGIT NUMERIC MODIFIERS
ONLY ARE COPYRIGHT 2006 AMERICAN MEDICAL ASSOCIATION.

5/31/07
CR 5614
```

Figure 4-4 Example of Medicare fee schedule in area 99 (Delmar/Cengage Learning)

Effective January 1, 2007									
PROC/MOD	**Amount**	**PROC/MOD**	**Amount**	**PROC/MOD**	**Amount**	**PROC/MOD**	**Amount**	**PROC/MOD**	**Amount**
G0027	$ 9.09	82550	$ 9.10	83986QW	$ 5.00	86005	$ 7.47	87185	$
G0103	$ 25.70	82552	$ 18.71	83992	$ 20.54	86021	$ 19.10	87186	$
G0123	$ 28.31	82553	$ 16.13	84022	$ 21.76	86022	$ 25.66	87187	$
G0143	$ 28.31	82554	$ 16.58	84030	$ 7.69	86023	$ 17.40	87188	$

Figure 4-5 Medicare clinical lab fee schedule (Delmar/Cengage Learning)

A Medicare Clinical Laboratory Fee Schedule for Northern California

In this example

- The lab codes are mixed with HCPCS codes, CPT codes, and modifiers that apply to one fee
- The fees are clinical lab fees only
- The fees are specified by geographic area
- This fee schedule does not have choices of participating, nonparticipating, or limiting physicians

  Figure 4-5 shows a Medicare clinical laboratory fee schedule.

Medicare Portable X-Ray Fee Schedule Used Mostly in a Skilled Nursing Facility

In this example

- The fees are grouped by state
- The fees are grouped into the number of patients seen at one facility for one trip

- The schedule includes the proper HCPCS modifiers applicable for each additional patient

Figure 4-6 shows Medicare X-ray fee schedules used for nursing facilities.

Chiropractors' Fee Schedule, Year 2007, California

Notice how in Figure 4-7

- The year is specified

- The grouping of codes are labeled by locality in numeric form or geographic locality by number

- The codes have different fees depending on the physician (participating or nonparticipating) and limiting charge

Medicare Durable Medical Equipment Fee Schedule

In Figure 4-8, notice

- All codes are HCPCS codes

- Some codes contain more than one modifier

- One modifier can potentially change reimbursement amounts

2007 Portable X-Ray Transportation Fees for California	
Effective January 1, 2007	
R0070 (One Patients)	$186.62
R0075 UN (Two Patients)	$93.31
R0075 UP (Three Patients)	$62.20
R0075 UQ (Four Patients)	$46.66
R0075 UR (Five Patients)	$37.32
R0075 US (Six or more)	$31.11

Figure 4-6 Medicare portable X-ray fee schedule (Delmar/Cengage Learning)

Revised 2007 Chiropractors Fee Schedule - California							
Effective January 1, 2007 (revised 12/21/06)							
Chiropractor Locality 03				Chiropractor Locality 17			
Code	Par Amount	Non-Par Amount	Limiting Charge Amount	Code	Par Amount	Non-Par Amount	Limiting Charge Amount
98940	$27.63	$26.25	$30.19	98940	$26.15	$24.84	$28.57
# 98940	$22.04	$20.94	$24.08	# 98940	$21.23	$20.17	$23.20
98941	$37.74	$35.85	$41.23	98941	$35.85	$34.06	$39.17
# 98941	$31.64	$30.06	$34.57	# 98941	$30.48	$28.96	$33.30
98942	$49.39	$46.92	$53.96	98942	$47.06	$44.71	$51.42
# 98942	$42.78	$40.64	$46.74	# 98942	$41.24	$39.18	$45.06

Figure 4-7 Chiropractic fee schedules (Delmar/Cengage Learning)

2007 April Updates to Durable Medical Equipment, Prosthetic, Orthotics, and Supplies For California Effective January 1, 2007					
PROC/MOD	Amount	PROC/MOD	Amount	PROC/MOD	Amount
A4561	$ 19.43	A6248	$ 16.24	L8624	$ 132.42
A4562	$ 48.37	A6251	$ 1.99	L8630	$ 281.81
A6010	$ 30.96	A6252	$ 3.25	L8631	$ 1,871.80
A6011	$ 2.28	A6253	$ 6.34	L8641	$ 296.14
A6021	$ 21.02	A6254	$ 1.21	L8642	$ 289.75
A6022	$ 21.02	A6255	$ 3.03	L8658	$ 255.29
A6023	$ 190.30	A6257	$ 1.53	L8659	$ 1,584.56

Figure 4-8 Medicare durable medical equipment fee schedule (Delmar/Cengage Learning)

Case Studies

The following two cases illustrate like diagnoses that are commonly interchanged by a patient, yet paid and treated differently.

Case Study – Spider Veins versus Varicose Veins

Sometimes patients discuss diagnoses and unwittingly interchange diseases that are separate and distinct from one another. In such cases, billers see procedures that are correct treatments for the diagnoses. One is covered and included on the fee schedule, the other is not.

Case 4-1 – When a Code Is Not on the Fee Schedule

Spider veins are not varicose veins. The correction of spider veins is cosmetic and usually not covered by the insurance. In this situation, the codes were billed correctly but there is no medical necessity. The following case demonstrates coding for spider veins.

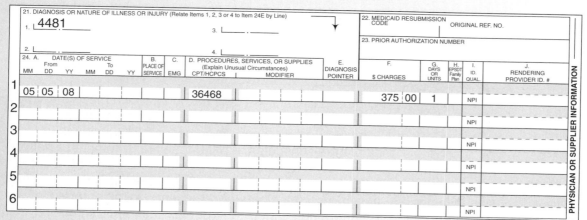

Figure 4-9 Case 4-1 – when a code is not on the fee schedule (Delmar/Cengage Learning)

(Continued)

```
448.1   Nevus, nonneoplastic - telangiectasia
36468   Single or multiple injections of sclerosing solutions. Spider
        veins (telangiectasia): limb and trunk
```

Case 4-2 – When a Code Is Covered on the Fee Schedule

Varicose veins are many times enlarged, swollen, and painful. They may affect the health and well-being of a patient. Correction would not be purely cosmetic. These codes were included in the fee schedule.

The following example demonstrates coding for varicose veins.

24. A. DATE(S) OF SERVICE From / To						B. PLACE OF SERVICE	C. EMG	D. PROCEDURES, SERVICES, OR SUPPLIES (Explain Unusual Circumstances) CPT/HCPCS	MODIFIER	E. DIAGNOSIS POINTER	F. $ CHARGES		G. DAYS OR UNITS	H. EPSDT Family Plan	I. ID. QUAL.	J. RENDERING PROVIDER ID. #
MM	DD	YY	MM	DD	YY											
1 05	05	08						36475			2140	75	1		NPI	
2 05	05	08						36476			416	12	1		NPI	
3															NPI	
4															NPI	
5															NPI	
6															NPI	

Figure 4-10 Case 4-2 – when a code is covered on the fee schedule (Delmar/Cengage Learning)

```
454.8    Varicose veins of lower extremities, with other complications
36475    Endovenous ablation therapy of incompetent vein, extremity,
         inclusive of all imaging guidance and monitoring, percutaneous,
         radio frequency, first vein treated
+36476   Second and subsequent veins treated in a single extremity, each
         through separate access sites (list separately, in addition to
         code for primary procedure)
```

Summary

A fee schedule gives listed information of what the payer and provider have agreed a service is worth and how it will be paid.

Sometimes other circumstances come into play, which make the procedure not payable. These circumstances may have very little to do with the process of billing and coding, such as procedures not included in the fee schedule, multiple fee schedules, a patient self-referring out of network, and medical necessity requirements. It is important for all employees in an office setting to understand their roll in obtaining and submitting the correct paperwork to eliminate nonpayment. Documentation of what services were performed is important, but just as important for payment is how the patient qualifies for the service. A biller and coder may need to deal with these issues long after the service has been provided.

Web Sites

Many payers publish their fee schedules on their Web sites. Sometimes a password is needed to access them. Medicare fee schedules can be obtained through the Medicare fee schedule site at www.medicarenhic.com.

Review

Fill in the Blank

1. A _____ is a list of all services and procedures coded using CPT, HCPCS, and ICD-9 notation.

2. A fee schedule is common for participating providers who contract with _____ and _____.

3. Many commercial payers begin their fee schedule negotiations at _____ rates.

4. The fee schedule should specify _____ dates and _____ periods when the fee schedule is in _____.

5. Capitated providers report claims at a _____ rate.

6. Reporting a dollar amount on a statistical claim helps the payer to realize the _____ _____.

7. If there is no contracted rate for the procedures, the provider may be asked to submit _____ to the payer from other insurances or _____.

8. In a contract, there can be _____ or more fee schedules _____ into the contract based on what the provider and _____ negotiate.

9. Plans do not always pay for _____ procedures. Hospitals pay for these procedures out of special funds from other sources that are used/dedicated to the clinical _____.

10. Sometimes payers divide their fees per _____ area if their plans cross _____ boundaries, _____ boundaries, and/or _____ boundaries.

Review Questions

1. What are three types of fee schedules? _____
   _____
   _____
   _____

2. What types of fees schedules have fixed rates? _____
   _____
   _____
   _____

3. Should billers have access to the fee schedules? _____
    _____
    _____
    _____

4. Do all fees schedules have the same rates? _____ yes _____ no
    Why or why not? _____
    _____
    _____

5. Fee schedules specify a beginning and an ending date?
    _____ yes _____ no
    Why or why not? _____
    _____
    _____

6. What types of information do fee schedules specify? _____
    _____
    _____

7. When fee schedules change, who should be aware of the changes?
    _____
    _____
    _____

8. When a statistical claim is being reported, how is the provider getting
    paid?
    _____ capitated basis
    _____ fee for service
    _____ percentage of billed
    _____ fee schedule

9. Why is it a good idea to report the cost of services on a statistical
    claim? _____
    _____
    _____

10. How might reporting zero-dollar-amount claims hurt future charges of
    payment schedules? _____
    _____
    _____

11. If a provider wishes to perform a service not covered on the plan,
    what should the provider explain to the patient? _____
    _____
    _____

12. How might the provider be prohibited from offering service outside of
    the fee schedule or covered services? _____
    _____
    _____

13. Under what circumstances might the plan pay if the patient self-refers out of network and the plan prohibits this? _____

_____

_____

_____

_____

14. If a code is unlisted and sent to Medicare, what will Medicare do with it? _____

_____

_____

_____

_____

15. Can a provider and payer contract for more than one fee schedule on the same contract? Explain. _____

_____

_____

_____

_____

Critical Thinking Exercise

Some payers list their fee schedules online. In performing this exercise, you will see that many of these schedules are specific to the group the provider participates in as well as specific to services listed via CPT or HCPCS. Sometimes fee schedules can find their way to Web sites and the logic of adopting them is explained.

This exercise will help readers understand various fee schedules used in their geographic area by the payer who chose to post them on the Internet. Sometimes, payers only make older, out-of-use fee schedules available to the general public.

Materials Needed

2 different-colored highlighters
1 blue pen
2 fee schedules found on the Web

Directions

1. Use your Web browser or search engine and look for a fee schedule in your state and your favorite health insurance company's fee schedule.

2. Print the fee schedules.

3. Use one color highlighter for generalized codes such as E/M codes; use the other for codes specific to a specialty. Note rates that differ in payment and the dollar amount differential.

4. Discuss the differences and similarities of the fee schedules with your professor.

Professional Corner

The following are some questions you may wish to address in your professional career:

- *As a coder do you code to the highest specificity based on medical records?*
- *As a coder, do you know what codes specifically apply to each physician's specialty in your practice?*
- *As a coder/biller, do you know if your physician is contracted with a certain insurance? If so, do you have access to the fee schedule?*
- *As a coder/biller, if your physician is contracted, do you understand the appeals process for the provider disputes?*
- *As a coder/biller, do you have set fee ranges of specialty codes for the group?*
- *As a coder/biller, do you have one fee schedule based on Medicare and another based on usual and customary fees?*
- *As a coder/biller, do you have various fee schedules that apply to the physician's practice?*
- *What percentage of the time does your provider perform an unlisted service, which requires gathering notes and reports with the claims?*
- *If you have access to fee schedules, what are your provider's top-20 performed procedures listed? If some of these procedures are not listed, are you able to get a special code from the payer, so you can report such codes specifically on the claim and not have to report unlisted procedure codes every time?*
- *What percentage of the time does your physician perform services not listed on the payer's fee schedule?*

References

Centers for Medicare and Medicaid. (2008). CMS, Fee Schedule, General Information Overview. Washington, D.C: U.S. Department of Health and Human Services.

NHIC. (2006, 2005). Part B Fee Schedules and Related Information. Hingham, MA: NHIC Corp.

Centers for Medicare and Medicaid. (April 12, 2007). "Medicare Physician Fee Schedule, (MPFS), Connecticut and Florida." Centers for Medicare and Medicaid, Federal Registrar.

Arizona State Rate Codes. (2007). "Physician Fee Schedules, AHCCS Fee for Service Rates." Medicare, CMS, Federal Registar, Vol. 71, No. 231.

Medicare, CMS. (April 2008). "ASP Drugs, First Coast Service Options, Florida Medicare and CMS." Jacksonville, FL: Medicare.

Upstate Medicare Division, New York. (2007). Physician Fee Schedule Payment Policies.

Medicare

Chapter Objectives

Upon completion of this chapter, you should be able to

- Recognize the Social Security Administration's role regarding Medicare
- Understand Medicare Part A, Part B, Part C, and Part D
- Identify the difference between participating and nonparticipating providers
- Identify the Medicare limiting charge and how it affects the patient's payment
- Recognize how Medicare relates to other insurances
- Understand how a common working file can affect claims
- Interpret what information a biller/coder can get from local medical review policies
- Identify how various Medicare acts and programs affect payment and coding
- Explain various payment mechanisms in Part B drugs
- Identify some examples of claims payment issues

Key Terms

Administrative
 Simplification
 Compliance Act (ASCA)

average sales price (ASP)

average wholesale price
 (AWP)

Benefits Improvement
 and Protection Act
 (BIPA)

carrier advisory
 committee (CAC)

Centers for Medicare
 and Medicaid
 Services (CMS)

common working file
 (CWF)

Comprehensive Error
 Rate Testing Program
 (CERT)

Medicare Advantage
 Plans (MA-PD)

Medicare
 demonstration
 project

Medicare
 Modernization Act

Medi-Medi

user fee proposal

Introduction to Medicare

This chapter explains various aspects of Medicare as they relate to coding and payment, finding codes through Local Medical Review Policies, Carrier Advisory Committees, Local Coverage Determinations, Medicare Common Working Files, Comprehensive Error Rate Testing programs, Medicare tracking and implementation codes, and examples of category III code use.

There are various factors that decide payment of codes through Medicare; this chapter explores a variety of reasons those factors play a hand in reimbursement.

Center for Medicare and Medical Services (CMC) Centers for Medicare and Medicaid, is an agency within the Health and Human Services Department of the federal government. Medicaid, Medicare, HIPAA and CLIA are all regulated through CMS.

Medicare programs are administered through **Centers for Medicare and Medicaid Services, CMS**. Medicare is a national program that touches every facet of the health industry. Because of the needs of its enrollees, Medicare must have policies, rules, and regulations regarding the payment and services the enrollees will receive. The list of providers is not just physicians and hospitals but nonphysician practitioners, therapists, and dentists, and so on. All providers of service need to adhere to the rules of Medicare if they serve Medicare enrollees. Even providers of service who do not participate in Medicare must follow the rules of Medicare when providing service to Medicare patients. A nonparticipating provider must charge Medicare nonparticipating provider rates, limiting charges, for its services and not its regular rates when it provides services to a Medicare beneficiary.

There are 10 regional offices for CMS, each covering a geographic region in the United States. For example, California, Arizona, and Nevada are in region 09. San Francisco is the regional headquarters for region 09. The central office for the country is located in Baltimore, Maryland, and there are different fiscal intermediaries for each location. Figure 5-1 shows the 10 regional offices and their codes.

For the regional offices, there is also a Web site listing the areas these offices cover and their headquarters. Each regional office is responsible for maintaining records, and controls and guidelines for the various functions it performs. These offices take any necessary action against fraud or abuse, or excessive use of codes outside of statistical norms. These offices also conduct audit reviews and provide payments of claims to the providers who provide services to the various Medicare beneficiaries. Additionally, they provide information to both participating providers and beneficiaries as needed.

- Atlanta-04
- Chicago-05
- Denver-08
- New York-02
- San Francisco-09
- Boston-01
- Dallas-06
- Kansas City-07
- Philadelphia-03
- Seattle-10

Figure 5-1 Medicare regional offices and their codes (Delmar/Cengage Learning)

The Role of the Social Security Administration

The Social Security Administration, or SSA, provides benefits in the following areas: retirement, disability, family, medical, survivors, and Medicare. SSA also provides the first enrollment package for Medicare and then issues a Medicare card.

The administration also maintains the deductible status, handles replacements of lost or stolen Medicare cards, updates address changes, establishes and maintains a person's enrollment, collects premiums from people who have retirement or disability benefits, educates beneficiaries concerning coverage and insurance choices, and issues Social Security cards.

Medicare Part A and Part B came into existence from the passing of the Social Security Act of 1965. This was referred to as the Mills Bill; it was introduced in March and passed in July 1965.

EXAMPLE: The Social Security Act was passed in 1965. On March 23, 1965, the Committee on Ways and Means in the House of Representatives passed the Mills Bill. And, on July 30, 1965, President Johnson signed H.R. 6675. This is Title XVII of the Social Security Act. Its two parts are Medicare Part A and Medicare Part B.

Also during this time, the government decided to have fiscal intermediaries under Part A and Part B carriers. Intermediaries and carriers are usually private insurance companies that contract with the government to provide administrative services. Intermediaries process Part A claims and carriers process Part B claims. Figure 5-2 shows intermediaries and carriers provide certain administrative services for the government.

Medicare's Future and Information to Access

The Kaiser Foundation publishes the *Medicare Fact Sheet,* which can be accessed through its Web site. The foundation is excellent at reporting trends, the cost of Medicare, and its future. Figure 5-3 shows a Kaiser Permanente Medicare fact sheet. For more information, go to http://www.kff.org/medicare.

Intermediaries and Carriers	
• Beneficiary appeals	• Beneficiary hearings
• Claims processing	• Claims review
• Final cost settlements	• Financial account
• Provider audits	• Period interim payments
• Provider reimbursement	• Professional relations

Figure 5-2 Intermediaries' and carriers' administrative services (Delmar/Cengage Learning)

FACT SHEET

MEDICARE

MEDICARE AT A GLANCE

February 2007

OVERVIEW OF MEDICARE

Medicare is the federal health insurance program created in 1965 for all people age 65 and older regardless of their income or medical history. The program was expanded in 1972 to include people under age 65 with permanent disabilities. Medicare now covers nearly 43 million Americans. Most people age 65 and older are entitled to Medicare Part A if they or their spouse are eligible for Social Security payments and have made payroll tax contributions for 10 or more years. People under age 65 who receive Social Security Disability Insurance (SSDI) generally become eligible for Medicare after a two-year waiting period, while those with End Stage Renal Disease and Lou Gehrig's disease become eligible for Medicare when they begin receiving SSDI payments.

Medicare plays a vital role in ensuring the health of beneficiaries by covering many important health care services, including a new prescription drug benefit. However, there are also gaps in coverage, notably dental, vision, and long-term care. Medicare benefits are expected to total $374 billion in 2006, accounting for 14% of the federal budget (CBO, 2006).

CHARACTERISTICS OF PEOPLE ON MEDICARE

Medicare covers a diverse population: 36% have three or more chronic conditions, 29% have a cognitive or mental impairment, 17% are African American or Hispanic, and 12% are age 85 and older (Figure 1). Many people on Medicare have modest incomes and resources: 47% have incomes below 200% of poverty ($20,420/single and $27,380/couple in 2007). Fifteen percent – nearly 7 million in 2006 – are under age 65 and permanently disabled.

MEDICARE'S STRUCTURE

Medicare is organized into four parts (Figure 2).

Part A pays for inpatient hospital, skilled nursing facility, home health, and hospice care. Accounting for 41% of benefit spending in 2006, Part A is funded mainly by a dedicated tax of 2.9% of earnings paid by employers and workers (1.45% each).

Part B pays for physician, outpatient, and home health visits and preventive services. Part B is funded by taxpayers through general revenues and beneficiary premiums and accounts for 35% of benefit spending in 2006. Medicare beneficiaries pay a monthly Part B premium of $88.50 in 2006 (estimated to increase to $98.40 in 2007). Starting in 2007, those with annual income over $80,000 ($160,000 per couple) will pay a higher, income-related monthly Part B premium.

Part C refers to the Medicare Advantage program, through which beneficiaries can enroll in a private managed care plan, such as an HMO, PPO, or private fee-for-service (PFFS) plan. These plans offer combined coverage of Part A, Part B, and in most cases, Part D (prescription drug) benefits. Part C accounts for 14% of benefit spending in 2006.

Part D is the new outpatient prescription drug benefit, delivered through private plans that contract with Medicare. The benefit includes additional assistance with plan premiums and cost-sharing amounts for low-income beneficiaries. Part D, which is funded by general revenues, beneficiary premiums, and state payments, accounts for 8% of benefit spending in 2006. Enrollees in Medicare drug plans pay a monthly premium that averages $25 across plans in 2006.

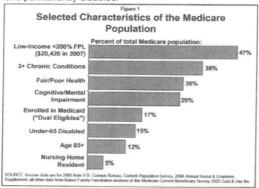

Figure 1
Selected Characteristics of the Medicare Population

Percent of total Medicare population:

- Low-Income <200% FPL ($20,420 in 2007): 47%
- 3+ Chronic Conditions: 36%
- Fair/Poor Health: 30%
- Cognitive/Mental Impairment: 29%
- Enrolled in Medicaid ("Dual Eligibles"): 17%
- Under-65 Disabled: 15%
- Age 85+: 12%
- Nursing Home Resident: 5%

SOURCE: Income data are for 2005 from U.S. Census Bureau, Current Population Survey, 2006 Annual Social & Economic Supplement; all other data from Kaiser Family Foundation analysis of the Medicare Current Beneficiary Survey 2003 Cost & Use file.

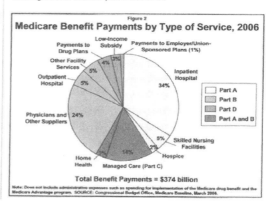

Figure 2
Medicare Benefit Payments by Type of Service, 2006

- Inpatient Hospital: 34%
- Physicians and Other Suppliers: 24%
- Managed Care (Part C): 14%
- Home Health
- Hospice: 2%
- Skilled Nursing Facilities: 5%
- Outpatient Hospital: 5%
- Other Facility Services: 5%
- Payments to Drug Plans: 4%
- Low-Income Subsidy: 3%
- Payments to Employer/Union-Sponsored Plans (1%)

Part A
Part B
Part D
Part A and B

Total Benefit Payments = $374 billion

Note: Does not include administrative expenses such as spending for implementation of the Medicare drug benefit and the Medicare Advantage program. SOURCE: Congressional Budget Office, Medicare Baseline, March 2006.

The Henry J. Kaiser Family Foundation: 2400 Sand Hill Road, Menlo Park, CA 94025 (650) 854-9400 Facsimile: (650) 854-4800
Washington, D.C. Office: 1330 G Street, N.W., Washington, DC 20005 (202) 347-5270 Facsimile: (202) 347-5274 Website: www.kff.org
The Henry J. Kaiser Family Foundation is an independent national health philanthropy and is not associated with Kaiser Permanente or Kaiser Industries.

Figure 5-3 Kaiser Medicare Information Fact Sheet. Medicare at a Glance – Fact Sheet (#1066-10), The Henry J. Kaiser Family Foundation, February, 2007. This information reprinted with permission from the Henry J. Kaiser Family Foundation. The Kaiser Family Foundation, based in Menlo Park, California, is a nonprofit, private operating foundation focusing on the major health care issues facing the nation and is not associated with Kaiser Permanente or Kaiser Industries.

BENEFICIARY COST SHARING AND OUT-OF-POCKET SPENDING

Medicare has relatively high cost-sharing requirements and covers less than half (45%) of beneficiaries' total costs. Medicare premiums and cost-sharing requirements are indexed to rise annually; the monthly Part B premium has nearly doubled between 2000 and 2006. In 2006, the Parts A, B, and D (standard) deductibles are $952, $124, and $250, respectively. Unlike most employer-sponsored plans, Medicare has no cap on out-of-pocket spending.

A significant share of beneficiary out-of-pocket spending in 2002 was for long-term care (36%) and prescription drugs (22%). Even with the new drug benefit, beneficiaries are likely to face significant out-of-pocket costs in the future to meet their long-term care needs.

THE ROLE OF PRIVATE PLANS IN MEDICARE

Private plans are playing a larger role in Medicare through a revitalization of the Medicare managed care program, now known as Medicare Advantage, as well as through the new Part D drug benefit.

Medicare Advantage. Medicare HMOs have been an option under Medicare since the 1970s, although the majority of beneficiaries have remained in the traditional fee-for-service program. The Medicare Modernization Act of 2003 (MMA) included several provisions to encourage private plan participation and beneficiary enrollment. In 2006, virtually all beneficiaries have a choice of one or more Medicare Advantage plans, with enrollment now at 16% of the total Medicare population. Medicare pays HMOs and other plans to provide all Medicare-covered benefits. The average Medicare payment to Medicare Advantage plans for Part A and B services is 111% of the cost of similar benefits in the fee-for-service program (MedPAC, 2006).

Medicare Prescription Drug Plans. Beneficiaries can obtain the new Medicare drug benefit through private stand-alone prescription drug plans (PDPs) and Medicare Advantage prescription drug plans (MA-PDs). Medicare pays plans to provide the standard drug benefit, or one that is actuarially equivalent.

As of June 2006, 22.5 million beneficiaries were enrolled in Medicare Part D plans, including 16.5 million in PDPs and another 6 million in MA-PDs (HHS, 2006) (Figure 3).

ADDITIONAL SOURCES OF COVERAGE

In addition to Medicare, most beneficiaries have some form of supplemental coverage.

Employer-sponsored plans. Employers are a key source of supplemental coverage, assisting about 11 million retirees on Medicare. However, retiree health benefits are on the decline; only 33% of large firms offered retiree benefits in 2005, down from 66% in 1988 (KFF/HRET, 2005). An additional 2.6 million Medicare beneficiaries are active workers (or spouses) for whom employer plans are the primary source of coverage.

Medicaid. More than 7 million low-income beneficiaries are dually eligible for Medicare and Medicaid. Most qualify for full Medicaid benefits, including long-term care and dental, and get help with Medicare's premiums and cost-sharing requirements. Some do not qualify for full Medicaid benefits, but get help with Medicare premiums and some cost-sharing requirements under the Medicare Savings Programs, administered under Medicaid.

Medigap and other coverage. Many beneficiaries purchase private supplemental policies, known as Medigap (nearly 9 million in 2002). Another 3 million beneficiaries receive supplemental assistance through the Veterans Administration or some other government program, according to HHS.

MEDICARE SPENDING AND OUTLOOK

With the aging of the population and the new drug benefit, net federal spending on Medicare is estimated by CBO to grow from $331 billion in 2006 to $524 billion in 2011. Annual growth in Medicare spending is influenced by factors that affect health spending generally, including increasing volume and utilization of services and higher prices for health care services. Although Medicare spending increases each year, the average per capita spending growth rate between 1970 and 2004 was lower for Medicare (8.9%) than for private health insurance (9.9%) for common benefits (excluding prescription drugs) (CMS Office of the Actuary, 2006).

Looking to the future, Medicare faces many challenges, but none greater than financing care for an aging population with a declining ratio of workers to beneficiaries. Medicare spending as a share of GDP is expected to increase from 2.7 percent in 2005 to 4.7 percent in 2020. The Part A Trust Fund reserves are projected to be exhausted in 2018, and a "Medicare funding warning" is expected to be triggered next year by the Medicare Trustees, as required by law. Maintaining benefits for future beneficiaries will require more resources over time. In addition to these fiscal challenges, others include: ensuring the successful implementation of the drug benefit; setting fair payments to providers and plans; improving care for those with multiple chronic conditions; and providing adequate financial protections for those with low incomes and health security for an aging U.S. population.

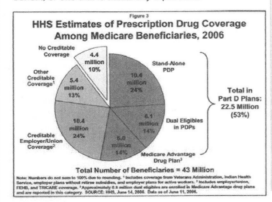

Figure 3

HHS Estimates of Prescription Drug Coverage Among Medicare Beneficiaries, 2006

Total Number of Beneficiaries = 43 Million

Additional copies of this publication (#1066-10) are available on the Kaiser Family Foundation's website at www.kff.org.

The Kaiser Family Foundation is a non-profit, private operating foundation dedicated to providing information and analysis on health care issues to policymakers, the media, the health care community, and the general public. The Foundation is not associated with Kaiser Permanente or Kaiser Industries.

Figure 5-3 Continued

Medicare Part A is for facility services, skilled nursing services, and home health services. Part A pays for the facility charges, inpatient hospital stays, outpatient use of services for hospitals, facility charges for outpatient, and ED in hospitals as well. It does not pay for urgent care facilities. It is a hospital-based insurance program paid into from taxes. Employers and the self-insured, not just the employee/patient, pay into this program as well.

Medicare Part B is the insurance program for physician's services, outpatient diagnostic services, ambulatory surgical services in an ASC facility, and ancillary services such as durable medical equipment. When a patient chooses Medicare Part B, he is charged a monthly premium that is deducted from his Social Security check every month. The physician can perform his services in various places, such as hospitals, nursing homes, the insured's home, the physician's office, and so on.

Under Part B, providers are paid from a specific fee schedule. Charges are based on three key components of the Resource Based Relative Value Scale. This is a national matrix, and each procedure has value based on this system. It covers the clinician's time, intensity, and technical skill required for the particular service provided. It also takes into account the practice's overhead expenses, including office, rents, equipment, staff, supplies, and malpractice insurance.

Medicare Part C, the Medicare Advantage Plan, offers more than the original Medicare plan. Variations of managed care may depend on the geographic area and may include the following elements:

- Medicare managed care plan
- Managed care plan with a point of service, or POS
- Fee-for-service plan
- Preferred provider
- Provider-sponsored organization

On January 1, 2006, Medicare began providing outpatient prescription drugs to its beneficiaries through private health plans, as part of Medicare Part D. The pharmacy benefit formulary can be accessed online. Private prescription drug plans, or PDPs, offer either the prescription drug coverage only or offer patients the opportunity to get prescription drugs through **Medicare Advantage Plans**, **MA-PD**, that are integrated into their plans with flexibility in the design of the plan.

Participating and Nonparticipating Providers

When a provider contracts with Medicare and becomes a participating provider in the program, it has access to Medicare and can call and ask questions about the program. A participating provider is informed of changes by CMS through a newsletter. The newsletter informs the participating provider about applicable time frames and dates when changes take place in regulations, laws, coding, and administrative handling. The provider must begin using the changes directed in the newsletter on the effective date. If it does not, the provider may have claims denied.

If a provider is nonparticipating, it does not have the same kind of access as a participating provider, nor is Medicare obligated to answer questions. In a nonparticipating situation, the provider bills Medicare for

Medicare Advantage Plans (MA-PD) These plans basically cover the patient from head to toe. Theoretically, the patient will not need any other plan. A patient who chooses these kinds of plans get Medicare Part A and Part B. There may be an additional charge to belong to this plan.

the patient, but the patient is reimbursed the money and the "nonpar," or nonparticipating, provider receives payment from the patient.

Nonparticipating Providers' Limiting Charge Increases the Patient Level of Responsibility

When a nonparticipating provider charges the limiting charge, it is greater than Medicare participating provider fees. Medicare only pays what it is responsible for, which is a percentage of the nonparticipating Medicare fees. Medicare's nonparticipating, or limiting, charge is 115 percent of participating rates. In Figure 5-4, we see how rates are different for participating and nonparticipating providers.

Medicare and Other Insurances

Medicare Advantage – The Balanced Budget Act of 1997 heralded the joining of HMOs into Medicare. The patient receives services and is covered under the rules of the HMO plan. The HMO must provide the same coverage as Medicare; however, it does offer richer benefits or fuller benefit packages, which is beyond what straight Medicare would normally cover. Not all plans cover or offer the same services beyond Medicare benefits.

Medicare secondary payer programs – This is when Medicare is the secondary payer and another commercial insurance is primary. The primary insurance is billed and pays its rate for the service. Then, Medicare considers what is left over under its guidelines of the services covered under the government plan.

Medicare supplemental plans, MediGap – A senior can purchase a MediGap plan that pays for what the traditional or "original" Medicare plan does not. Medicare is the primary insurance and is billed first; the MediGap plan is billed second. The physician must provide services covered by Medicare in order to be considered for payment by the MediGap payer. MediGap plans traditionally have deductibles, and the patient pays the premiums of the MediGap plan as well.

Original Medicare rates for participating providers	
Medicare rate	$80
Medicare pays 80% of Medicare rates	$64
Patient pays	$16
Medicare rates for the same procedure for nonparticipating providers	
Medicare rate	$92
Medicare pays 80% of Medicare rates	$64
Patient pays	$28

The patient pays the difference between the limiting charge and Medicare's provider percentage charge.

Figure 5-4 Example – participating provider and nonparticipating rates (Delmar/ Cengage Learning)

Medi-Medi These are patients who have both Medicare and Medicaid. The patients should not have any out-of-pocket expense/share of cost unless it is a monthly share cost stipulated by the plan.

Medicare and Medicaid – In **Medi-Medi** plans, a combination of Medicare and Medicaid plans, Medicare is primary and Medicaid is secondary. Medicaid programs are federal programs run by the states and allow medical services to whomever meets the state requirements for eligibility.

Patient Deductibles

Medicare is at the forefront of change. And it must be! A percentage increase in spending for medical services can add up to billions of dollars in reimbursement. Figure 5-5 shows the changes in deductibles and premiums over the past few years.

This amount should not be billed to the patient prior to receiving the applicable explanation of benefits, or EOB, directing the provider as to the proper amount due directly from the patient. The providers, theoretically, may not know of other health care professionals the patient has seen during this time. The provider should not bill a Medicare patient a presumed amount of deductible not documented by Medicare itself. Instead, the provider should wait for direction from the Medicare EOB, then bill the patient the coinsurance and deductible stated on the EOB.

Medicare's Common Working File

common working file (CWF) A form of verifying eligibility of the patient for services. This verification is done before the claim(s) is paid.

Medicare needs to validate when a beneficiary is eligible for benefits, what kind of benefits, and so on. But how is the system to do this? A **common working file**, or **CWF**, was developed to show information Medicare has about a beneficiary and to confirm eligibility. The eligibility is confirmed before the claim is paid. If a claim is rejected, information is given as to why. Claims are considered in the order they are received and not necessarily by the date of service. If the claim is rejected, it does

Medicare deductible and standard premium for patients in 2006	
Medicare Part A deductible	$952.00
Medicare Part B standard premium	$88.50
Medicare Part B deductible	$124.00
Medicare deductible and standard premium for patients in 2007	
Medicare Part A deductible	$992.00
Medicare Part B standard premium	$93.50
Medicare Part B deductible	$131.00
Medicare deductible and standard premium for patients in 2008	
Medicare Part A deductible	$1024.00
Medicare Part B standard premium	$96.40
Medicare Part B deductible	$135.00

Figure 5-5 Example – changes in deductible and premiums from year to year (Delmar/Cengage Learning)

not affect the beneficiary's utilization data and an error code is given. Utilization is the services used by the patient during a period of time.

The information about each beneficiary is given to one of nine regional hosts that keep and date the data. The intermediaries and carriers must pay services the patient qualifies for and the plan deems medically necessary. The CWF updates individual patient information. The payer uses the information/data given by the CWF to make its final decision to pay the claims or not. The payer also decides the services the patient qualifies for under the plan the payer administrates. In other words, the CWF keeps the data correct and timely; the payer decides if the claim is valid. The CWF does not make judgments but gives the correct data regarding an individual patient to the payer, so the payer can make correct and timely payments. Figure 5-6 provides information about the CWF.

The common working file does the following:

- Coordinates benefits
- Tracks deductible status
- Validates prepayment claims
- Maintains Part A and B crossover edits
- Medicare secondary payer data
- Tracks Medicare volume performance standard
- Manages a database for research development
- Provides quick information access by intermediaries and carriers
- Looks for Medicare secondary payer claims
- Manages the database for program changes
- Provides primary insurance data when Medicare is secondary
- Performs end stage renal disease computations
- Provides certificate of necessity
- Keeps up to date with codes from ICD, CPT, DRGs, and groupers

The common working file keeps and updates the following data:

- Claims history of an individual beneficiary
- Beneficiary's entitlement
- What services a beneficiary uses

The common working file prevents the following:

- Overpayments
- Payment of noncovered services
- Duplicate claims payment

Figure 5-6 Common working file information (Delmar/Cengage Learning)

Local Medical Review Policies

Local Medical Review Policies, or LMRPs are decisions made by an intermediary or a carrier to cover a service or not; they contain category and statutory provisions. The emphasis is on the provider knowing the Medicare review policies and other guidelines, based on coverage and specific payment criteria. Benefits may vary from area to area depending on how urban or how rural the area is because of population. Less of a population could cost more, depending on how rural the area is.

LMRPs provide an explanation of how to bill a particular service or provide a determination by Medicare, describing how the service needs to be provided and in what setting. LMRPs provide a clarification of what services are covered and under what conditions. The provider of service needs to understand what its local area covers under the benefit, how it needs to be billed, how it will be paid, and in what setting it needs to be provided to the patient.Since the LMRP lists the criteria for which a claim will get paid, the provider who follows the direction of the LMRP should have its claim paid in a timely manner with clean claim status. The following information can be found in an LMRP:

- Contractor name
- Contractor number
- Contractor type
- LMRP ID number
- LMRP title
- Original policy effective date
- Original policy ending date
- Revision dates
- CPT codes
- Geographic area jurisdiction
- Oversight region
- LMRP description
- Limitations of coverage
- Coverage topics
- Revenue codes
- ICD codes
- Coding guidelines
- Documentation requirements
- Start date of comment period
- Last date of review
- Other version of the LMRP
- Disclaimers

Local Coverage Determinations

A Local Coverage Determination, or LCD, specifies how a service is covered and how it is coded correctly. This helps in the submittal of correct claims because each LCD must comply with the regulations of national coverage, coding guidelines, and regulations set forth if it meets title XVIII of the Social Security Act. (At the end of this chapter, Web sites for LCDs are listed.) Coding and billing are ever changing because of technology and the needs of the community. The following are some examples that may have an impact on local coverage determination:

- The needs of the community

- New technology, usually introduced at a high cost

- When a service or equipment is never covered but needed and claims are frequently denied because of it

- When the patient needs the service but cannot qualify for it under the plan

In these instances, the criteria have been formed to review the need, cost, and so on, of a procedure or an item. An LCD searches for public data that is scientific, such as research, medical opinion, or an acceptance of medical validity by the medical community. When this is found, a policy in draft form is sent out for review to an advisory committee. The advisory committees are called carrier advisory committees, or CAC, and are mandated by the Center for Medicare and Medicaid Services, CMS.

These committees are important because they link the carriers with the physicians, and the policies of the LCDs can be developed by discussing the potential policies and thereby improving them.

Carrier Advisory Committees

Carrier advisory committees (CAC) Usually one committee is established per state to make recommendations about policy and educate peers on LMRPs. The committee reviews local medical review policy issues relevant to its state and can make recommendations to the state carrier medical directors regarding policy.

Carrier Advisory Committees, CAC, review local medical review policy issues relevant to their state and can make recommendations to the state carrier medical directors regarding policy. Each state has its own committee. The committees meet quarterly to talk about how to educate other physicians in the development of LMRPs, pinpoint improvement/needs of Medicare, and work as a liaison between physician and carriers.

The professionals who sit on such a committee are

- Physicians

- Specialists

- Allied health professionals

- Administrators

- Beneficiaries

The Need for Complete Documentation of the Evaluation and Management Level of Service Chosen by the Physician or Coder

The codes chosen to report evaluation and management services are based on the documentation in the medical record. The medical record tells the medical story of the patient in chronological order, giving the dates of service, type of service, place of service, health risk, progress and changes in treatment and/or diagnosis, rationale for treatment, and so on.

Since coders are not in the room at the time of the patient's visit, they must be able to read the documentation about the visit to assign a code. In evaluation and management, they choose a code level based on history, exam, and medical decision making. There needs to be documentation supporting the coder's decision, even though the ultimate burden of documentation is the responsibility of the provider of service who documents the medical record.

In medical documentation, the signature and date of the person providing the service is required because this shows when the provider reviewed/documented the record. In this way, the correct choice of evaluation and management code(s) can be supported in the documentation itself, no matter who codes the chart.

Comprehensive Error Rate Testing Program

Comprehensive Error Rate Testing Program (CERT) These are error rates based on a random sampling of paid claims broken into service type and provider type. A random sampling could mean every 10th claim the system has or a time period of claims in the database itself.

Comprehensive Error Rate Testing, or **CERT**, is an error-rate program based on a random sampling of paid claims, broken into service type and provider type. A random sampling could mean every tenth claim the system has or a time period of claims in the database itself. The data may be too vast to investigate each claim; therefore, a sampling is performed to get an idea of the overall performance or accuracy of the provider or service type being examined.

The program targets improvement based on identified errors that lead to improper payment. The program may find a larger percentage of improper payment of claims due to providers of service not understanding a regulation, a law, or coding guideline. In the search for correct payment, the system must learn, understand, and identify errors in how the data is reported to achieve a higher percentage of accurate data.

The program requests documentation from providers and compares the medical records with what is reported. If the provider does not send the requested documentation, these are looked at as overpayments because the provider of service is not taking the time to prove its accuracy of information on the claims submitted to Medicare.

Each fiscal year, the categories looked at are

- Insufficient documentation
- Nonresponse
- Procedures medically unnecessary
- Incorrect coding
- Other information that may be requested

Some key factors when CERT requests documentation from the provider of service are

- Request for information should be responded to in a timely manner
- Medical records should not be altered
- Medical records should fully support billing/coding submitted for payment
- Dates and times of service are important

Not responding to such a request may result in Medicare wanting its payment back from the provider of service. Medicare may not ask for a refund but notify the provider and retract the payment of claims paid electronically. Proving through correct documentation that the coding and billing were justified will help prevent refunding money to Medicare for services billed correctly. (CERT has a telephone number for general questions, 804-264-1778, extension 164; and a Web site, www.cms.hhs.gov/cert).

The Tracking of Codes for Utilization

Medicare tracks various codes and claims processed through its system, for example, drug administration codes. When the claims are processed into the system, Medicare can run reports and trends. This is how an individual trend of physician, geographic areas, and specialties are tracked. Medicare also tracks codes for up-coding and down-coding, for example, how many surgeries a surgeon performs in a matter of hours. Providers billing Medicare should attend annual workshops about Medicare, to be aware of changes and to be able to apply changes in a timely manner. Providers may receive their updates from various newsletters, electronic bulletins, lists of services, magazines, and mailers.

Implementation of Codes

A grace period is the time between an announcement of change and the actual change itself. Medicare is shortening grace periods when a code is discontinued for use. The biller/coder should note the dates for discontinued use that apply to his physician's specialty and practice because these dates will be adhered to. If a code is used after the discontinued date, the claim will be rejected, causing resubmission and/or provider dispute issues. Tracking changes and the timing of grace periods for codes will promote the smooth flow of information and prevent undue denials.

average sales price (ASP) From the Medicare drug list. This pertains to Medicare Part B drugs. Payments are allowed for drugs not included in the ASP Medicare file.

Medicare Modernization Act (Public Law 108-173) This act is to help bring more up to date services or modernize the service offered to Medicare patients.

Average Sales Price List for Medicare Part B Drugs

The **average sales price**, **ASP**, is from the Medicare drug list. These prices became available as a result of the **Medicare Modernization Act**, of 2003, in section 303, enforced January 1, 2005. The act states all drugs and biologicals that are not paid at cost or following the perspective payment system will be paid on an average sales price plus 6 percent. This requirement pertains to Medicare Part B drugs.

CMS will supply their carriers with an ASP drug listing case file on a quarterly basis for the Medicare Part B drugs. The ASP is based on quarterly drug information supplied to CMS by the drug manufacturer. An exception to this is they are to be covered at 90 percent of the average wholesale price that is reflected in the compendia of October 1, 2003. The most common drugs included in this list are

- Blood products
- Transfusion drugs associated with DME with a covered item
- Influenza drugs
- Pneumococcal drugs
- Hepatitis B vaccines

average wholesale price (AWP) In drug pricing, it is the wholesale price, or the price that the drug is sold for to pharmacies, physicians, or hospitals, which are not the end users of the drugs. The cost to the patient, the actual end user, for the medications is not the same price.

The **average wholesale price (AWP)** in drug pricing is the wholesale price, or the price that the drug is sold for to pharmacies, physicians, or hospitals (which are not the end users of the drugs). The cost to the patient, the actual end user, for the medications is not the same price.

Payments are allowed for drugs not included in the ASP Medicare file. Providers need to confirm if the drug is included in the ASP list; if not, payment is switched to the average wholesale price, or AWP.

Drugs Listed Separately

Now available from Medicare is a list of new services that are included in the procedures and should not be reported separately on supplies. This includes

- Local anesthesia
- Subcutaneous catheter
- Exclusion, inclusion, or infusion of standard tuning syringes and supplies

Drug Infusions

Drug infusions are procedures that would not be covered separately from another service. Many providers billed such procedures á la carte. This has to do with all new drug infusions. When providers perform multiple infusions and injections, or a combination of some, only one initial drug administration service may be reported currently. This may change over time. Unless there is a protocol that requires two separate codes to be used, only the service that best describes the primary service should be used; if any additional codes are necessary, they will be secondary.

Ambulance Providers and Medicare

Medicare pays for some ambulance services. This is designed to encourage the ambulance providers and suppliers to communicate what the condition of the patient was to the Medicare contractors, as reported by the dispatch center or by the ambulance crew. This will provide a crosswalk from ICD-9 codes used to describe a patient's clinical condition during a transport to the appropriate HCPCS code. This really benefits the ambulance company because providers and suppliers should use the ICD-9 codes, not the ambulance codes, on the claim form to define a patient's condition. The ICD-9 diagnosis and medical condition crosswalk codes and the HCPCS codes will not guarantee payment for a certain level of service.

Most claims for ambulances are for 911 calls. Other transports may be from a hospital to a skilled nursing facility, SNF, and/or transportation home may not be a covered benefit but may be approved based on medical necessity and documentation.

The ambulance service documentation should contain the following elements:

- The dispatch instructions
- What the patient's condition was
- Information or details of the transport—where the patient was picked up and taken
- Medication administered
- What the change in the patient's condition was
- How many miles the patient traveled
- What services were provided in the ambulance

All of these may be subject to medical review by the Medicare contractor or by an oversight authority. In the case of the HMO, if the call is not a 911 call, then the claim, unless it is a diagnosis that meets an approved criteria, would have to be reviewed by a utilization management review board to ensure that the service was medically appropriate. Also, payers are going to rely on medical records and documentation, not just an HCPCS code, to justify the coverage.

Benefits Improvement and Protection Act

Benefits Improvement and Protection Act (BIPA) BIPA has to do with the appeals process of claims and a proposed cost to appeal those claims. Also, a fee for claims that cannot be processed would be paid by the provider of service per unprocessable claim. This is called a user fee proposal. For Medicare Part B claims, a provider has a time limit of 120 days to file an appeal after the initial claim has been filed.

Benefits Improvement and Protection Act, or **BIPA**, is important because it has to do with the appeals process of claims and the proposed cost to appeal those claims. This may be a fee for claims that cannot be processed would be paid by the provider of service per unprocessable claim. This fee is called a **user fee proposal**. For Medicare Part B claims, a provider has a time limit of 120 days to file an appeal after the initial claim has been filed.

BIPA is currently standardizing the appeals process of a claim. The provider will be given a Medicare Redetermination Notice, MRN, regarding the decision of the appeal. A copy of an MRN can be found at http://www.cms.hhs.gov/manuals/pm_trans/R97CP.pdf.

User Fee Proposal User fees are charged when people use services that have a fee for public use. Here, the proposal fee may be set by federal or state government.

Providers should keep up to date on all Medicare rules and be aware of any changes in the appeals process, including changes in BIPA. A fee for duplicate claims, appealing claims, and submissions of claims levied on providers is a possibility BIPA is considering.

Medicare Demonstration Projects

Medicare Demonstration Project This project looks at how traditional Medicare compares to Medicare Advantage Plans and will not begin until 2010.

Medicare demonstration projects are conducted by Medicare to test what kind of care a patient may receive for designated services, the cost of such care, and the cost for future health improvements to those who participate in Medicare. The Medicare demonstration projects come under the jurisdiction of the Medicare Modernization Act. For providers to participate, usually the data the project requests must be forthcoming with the claim. Usually the project answers a question by testing it under the demonstration project, so billers may need to gather information from various office staff and fill out forms required by the project manager. (For a Web site listing of all upcoming demonstrations, see the end of the chapter.)

Any physician's office thinking about participating in a Medicare demonstration project should consider the time constraint on staff members who would be required to participate and how cost effective taking on such a project would be. Factors to consider are

- Duration of project
- Start date
- Who may participate
- Paperwork and reporting requirements

These will vary depending on the project.

The Administrative Simplification Compliance Act

Administrative Simplification Compliance Act (ASCA) The Act requires claims to be submitted electronically to Medicare. The requirement date was October 16, 2003. The exception is small practices.

According to the **Administrative Simplification Compliance Act**, **ASCA**, Medicare cannot make payments of claims not submitted electronically after October 16, 2003. Under amendment section 1820 62-A of the act, this also includes Part A and Part B claims. Medicare wants all claims to be submitted electronically. If the provider is in violation and it is ruled it is in violation, the provider will need to give back the payment with interest or Medicare will recover what it calls an "overpayment." This can be determined when paper claims submitted by the provider are analyzed. The providers who are submitting the highest number of claims will be asked to submit information about why they may be exempt from submitting electronic claims.

There are exceptions to filing claims electronically: less than 25 full-time employees for fiscal intermediaries and fewer than 10 for carriers (remember, carriers serve Part B and intermediaries serve Part A), unusual circumstances, disruption of electricity, provider gives services only outside of the United States, a payer is responsible for prior payment, mass immunizations, and participation in a Medicare demonstration project.

Medicare Fee Schedule

Many commercial, HMO, and PPO plans use the Medicare fee schedule as the basis for reimbursement levels, not just for Medicare reimbursement alone. Other insurances use it and may follow the same guidelines. Very few physicians or groups are nonparticipating. It is very difficult to not be a participating provider or group. The following are various considerations of payments and nonpayments relating to the Medicare fee schedule.

New Procedure Not on the Medicare Fee Schedule

New procedures not on the Medicare fee schedule have no assigned values. If Medicare allows new technology a provider is performing, the biller should save the EOBs that state at what amount the procedure is going to be paid.

When negotiating rates not yet established, such as emerging technology, watch for these deciding factors. Some PET scans, MRIs, and MRAs now have G codes listed in the HCPCS manual, and they do not all have an assigned payment value with Medicare. Medicare assigns its own rate based on what it feels is the appropriate medical level of care and the complexity of the procedure itself. Medicare HMOs may establish values of their own, and these are usually established at a negotiated rate.

Clinical Labs

Most clinical labs are covered under Medicare. Tests required for diagnosing an illness would be covered if requested by a licensed provider. Panels, blood tests, urinalysis, and a condition or disease would warrant such testing. If the diagnosis does not justify the lab tests, this will be recognized as a wellness checkup, which Medicare itself did not pay for prior to 2005. Providers can do a cursory welcome physical, called an initial preventive physical examination, IPPE, during the first six months of enrollment after or since January 1, 2005; lab tests are not included in this type of physical.

EXAMPLE: Interest Due Providers for Untimely Claims

The following is an example of Medicare owing interest on a claim not paid in a timely manner by the Medicare fiscal intermediary.

Interest due the provider from a claim not paid in a timely manner begins 30 days after receipt of the clean claim. For example, the payer received the claim December 1. The payer has 30 days to pay the claim, but it was paid 40 days later instead. After the 30th day, the claim begins to accrue interest on the annual percentage rate. The claim must be a clean claim and payable. The interest is only paid on clean claims not being paid in a timely manner.

Annual interest rate is 4.5%. This rate may change; check for yearly change.

Amount of reimbursement	$100.00
Annual interest rate	× 4.5%
Total of interest per year	$4.50
Determine the daily interest rate by dividing total by days in a year	$4.50 ÷ 365 = $.011
Interest due date started January 1 and ended January 10. Multiply by number of days	$.011 × 10 = $.11
Total due provider of service, including interest	$100.11

A Deceased Patient

A supplier such as a DME provider may not be given notice of a deceased patient and thereby continue to bill for durable medical equipment after the patient has expired. The DME company is obligated to return any monies it is paid if it had continued to bill for services after the date the patient expired.

Case Study – A Consulting Physician Initiates Care of a Medicare Patient, Uses Category III Code

The patient feels popping and snapping in her knee. This has gone on for six months. The general practitioner refers the patient to an orthopedist for a consultation to rule out arthritis and torn meniscus.

When the patient is referred to the specialist, an E&M consult is performed. The orthopedist decides to initiate treatment in the office (such as aspiration or injection of the joint).

The patient needs temporary relief from the pain. An injection of lydocaine and Synvisc® is given.

The specialist performs the procedure, generates a report, and sends the patient back to her general practitioner. The orthopedist can have the patient return for future treatment.

The E&M must be modified with a -25 in order to get the procedure and the E&M/consult paid. The following shows what the CMS-1500 looks like.

24. A. DATE(S) OF SERVICE From MM DD YY To MM DD YY	B. PLACE OF SERVICE	C. EMG	D. PROCEDURES, SERVICES, OR SUPPLIES CPT/HCPCS MODIFIER	E. DIAGNOSIS POINTER	F. $ CHARGES	G. DAYS OR UNITS	H. EPSDT Family Plan	I. ID. QUAL.	J. RENDERING PROVIDER ID. #
1 05 05 08			99243 25		250 00	1		NPI	
2 05 05 08			20610		69 25	1		NPI	
3 05 05 08			Q4084		198 08	1		NPI	
4								NPI	
5								NPI	
6								NPI	

21. DIAGNOSIS OR NATURE OF ILLNESS OR INJURY (Relate Items 1, 2, 3 or 4 to Item 24E by Line)
1. 71536

Figure 5-7 Claim form (Delmar/Cengage Learning)

DIAGNOSIS

715.36   Osteoarthritis, localized, not specified whether primary or secondary, lower leg

PROCEDURES

99243-25   Consultation of a new or established patient which requires these three components: a detailed history, a detailed examination, and a medical decision making of low complexity

20610   Arthrocentesis, aspiration, and/or injection: major joint or bursa (e.g, shoulder, hip, knee joint, subacromial bursa)

Q4084   Synvisc®, per dose injection. The payment allowance is subject to the ASP, the category III code

The specialist must write the report and send the patient back to the requesting physician.

If the consultant does not use modifier 25, the consult is going to be denied as inclusive in the procedure.

Medicare Remittance Advice

Claim # _____

Processed Voucher # _____

Vendor # _____

NAME Date of service	HMO CPT code	MEMBER # Description	ACCOUNT # Billed
05/05/2008	99243-25	Office consultation, low cmplx	$250.00
		Approved for payment	$200.00
		Patient responsibility	$50.00
05/05/2008	20610	Injection	$69.25
		Approved for payment	$55.00
		Patient responsibility	$14.25
05/05/2008	Q4084	Synvisc, I Dose	$198.08
		Approved for payment	$158.46
		Patient responsibility	$39.62

Billed:	Approved:	Withhold:	Interest:
$517.33	$413.46	$0.00	$0.00

Figure 5-8 Explanation of benefits (nonparticipating) (Delmar/Cengage Learning)

Summary

As Medicare prepares for the baby boomers to become Medicare eligible within the next 10 years, billers and coders will experience many changes in reporting requirements pertaining to different program types while servicing existing provider claims.

The provider will need to make a determination if paying for an appeal on a claim is truly worth the expense, or the provider may want to have the patient more involved in the appeal. A provider should have in-house criteria of appealing claims if there is a cost involved. Paying a fee for an appeal is a definite possibility in the future, and, of course, an employee-hour cost also would be involved. At this time, patients do not have to pay anything if they appeal claims.

Various programs and rates depend upon fee schedules and geographic area rates requested by carriers and intermediaries who administrate such claims.

Web Sites

Medicare participating providers and physicians, http://www. medicareenhic.com

BIPA, *http://www.hhs.gov (click on Government, BIPA)*

CMS, *http://www.cms.hhs.gov*

LMRPs, *http://www.CMS.hhs.gov (search LMRP)*

Medicare demonstration projects, *http://www.cms.hhs.gov (click on Research then Demos)*

Medicare redetermination notice, *http://www.cms.hhs.gov/manuals (click on Redetermination Notice)*

> **Note:**
>
> *Billers/coders should always be aware of the Medicare programs their providers participate in and the reporting requirements of those programs.*

Review

Fill in the Blank

1. Medicare Part A is for _____, _____, and _____.

2. Under Medicare Part B, physicians are paid from a _____ _____ _____.

3. Medicare Part C, the _____ _____ _____ offers _____ _____ the original _____ plan.

4. Medicare Part D has _____ _____ _____, or PDP. Patients can also get prescription drugs through Medicare _____ Plans, or MA-PD.

5. A _____ _____ _____ is used to validate what a beneficiary is eligible for.

6. A Medicare common working file updates _____ _____ _____.

7. The Medicare common working file prevents _____, _____, and _____.

8. Local coverage determination specifies how a _____ is covered and how it is _____ _____.

9. CERT stands for _____ _____ _____ _____.

10. What documentation is needed for medical necessity/medical review if the ambulance service is asking Medicare to pay for a non-911 emergency?

    _____

    _____

    _____

    _____

    _____

    _____

    _____

Review Questions

1. Nonparticipating providers of Medicare can use what rates? _____

   _____

   _____

2. How many regional offices in different locations of the country, fiscal intermediaries service these locations? _____

   _____

   _____

3. Who issues Medicare cards? _____

   _____

   _____

4. Who decides deductible status? _____

   _____

   _____

5. What Medicare part is for physician services? _____

   _____

   _____

6. What Medicare part is for hospital services? _____

   _____

   _____

7. What year was the Social Security Act introduced? _____

   _____

   _____

8. Was the Social Security Act ever denied? _____
    _____
    _____
    _____

9. In what part of Medicare would you find intermediaries?
    _____
    _____

10. In what part of Medicare would you find carriers? _____
    _____
    _____

11. Carriers and intermediaries provide which of the following services?
    Mark all that apply:
    _____ Beneficiary appeals   _____ Beneficiary hearings
    _____ Claims processing   _____ Claims review
    _____ Final cost settlements   _____ Financial account
    _____ Provider audits   _____ Periodic interim payments
    _____ Provider reimbursement   _____ Professional relations
    _____ Recouping overpayments   _____ Statistical activities
    _____ Utilization review

12. What part of Medicare applies to each item?

    Part A   Part B   Part C   Part D

    _____ : Medicare Advantage Plan—offers managed care to various
                 beneficiaries in geographic areas that offer such plans
    _____ : Beginning January 1, 2006, Medicare will provide
                 outpatient prescription drugs to its beneficiaries.
    _____ : Represents inpatient services for hospitals, skilled nursing
                 facilities, and home health services, paid into from taxes
    _____ : The supplemental insurance programs for physician's
                 services, outpatient service, and ancillary services

13. What is a nonparticipating provider's limiting cost charge? _____
    _____
    _____

14. What is the Medicare deductible for 2008? _____
    _____
    _____

15. Can the provider bill the patient a presumed amount of deductible?
    _____ yes _____ no

Critical Thinking Exercise

Many local medical review policies are posted on the Web. In this lesson
find two examples on the Internet. Compare and highlight what is the
same or similar about both LMRPs (for example: both may have a defined
service area mentioned).

Materials Needed

2 different-colored highlighters
1 blue pen
2 PPO contracts found on the Web

Directions

1. Use your Web browser and search engine and type in phrases such as

   LMRPs for _____ (type in your city)

   LMRPs for _____ (type in your county)

   LMRPs for _____ (type in your state)

   LMRPs for _____ (type in a specialty that interests you)

   LMRPs for _____ (type in a procedure that interests you)

2. Print two of the LMRPs that interest you.

3. Use one color highlighter for generalized information; use the other for specified information (that is, dates, lists, schedules, and so on) Highlight the following information (if stated):

   - Any problems the LMRP has identified
   - Any stages of revision
   - Any expectation for improvement
   - Any meeting dates (this may be a good field trip or extra credit idea)

4. Discuss the differences and similarities in the contracts with your professor.

Professional Corner

1. Does your physician only perform services covered by Medicare for Medicare beneficiaries?

2. What percentage of the time does your office appeal claims to Medicare? Does your office make time for the appeals process?

3. Do you have a tracking procedure or strategy for appeals to Medicare?

4. Are the Medicare fee schedules that apply to your practice/specialty readily available to view or for use in your software program or hardcopy?

5. Has your office billed for services not yet established by Medicare? What was the outcome?

6. Has Medicare ever paid your office interest on a claim because of nontimely payment?

7. Does the biller know who the Medicare intermediary/carrier is for the area providing services?

8. Does your office have procedures for claims tracing of payments and appeals?

9. Does your office have policies and procedures in place to follow up on claims that have not been paid timely, not been paid at all, or that were denied?

10. Does your office attend yearly workshops?

References

Kazon, Peter & Martin, Cathy. (2008). 2008 and Beyond: Outlook for In-Office Pathology Arrangements. Washington, DC: Alston & Bird.

Aetna. (2/22/08). Medicare Open Plan, Provider Terms and Conditions of Participation Deemed Providers. (22-5-177) El Paso, TX: AETNA.

Blue Cross, Medicare, PFFS. (2008). Medicare Advantage Terms and Conditions. Grand Rapid, MI: Blue Cross.

Federal Registrar. (May 23, 2008). Part II (Department of Health and Human Services, 42 CFR Parts 405, 413, 417). Washington, DC: Federal Registrar.

Practice Management Information Corporation. (January 2007). Medicare Compliance Manual. Los Angeles, CA: PMIC.

Practice Management Information Corporation. (2008). Medicare Rules and Regulations. Los Angeles, CA: PMIC.

Medicaid

Chapter Objectives

Upon completion of this chapter, you should be able to

- Interpret timeliness issues handled by state Medicaid
- Recognize clearinghouse acceptance
- Understand billing service disclosure
- Identify payer of last resort
- Recognize why entities adopt national codes
- Understand how new HCPCS codes are requested for state Medicaid programs
- Recognize pricing criteria
- Understand conversion tables for changed ICD-9-CM codes

Key Terms

comprehensive
  medical care

Health Insurance
  Portability and
  Accounting Act (HIPAA)

local codes

pricing criteria

Introduction to Medicaid

This chapter looks at pricing criteria and how new HCPCS codes are requested by state Medicaid programs, how timeliness issues can affect the provider bottom line, Medicaid as the payer of last resort, and dollar amounts in a coding series. Some states' physician groups and clinics have mostly Medicaid patients, while others have very few. Pricing criteria and what to expect from a state's Medicaid program will help decide how to handle claims and coding issues. This chapter explores those subjects and more.

Medicaid Program Funding Process

comprehensive medical care Complete medical care.

We find Medicaid's beginnings under the Social Security Act of July 1965 in title XIX. If a state offered **comprehensive medical care**, the federal government would give matching funds to provide services to families on public assistance. The services are meant to be comprehensive in their scope and may include drugs and dental services, long-term care, and many services Medicare does not cover. The matching funds, the federal medical assistance percentages, are determined annually per state. The Web site to view your state is http://aspe.hhs.gov/health/fmap.htm.

In the Medicaid program, each state receives funding on a federal level to give services to its constituents in need. The state identifies the need through numerous programs. Each program specifically defines benefits and share of cost for its participants. However, many plans have no share of cost.

In Figure 6-1, we see how the program process works to identify a need, develop a program, define benefits, and determine if there will be a share of cost.

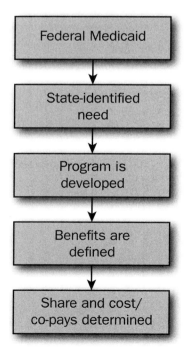

Figure 6-1 Medicaid program process (Delmar/Cengage Learning)

The Program: Described specifically for a population (example Aid to the Blind), Medically Needy (FFP) (code 24). This covers persons who meet the federal criteria for blindness and who do not wish to receive or who are not eligible for a cash grant but are eligible for the state-defined Medicaid service only.

The Benefits: The program will define at what level the patient qualifies for benefits. For example, through the program a patient may be eligible for full benefits, for benefits at a restricted level, or for emergency services only. The program itself will define the benefits for everyone who participates in the plan. If the program restricts recipients in some way, it will be clearly stated.

Share of Cost: A share of cost is when the patient must pay a portion of the cost of the service for using the plan. The patient usually does not pay for this service until it is used. Most plans will state this in a list of program descriptions. Many states have exemptions for share-of-cost responsibility. The most common are: under the age of 21, pregnant, resident of an adult care facility, resident of nursing home, long-term care, immigrant status, OB care, emergency and trauma care.

Figure 6-2 shows some common exemptions for cost sharing.

Co-payments: Some states ask their patients to make co-payments. The co-payment is a set amount for the service, and the patient only pays that amount and no more for that service. (Note that some states do not

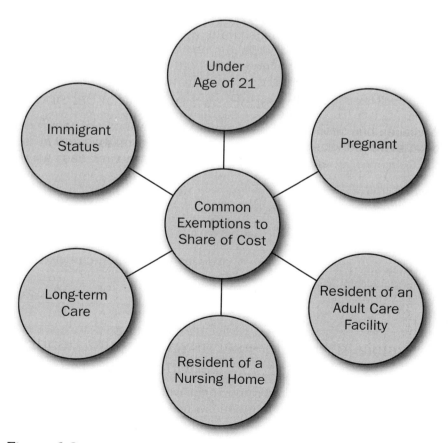

Figure 6-2 Common exemptions to share of cost (Delmar/Cengage Learning)

ask this of their enrollees.) If the state wants co-payments collected from the patient, there is usually an out-of-pocket maximum stated.

Many states give their programs a code to verify eligibility of benefits and share of cost for that program. When verifying eligibility under the plan, this code may be used as a reference. Most states have an eligibility/claims inquiry set in real time, meaning the inquiry can be judged for what the patient qualifies for on that day.

Timeliness Issues Are Handled by Each State

Each state has rules and/or gives its own state code regulations as to the timeliness of submitting claims, settling debt, adjustments, tracers, denied claims, and so on. The state code will usually be quoted in a state assembly bill of title and section defined in the state code of regulations.

Clearinghouse Acceptance

Some states will only accept electronic claims from specific clearinghouses they have contracted with and who therefore know their systems. This stipulation should be stated by the Medicaid program. Some states also distinguish their clearinghouse participation by inpatient and outpatient contractors.

Disclosure of Outside Billing Services

Health Insurance Portability and Accounting Act (HIPAA) Enacted by Congress in 1996, HIPAA addresses such issues as confidentiality, security, and standards of how health care information needs to be handled. It also looks at patients applying for benefits from health care plans like limiting preexisting conditions clauses for the patients and protecting their rights to health care when they change jobs.

Providers are asked to disclose their outside billing service if they use one. This may be requested because of state laws and requirements or because of regulations from the **Health Insurance Portability and Accounting Act (HIPAA)**. HIPAA was enacted by Congress in 1996 and addresses such issues as confidentiality, security, and standards of how health care information needs to be handled. It also looks at patients applying for benefits from health care plans and considers such issues as limiting preexisting conditions clauses for the patients and protecting their rights to health care when they change jobs.

The state may also want a copy of the agreement between the provider and the billing company, in order to gain the following information:

- Confidentiality agreements
- Restrictions about what can be submitted from the billing service
- Audit issues
- Terms of acceptance
- Notification of change-of-services rules
- A list of providers and vendors to whom information will be given

The Payer of Last Resort

Federal law does not allow any Medicaid program to pay as the primary for services when the patient is enrolled in other insurance plans that cover the service. The other insurance or health plans need to be billed first;

then Medicaid is billed as a secondary payer. Thus Medicaid is known as the payer of last resort.

Medicaid may require one of two options: 1) Bill the commercial carrier for a denial relative to the disease/condition covered; the patient then qualifies for claim submission to Medicaid; or 2) Allow the direct submission due to the fact that the primary commercial carrier has no benefit for the disease/condition.

In the following example, a pregnant woman works full time but still qualifies for Medicaid benefits because of her disease/condition.

EXAMPLE: A 39-year-old pregnant female works full time at a restaurant chain, where employees are offered an insurance policy that covers only basic services at a cost to the employee of $250.00 per month with no dependent coverage. The employer chose its own benefits, which do not include maternity. Because the patient is considered high risk for being pregnant at her age, she qualifies for "maternity benefits" only through the state Medicaid system. Upon delivery, her child will be eligible for state Medicaid benefits, in lieu of any other private commercial policy options.

In this example Medicaid allowed the claim to be billed directly and paid the claim according to its allowed amount.

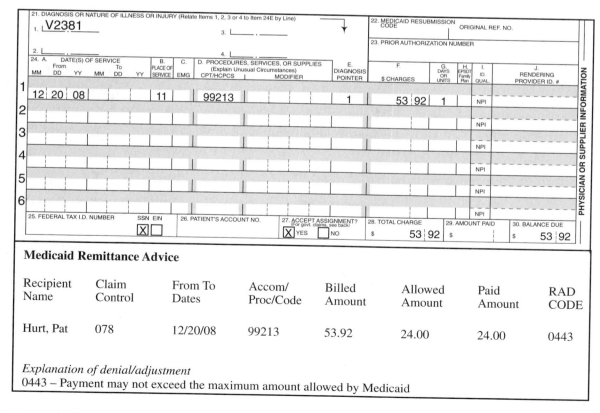

Figure 6-3 Example of payer of last resort (Delmar/Cengage Learning)

Adopting National Codes

As a result of HIPAA, most states have discontinued their use of **local codes** to officially adopt current procedural terminology (CPT) and the Healthcare Common Procedure Coding System (HCPCS) codes to establish, respectively, uniform reporting and payment. Added to these are modifiers and codes for place of service that are acceptable for payment consideration as well. State Medicaid HMO programs are also expected to follow protocols set by HIPAA.

Requesting New HCPCS Codes for a State Medicaid Program

The states should have discontinued use of local codes to report new services, services not covered by Medicare, or services for which there are no codes to choose from. HIPAA wants only national HCPCS codes assigned for services or products that cannot be identified by CPT codes. Following this protocol makes for continuity and uniformity in reporting.

When there is a need for a new code, the state Medicaid submits a request, after review for a HCPCS code(s), to the CMS operations arm, or CMSO. Then the request travels on to the HCPCS work group. If the HCPCS work group decides there is a need, it will assign a HCPCS code, and implications for private payers will be looked at by a national panel.

T codes are HCPCS codes not covered by Medicare but needed by states for their coding and billing process.

Most states give coding information, corrections, changes, updates, and reviews in their monthly bulletins. In some offices, the coding and/or billing staff has access to these, but in others it is the duty of the operations managers, office managers, or physicians to interpret and implement informational changes to be applied, and to comply with dates necessary for reporting and payment purposes.

Medicaid bulletins give direction for various procedures, CPT codes that will be covered under the plan, codes covered with prior authorization, and noncovered codes.

Many states want diagnostic codes stated on their prior-authorization paperwork. These codes include the International Classification of Disease, Ninth Revision, clinical modification (ICD-9-CM) codes. Also, underlying conditions that may affect the outcomes and dates of onset of each diagnosis are expected and may be needed for the patient to qualify for full treatment consideration by the Medicaid program giving consent.

Some wish to have reportings similar to SOAP note or evaluation and management type reporting of past family and social histories as an attachment, for their overall consideration and verification of treatment and plan-of-treatment justification and understanding of the request.

Most prior authorization forms are available through PDF files accessible through the states' respective Medicaid Web sites. Some have PDF files that can be filled in, to use with Adobe Acrobat Reader.

These files may be completed and sent electronically or printed and sent with attachments. Some states call these treatment authorization requests, or TARs.

Pricing Criteria

Most programs will explain the **pricing criteria** by which they pay claims. The criteria for what services will be covered by claim type will be explained individually by each program. Claim type may be a certain category of service, for example, pharmacy, dental, inpatient, outpatient, and so on. Not every program will cover each claim type, but a program will cover services it deems necessary to maintain the population of the program.

Since Medicaid is the payer of last resort, it covers a wide range of services not picked up by the average health plan, for example, long-term care, hospice, dental, home health, or nursing home. Each state plan will explain how the patient qualifies for the services under that plan. Many times a state does not have an overall qualifying criteria unless it has decided to offer only one plan to all those who qualify for the services. The program and/or plan will describe how criteria apply to each patient who participates.

In some states, patients may see a case management provider who is a physician. These physicians usually only provide primary care and refer the patients to outside providers for specialty care, labs, inpatient hospital, and so on. This system is unlike that for a patient who participates in an HMO, where the physician is responsible for providing all medical service needs of the patient.

Conversion Tables for Changed ICD-9-CM Codes

Every year Centers for Medicaid and Medicare Services (CMS) and the National Center for Health Statistics post their changes for the ICD-9-CM diagnosis codes; these changes are to be used after the effective date stated. A biller/coder can find lists of the conversion codes and their effective dates at www.cms.gov. The pathway is: CMS home, Medicare, ICD-9 Provider Diagnostic Codes, Overview.

Diagnosis code categories have changed or evolved over a period of time. The benefit of this conversion table is you can clearly see the year of the change beginning October 1 in any calendar year.

In noting the changes, observe that many codes have the ability to become more specific with the addition of a fifth-digit choice, while only the fourth digit was the most specific in prior years. Or, codes become more defined as they are taken out of the generalized digits .8 or .9, with .8 being a catchall digit of the disease specified in written word but not bearing its own code for the coder to choose. Or, as in .9, generalized fourth digits advance to a mix of fourth and fifth digits, as in .98 to .99. Also note that dates in the "Effective October 1" column have the year of change. See Figures 6-4 and 6-5 for examples of ICD conversion tables.

Current Code(s) Assignment	Effective October 1	Previous Code(s) Assignment
288.60-288.65	2006	288.8
288.66	**2007**	**288.69**
288.69	2006	288.8
289.52	2003	289.59
289.53	2006	288.0
289.81-289.82	2003	289.8
289.83	2006	289.89
289.89	2003	289.8
291.81	1996	291.8
291.82	2005	291.89
291.89	1996	291.8
292.85	2005	292.89
293.84	1996	293.89
294.10-294.11	2000	294.1
300.82	1996	300.81
305.1	1994	305.10, 305.11, 305.12, 305.13 (codes deleted)
312.81-312.82, 312.89	1994	312.8
315.32	1996	315.39
315.34	**2007**	**315.31; 315.39**
320.81-320.89	1992	320.8
323.01-323.02	2006	323.0
323.41-323.42	2006	323.4
323.51-323.52	2006	323.5
323.61-323.63	2006	323.6
323.71-323.72	2006	323.7
323.81-323.82	2006	323.8

\# Code title restated
***Amended 10/02/2004

Conversion Table of New ICD-9 CM Codes, October 2007
Page 8 of 52

Figure 6-4 Example of conversion table stated by CMS and NCHS, October 2007 (Delmar/ Cengage Learning)

Diagnosis Codes

Current Code(s) Assignment	Effective October 1	Previous Code(s) Assignment
005.81	1995	005.8
005.89	1995	005.8
007.4	1997	007.8
007.5	2000	007.8
008.00-008.09	1992	008.0
008.43-008.47	1992	008.49
008.61-008.69	1992	008.6
031.2	1997	031.8
038.10-038.11	1997	038.1
038.19	1997	038.1

\# Code title restated
***Amended 10/02/2004

Conversion Table of New ICD-9 CM Codes, October 2007
Page 1 of 52

Figure 6-5 Example of the conversion table (Delmar/Cengage Learning)

Medicaid Case Study – How Rates Vary in Medicaid

Medicaid rates vary by geographic area, RBRVS, code series, amount billed, and fee schedules. The following are three forms of reimbursement offered in various states around the country.

Basic Medicaid Rates Offering One Fee for a Series of Codes

A provider may be reimbursed a basic rate for a group of codes, no matter what the level of service.

An example would be that E/M office visit codes 99201–99205 and 99211–99215 all receive the same rate of reimbursement, $53.92. The provider could bill its regular rates but, according to the contract, would receive only one rate.

Fee Schedule	
99201	$53.92
99202	$53.92
99203	$53.92
99204	$53.92
99205	$53.92
99211	$53.92
99212	$53.92
99213	$53.92
99214	$53.92
99215	$53.92

Figure 6-6 Medicare rates – one fee for a series of codes (Delmar/Cengage Learning)

Dollar Amounts in a Coding Series

Some Medicaid programs pay a specific dollar amount regarding the series code and the dollar amount billed.

In such cases, any visit having to do with a well-child checkup being billed at $90.00 will be reimbursed at $42.99, regardless of the code, as long as it is in the series.

In some states, Medicaid reimbursement is lower than Medicare rates, sometimes 45 percent to 60 percent lower. This has discouraged many physicians and hospitals from participating in state Medicaid programs altogether.

Sometimes providers receive more in reimbursement from where they perform their services. In other words, a facility may be reimbursed at a lesser rate than if the provider stays in the office on a *place of service 11.*

Managed Care Fee-for-Service Rates Vary in Medicaid Contracts

Rates may vary from carrier to carrier. Providers may contract for different or varied rates, depending on the Medicaid population who participate in their plans. Or providers may receive different rates, depending on the program the patient participates in. The following is an example of a rate for E/M 99213, a level three office visit, from two managed care companies.

Xxx Managed Care Company			
99213 OV	$75.00	Allowed $26.00	Write off $49.00
Yyy Managed Care Company			
99213	$85.00	Allowed $35.00	Write off $50.00

Figure 6-7 Coding series dollar amounts (Delmar/Cengage Learning)

Summary

Each state administers its own Medicaid program, and in doing so, provides services needed to those who participate in its programs. Some states have only one program, while others offer various programs catering to the specific needs of those enrolled. Each program announces the criteria by which a patient may become a participant. Many states have programs for specific groups of participants, for example, children, the blind, expectant mothers, and so on. In this way, the program specifies what codes/services will be covered and the pricing criteria at which it pays the claims. One group of participants may need to pay a co-payment or coinsurance, while others from the same state, but participating in a different program, may not.

Some communities in low-income areas decide to open clinics with a high Medicaid participation rate. These clinics give their best efforts to provide comprehensive care to those on Medicaid or without access to health care of any kind. Community clinics are sometimes the only alternative for participants who have a dwindling provider base in their area.

Web Sites

Latest updates of HIPAA and final rules (in this one you can download implementation guidelines), *aspe.hhs.gov/admnsimp*

Basic HIPAA news to keep up-to-date, *http://www.cms.gov/hipaa*

CMS Administrative Data Work Group – CMS DOQ Project Administration Work, *http://www.cms.gov*

National Quality Forum, *http://www.quality/forum.org*

Review

Fill in the Blank

1. _____ codes are HCPCS codes not covered by Medicaid but needed by states for their coding and billing process.

2. Most states give coding information, corrections, changes, updates, and reviews in their _____ _____.

3. Most prior-authorization forms are available through _____ _____, accessible through each state's respective Medicaid _____ _____.

4. Most Medicaid programs will explain the pricing _____ at which they pay claims.

5. Since Medicaid is the payer of last resort, it covers a wide range of service not picked up by the _____ _____ _____.

6. In some states, patients may see a _____ _____ _____ who is a physician.

7. Each Medicaid program announces the _____ by which a patient may become a _____.

8. Many states have programs for specific _____ of _____.

9. Some communities in _____ areas decide to open _____ with a high Medicaid participation rate.

Review Questions

1. Under what circumstances will the federal government give matching funds to the states that offer Medicaid programs? _____
    _____
    _____

2. What services might be included in a state Medicaid plan? _____
    _____
    _____

3. How does the state identify those in need of their Medicaid programs?
    _____
    _____

4. Who defines the benefits the participants will receive? _____
    _____
    _____

5. What are some share-of-cost responsibility exemptions? _____
    _____
    _____

6. What kind of information might you find in a provider billing agreement? _____
    _____
    _____

7. Explain what *payer of last resort* means. _____
    _____
    _____

8. Why are state Medicaid programs discontinuing local codes? _____
    _____
    _____

9. What is the process of requesting new HCPCS codes for Medicaid reporting needs? _____
    _____
    _____

10. Name some examples of information found in Medicaid bulletins. ___
    _____
    _____

Critical Thinking Exercise

Some providers look to serve Medicaid populations in their area; others have a sprinkling of patients from programs specific to their specialty. This Web search will give billers/coders an idea of programs/services offered in their areas to those who participate in their plans.

Materials Needed

2 different-colored highlighters
1 blue pen
2 printouts of Medicaid program services offered

Directions

1. Use your Web browser and search engine and type in phrases such as:

    Medicaid programs in _____ (your state)
    Medicaid or the name of the Medicaid program in your state (for example, TennCare, MediCal)
    Medicaid programs available for _____ (insert one of the following):

    - blindness,
    - children 7–12
    - skilled nursing

2. Does the program offer comprehensive services or services specific to an illness stated in the program?

3. Use one color highlighter to mark similar information in program services.

    Use the other to highlight service unique to the program offered.

4. Discuss the differences and similarities of services with your professor.

Professional Corner

Medicaid is one of the best types of programs to study outcomes of codes used by defined geographic populations. Data is gathered, compared, evaluated, and managed, by cost, common codes, payer types, and rates. The Medicaid population encompasses every age group and every disease in the community in which it serves. The data may be studied and compared to Medicare rates, to commercial fee for service, to commercial HMOs and PPOs, and so on.

*Since most states' Medicaid reimbursement is far below **usual, customary and reasonable** UCR rates, patients having access to the care they need is a concern. Some states pay more or a higher percentage to service areas (for example, well-child care) to assure those populations' needs are met. This encourages providers to accept patients from these programs and allows them to afford to see these patients.*

Some provider groups practice in low-income areas where Medicaid is a main source of income. Codes reported are used beyond reimbursement purposes. They help the program decide how it will ration payment, based on who in its system is in need of the most services and how those services are delivered.

If your physician/provider accepts Medicaid, you may have access to timely data that explain reimbursement rationale by code. Or, the Internet may have similar data, but it may be four to five years older. Searching for this data is easy. Type in your state name, and phrases such as "code payments" and "comparing CPT codes" with names of programs your providers participate in.

References

Naujokaitis. (2007). Provider Handbook. Lincoln, NE: Nebraska Department of Health and Human Services, Nebraska Medicaid Program.

Federal Registrar. (May 23, 2008). Part II (Department of Health and Human Services, 42 CFR Part 440, CMS-2132-F). Washington, D.C.: Federal Registrar.

Health and Human Services. (6/19/08). Montana Medicaid Provider Information. Helena, Montana: Department of Public Health and Human Services.

Medicare Rights Center. (January 2009). How Does Medicaid Work? Juneau: State of Alaska, Health and Human Services, Division of Public Assistance.

CPT Modifiers

Chapter Objectives

Upon completion of this chapter, you should be able to

- Understand definitions of modifiers as they relate to the codes
- Identify when these modifiers would be used
- Comprehend the reasons why modifiers are used
- Match the meaning of procedure codes to the modifiers
- Recognize diagnosis codes as they relate to the modifiers in examples
- Understand the case studies in the chapter
- Choose modifiers for use with CPT codes
- Distinguish between the need for a modifier and a CPT code

Key Terms

huffing addiction	medical necessity	modifiers	Mohs surgery
primary procedure			

Introduction to Modifiers

This chapter explores modifiers in detail and gives scenarios of appropriate use with CPT codes, distinguishes the need for a modifier, and explores various circumstances that substantiate and justify the use of modifiers.

> **modifiers** Modifiers explain how a procedure was modified or changed in some way but not enough to choose a new code.

CPT **modifiers** are codes added to current procedural terminology codes already selected by the coder. They tell the story of how the procedure described in the CPT code changed or needed to be modified from the procedure reported. Modifiers appear beside the CPT code, in block 24-D, on the CMS-1500 claim form when physician's services are reported. Modifiers should only be used when needed, and they have their own definitions to be taken into consideration along with the original code. Reporting modifiers correctly, when needed, will help the practice define special circumstances of the patients and sometimes of the practice.

Sometimes a procedure changes, but not enough to choose a different CPT code altogether. This is where modifiers can become invaluable because they tell another part of the story unique to the circumstance of that patient, on that date. Modifiers will help not only in getting correct payment to the provider but also in getting payment for future services considered for authorization and services to the patient. Modifiers also help code definitions stay statistically sound.

Many payers' computer systems do not have the capability of reading modifiers to make the decision for payment, and therefore the claims are set aside for staff review. Many consider their use by the provider a cause for review of the claim. Yet CCI edits will tell a payer if the modifier can be used with a particular CPT code. This editing process provides a mechanism for weeding out what would not be considered in basic coding conventions.

A defined set of CPT modifiers exist, and their definitions are written in the CPT manuals themselves. HCPCS modifiers can also be used with CPT codes themselves, but the biller/coder cannot interchange the CPT modifier codes with HCPCS codes. Figure 7-1 indicates the correct use of modifiers with CPT and HCPCS codes.

> CPT codes can use CPT modifiers and/or HCPCS modifiers.
>
> HCPCS codes cannot use CPT modifiers.

Figure 7-1 Correct use of modifiers with CPT and HCPCS codes (Delmar/Cengage Learning)

Modifiers, Scenarios of Use, and Their Definitions

The following are CPT modifier definitions with scenarios for their appropriate use, including proper and sometimes improper examples, noting the sequence and placement suitable for CMS-1500 claim forms.

Modifier -21 or 09921

The following describes the correct use of -21 modifier.

Definition of -21

Prolonged E/M services: When the face-to-face or floor/unit service(s) provided is prolonged or otherwise greater than that usually required for the highest level of E/M service within a given category. A report may be appropriate.

Scenario

New patient presents with family members who are concerned about the patient's health. The patient is 14 years old, has asthma, and wants to play high school football. The patient has a heart murmur, was a preemie baby, and previously in rehab for a **huffing addiction**. (A huffing addiction is inhalant abuse, where mostly chemical vapors are inhaled to get high.)

> **huffing addiction** Inhalant abuse, where mostly chemical vapors are inhaled to get high.

Explanation of Why the Modifier Is Used

Here the physician performs a level-5 E/M because of the patient's medical history and desire to play sports. The modifier -21 is added because of the family's concern for the patient's overall health, and discussions took place with the physician. The physician noted the time spent in the examining room began at 1:30 and ended at 3:00 p.m. Figure 7-2 shows the use of modifier -21.

DIAGNOSIS

493.00	Extrinsic asthma, without mention of status asthmaticus
785.2	Undiagnosed cardiac murmurs
V15.89	Other specified personal history presenting health hazards, other

PROCEDURE

99205-21   Office or other outpatient visit for the evaluation and management of a new patient, which requires these three key components:

- a comprehensive history
- a comprehensive examination
- medical decision making of high complexity

Figure 7-2 Example of CPT modifier -21 (Delmar/Cengage Learning)

Counseling and coordination of care with other providers or agencies are provided, consistent with the nature of the problems and the patient and/or the family needs. Usually the presenting problems are of moderate to high severity. Physicians typically spend 60 minutes face to face with the patient and/or family – prolonged E/M services.

Modifier -22 or 09922

The following is an example of the correct use of -22 modifier.

Definition of -22

Unusual procedural services: When the service(s) provided is/are greater than those usually required for the listed procedure. A report may be appropriate.

Scenario

Patient is admitted for a bilateral tubal ligation, or BTL, in an ambulatory surgery center. Patient has an obese abdomen, which requires extra time for the entry, and preventa prevous C-section scars and adhesions and endometriosis. An extra 45 minutes of time is needed to perform the BTL. The physician only does the bilateral tubal ligation.

Explanation of Why the Modifier Is Used

Here the time is greater because the patient is obese; the opening and closing of the patient would be included in a global surgery, and this is not billed separately. The modifier is appropriate to state the extra time because no new separately billable service has been performed. Figure 7-3 shows the use of modifier -22.

DIAGNOSIS

V25.2	Sterilization
617.9	Endometriosis, site unspecified
709.2	Scar conditions and fibrosis of skin

Figure 7-3 Example of -22 modifier used correctly (Delmar/Cengage Learning)

PROCEDURE

58670-22   Laparoscopy, surgical; with fulguration of oviducts (with or without transaction), unusual procedure services

Modifier -23 or 09923

The following is an example of the correct use of -23 modifier for the use of anesthesia.

Definition of -23

A procedure that usually requires either no anesthesia or local anesthesia must be done under general anesthesia because of unusual circumstances.

Scenario

The patient is an adult and mentally retarded. He presents for a tooth extraction and cleaning in the ambulatory surgical center or outpatient hospital setting. General anesthesia is given.

Explanation of Why the Modifier Is Used

Anesthesia is required due to patient/staff safety issues. Figure 7-4 shows the use of modifier -23.

DIAGNOSIS

319   Unspecified mental retardation
523.1   Chronic gingivitis
521.03   Diseases of hard tissues of teeth, dental caries extending into pulp

PROCEDURE

D7140   Extraction, erupted tooth or exposed root, elevation and/or forceps removal
D1110   Prophylaxis – adult, no minimum age

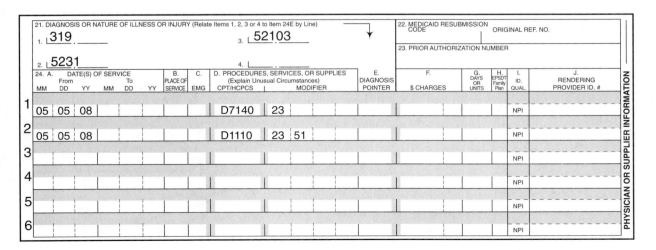

Figure 7-4 Use of -23 modifier with a procedure (Delmar/Cengage Learning)

Modifier -24 or 09924

The following describes the correct use of the -24 modifier in a procedure.

Definition of -24

Unrelated E/M service was performed by the same physician during a postoperative period. The physician may need to indicate that an E/M service was performed during the postoperative period for a reason unrelated to the original procedure.

Scenario

The patient presented for cataract extraction on Friday and over the weekend developed contact conjunctivitis in both eyes and had to be seen for an evaluation and management visit; an ointment was prescribed.

Explanation of Why the Modifier Is Used

In this example, the patient had a problem with her eye and returns to the surgeon thinking this may have something to do with the surgery, but it does not. Hence, there is a separate E/M by the same physician during a postoperative period. Figure 7-5 shows the use of modifier -24.

DIAGNOSIS

372.00   Acute conjunctivitis, unspecified

PROCEDURE

99212-24   Office or other outpatient visit for the
                evaluation and management of an established
                patient, which requires at least two of
                three key components:

                • a problem-focused history

                • a problem-focused examination

                • straightforward medical decision making

Figure 7-5 An example of the correct use of -24 for a procedure (Delmar/Cengage Learning)

Usually, the presenting problem(s) are self-limited or minor; unrelated E/M service is provided during the postoperative period by the same physican who performed the surgery.

Modifier -25 or 09925

The following scenario describes the correct use of the -25 modifier.

Definition of -25

Modifier -25 describes significant and separately identifiable E/M services performed by the same physician on the same day of the procedure or other services.

Scenario

The patient is in the hospital for acute renal failure due to toxic effects of therapeutic use of Digoxin® administered properly. After supervising dialysis, the patient complains of pain under her breast; the physician attends to the patient and finds a rash in the breast area under the bra line.

Explanation of Why the Modifier Is Used

The patient complains of an unrelated problem on the same day to the physician caring for her. After evaluating the problem, this is separate from the reason for the visit which is the renal failure, yet the physician performs the E/M service and does not wait. Figure 7-6 shows the use of modifier -25.

DIAGNOSIS

782.1	Rash and other nonspecific skin eruption
584.9	Acute renal failure, unspecified
E942.1	Agents primarily affecting the cardiovascular system; cardiotonic glycosides and drugs of similar action

Figure 7-6 An example of the correct use of -25 in coding (Delmar/Cengage Learning)

PROCEDURE

90935	Hemodialysis procedure with single physician evaluation
99231-25	Subsequent hospital care per day, for the evaluation and management of a patient, which requires at least two of these three key components:

- a problem-focused interval history
- a problem-focused examination
- decision making that is straightforward or of low complexity

Usually the patient is stable, recovering, or improving but requires significant, separately identifiable E/M service by the same physician on the same day of the procedure or other service.

Modifier -26 Professional Component or 09926

The following describes the use of -26 when coding a professional component of a procedure.

Definition of -26

Some procedures have a combined professional and technical component. When the physician component is reported separately, the service may be identified by adding a modifier -26.

Scenario

The homebound patient complains of pain in his wrist after falling at home while under the care of a home health worker. The general practitioner calls for a mobile X-ray; the films are taken and developed and then delivered to the doctor's office for interpretation. No evidence of fracture is found. The general practitioner codes for the interpretation with the -26.

Explanation of Why the Modifier Is Used

Here the physician does not take the films, the mobile X-ray does. Therefore, the physician can only charge for the professional component -26, which means the physician reads the films and reports the outcome of what is seen on the X-rays. Figure 7-7 shows the use of modifier -26.

DIAGNOSIS

719.43	Pain in joint, forearm
E885.9	Fall on same level from other slipping, tripping, or stumbling
E849.0	Place of occurrence, home

PROCEDURE

73110-26	Radiologic examination, wrist; complete, minimum of three views

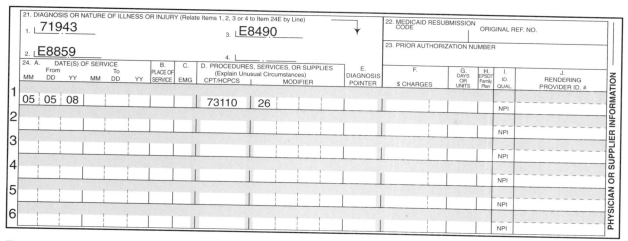

Figure 7-7 The use of -26 as a modifier in coding (Delmar/Cengage Learning)

Modifier -32 Mandated Services or 09932

The following scenario depicts the use of the -32 modifier in coding.

Definition of -32

Services related to mandated consultations and/or related services like PROs, third-party payers, governmental, legislative, or regulatory requirements.

Scenario 1 for -32

Patient with lab indication of prostate cancer but has no physical indications. The physician requests a referral for surgery, TURP, Transurethral Resection of the Prostate, but the HMO wants a second opinion before authorizing.

Explanation of Why the Modifier Is Used

> **medical necessity** A treatment, standard, or medically accepted procedure that is recognized or furnished to treat a symptom, disease, or condition. How an insurance company defines what is needed or necessary can be decided by state laws, federal laws, by contract or by limits to the medical plan.

This physician is being audited for past **medical necessity** issues, meaning the physician may be asking that procedures be performed for which their medical need is in question. The patient probably will not know or understand this, and the HMO does not want to pay for procedure(s) not medically necessary. Figure 7-8 shows the use of modifier -32.

DIAGNOSIS

600.91	Hyperplasia of prostate, unspecified
790.93	Elevated prostate-specific antigen (PSA)

PROCEDURE

99242-32   Office consultation for a new or established patient, which requires these three key components:

- an expanded problem focused history
- an expanded problem focused examination
- straightforward medical decision making

Usually the presenting problem(s) are of low severity. Physicians typically spend 30 minutes face to face with the patient and/or family – mandated services.

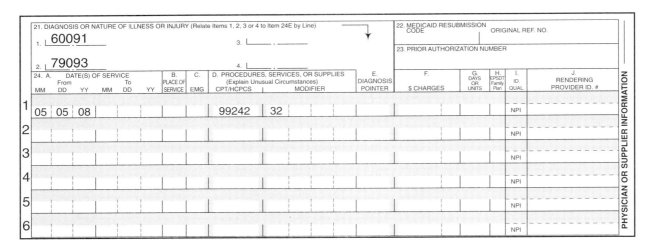

Figure 7-8 This shows an example of -32 used correctly when coding (Delmar/Cengage Learning)

Scenario 2 for -32

The following shows another use of the -32 modifier in coding.

Explanation of Why the Modifier Is Used

The physician is under investigation for cataract surgery on patients with immature cataracts. The insurance company wants a second opinion.

Usually such procedures need a preauthorization. The insurance company may have seen signs of requesting surgeries prematurely in the past and will request second opinions for a period of time for sampling purposes. Figure 7-9 shows the use of modifier -32.

DIAGNOSIS

    366.03   Infantile, juvenile, and presenile cataract; cortical lamellar, or zonular cataract

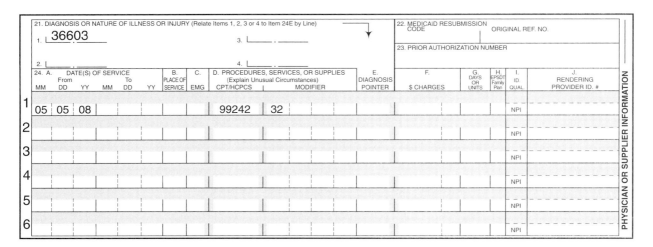

Figure 7-9 Another example of correct -32 coding (Delmar/Cengage Learning)

PROCEDURE

```
99242-32   Office consultation for a new or
           established patient, which requires these
           three key components:
           • an expanded problem focused history
           • an expanded problem focused examination
           • straightforward medical decision making
Usually the presenting problem(s) are of low severity.
Physicians typically spend 30 minutes face to face
with the patient and/or family - mandated services.
```

Modifier -47 or 09947

The following describes the correct use of modifier -47 when coding.

Definition of -47

Regional or general anesthesia provided by the surgeon. This does not include local anesthesia.

Scenario

The patient reports to the ambulatory surgery center per the physician's request to have a manipulation of a severe dislocation of the metacarpophalangeal MCP joint of the ring finger. The patient has no one to drive him home; he drove himself. The patient presented to the physician's office thinking he might have just a sprained finger. The patient was playing baseball at a family picnic when the injury occurred.

Explanation of Why the Modifier Is Used

Here the patient presents with a more serious problem than presumed earlier. The physician is obligated to tend to the patient and to do so properly; the physician must give a regional anesthesia (for example, Bier Block) without an anesthesiologist present. Figure 7-10 shows the use of modifier - 47.

21. DIAGNOSIS OR NATURE OF ILLNESS OR INJURY (Relate Items 1, 2, 3 or 4 to Item 24E by Line)
1. 834.01 3. E849.4
2. E917.0 4. .
22. MEDICAID RESUBMISSION CODE ORIGINAL REF. NO.
23. PRIOR AUTHORIZATION NUMBER

	24. A. DATE(S) OF SERVICE From MM	DD	YY	To MM	DD	YY	B. PLACE OF SERVICE	C. EMG	D. PROCEDURES, SERVICES, OR SUPPLIES (Explain Unusual Circumstances) CPT/HCPCS	MODIFIER	E. DIAGNOSIS POINTER	F. $ CHARGES	G. DAYS OR UNITS	H. EPSDT Family Plan	I. ID. QUAL.	J. RENDERING PROVIDER ID. #
1	05	05	08						26705	47					NPI	
2															NPI	
3															NPI	
4															NPI	
5															NPI	
6															NPI	

PHYSICIAN OR SUPPLIER INFORMATION

Figure 7-10 The correct use of -47 modifier in coding for a local anesthesia (Delmar/Cengage Learning)

DIAGNOSIS

834.01   Closed dislocation, metacarpophalangeal, joint

E917.0   Striking against or struck accidentally by objects or persons, in sports

E849.4   Place of recreation and sport

PROCEDURE

26705   Closed treatment of metacarpophalangeal dislocation, single, with manipulation; requiring anesthesia.

Modifier -50 or 09950

The following describes the use of -50 when coding a bilateral procedure.

Definition of -50

Bilateral procedures: Unless otherwise identified in the listing, bilateral procedures that are performed at the same operative session should be identified by adding a modifier -50.

Scenario

Patient presents for a blepharoplasty, contralateral side, due to "saggy" eyelids; says she looks tired and old when she looks in the mirror.

Explanation of Why the Modifier Is Used

This physician performs the procedure on both sides, but the procedure code only recognizes one eye. The -50 is used to recognize both sides. Figure 7-11 shows the use of modifier -50.

DIAGNOSIS

V50.1   Other plastic surgery for unacceptable cosmetic appearance; blepharoplasty each eye

PROCEDURE

15823-50   Blepharoplasty, upper eyelid; excessive skin weighing down lid

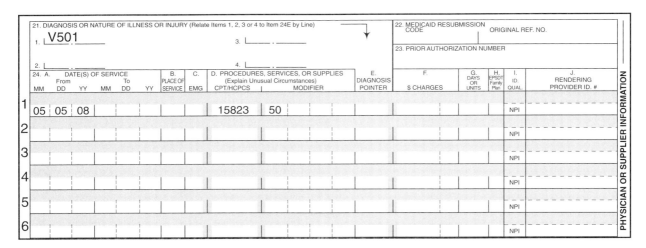

Figure 7-11 The correct use of -50 to code a bilateral procedure (Delmar/Cengage Learning)

Modifier -51 or 09951

The following describes the correct use of modifier -51 when coding.

Definition of -51

Multiple procedures: When multiple procedure(s) other than E/M services are performed at the same session by the same provider, the **primary procedure** or service may be reported as listed. A primary procedure is the first or main procedure.

Figure 7-12 shows what is exempt under modifier -51.

Scenario

The patient presents to the operating room of an ambulatory surgery center with a preoperative diagnosis of facial pain on the right side.

Explanation of Why the Modifier Is Used

The procedures performed are not bundled and are performed at the same surgical session. The modifier -51 is recognizing this for payment consideration. The payer may consider procedures identified with the modifier -51 at 50 percent of the negotiated fee. It would be a good idea to check the participating provider contract or fee schedule for payment of this modifier. Modifier -51 should be used with different procedures, not with same procedures performed at the same surgical session. (See modifier -50 or -59.) Such billing may be looked at as duplicate billing.

Medi-Cal looks for the modifier -AG to identify the primary procedure that may be considered at full fee, and the procedures with a modifier -51 may be considered at 50 percent reimbursement. Figure 7-13 show the correct use of modifier -51.

DIAGNOSIS

473.2	Chronic sinusitis, ethmoidal
784.0	Headache, facial pain

PROCEDURES

Sinus surgery for right-sided facial pain

Ethmoidectomy (A&P)	31255-RT
Maxillary antrostomy	31256-RT-51
Frontal exploration	31276-RT-51
Sphenoidotomy	31287-RT-51

What Is "Modifier -51 Exempt"?

In the CPT appendix, you will find a listing/summary of codes that are "-51 exempt," which means the rules for modifier -51 do not apply to the codes on that list. Since the codes may change from year to year, it would be wise to check the listing for codes routinely used in the medical office where you currently work or will work in the future.

Figure 7-12 Modifier -51 exempt summary explanation (Delmar/Cengage Learning)

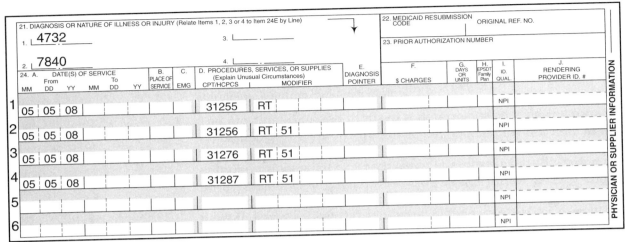

Figure 7-13 An example of using -51 in procedure coding (Delmar/Cengage Learning)

Modifier -52 or 09952

The following describes using -52 as a modifier with reduced services.

Definition of -52

Reduced services: Under certain circumstances a service or procedure is partially reduced or eliminated at the physician's discretion. The -52 signifies the service has been reduced.

Scenario

Patient presents to outpatient department of hospital for bilateral tubal ligation. Surgeon discovers during surgery that patient has a congenital anomaly of only one tube and one ovary. The physician ligates only one side, and the procedure takes less time than allocated.

Explanation of Why the Modifier Is Used

The physician begins to perform the service and finds he can only do one side. Here the process has not changed, just the physician's capability of performing it completely. This justifies the modifier -52. Figure 7-14 shows the use of modifier -52.

DIAGNOSIS

752.19	Anomalies of fallopian tubes and broad ligaments
752.0	Congenital anomalies of genital organs, anomalies of ovaries
V25.2	Encounter for contraceptive management, sterilization

PROCEDURES

58670-52	Laparoscopy, surgical; fulguration of oviducts (with or without transaction), reduced services

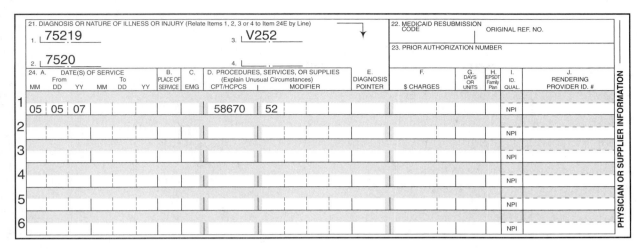

Figure 7-14 The correct use of -52 to show reduced services (Delmar/Cengage Learning)

Modifier -53 or 09953

The following shows the use of modifier -53 to describe a discontinued procedure.

Definition of -53

Discontinued procedure: Under certain circumstances the physician may elect to terminate a surgical or diagnostic procedure. Due to extenuating circumstances or those that threaten the well-being of a patient, it may be necessary to indicate that a surgical or diagnostic procedure was started but discontinued. This modifier is not used to report elective cancellation of a procedure prior to the patient's anesthesia induction and/or surgical preparation into the surgical suite.

Scenario

Patient is at the endoscopic center with a history of colon polyps. The patient presents for a colonoscopy but due to a twisted colon, the scope cannot be advanced to the cecum and only 60 percent of the colon can be visualized.

Explanation of Why the Modifier Is Used

Under the circumstances, the patient's colon will not let the procedure continue as would normally happen. The physician was planning to perform the full procedure, but the patient's twisted colon precluded the procedure from being completed. Figure 7-15 shows the use of modifier -53.

DIAGNOSIS

751.5   Other anomalies of intestine
V12.72   Diseases of digestive system, colonic polyps

PROCEDURE

45378-53 Colonoscopy, flexible, proximal to splenic flexure; diagnostic, with or without collection of specimen(s) by brushing or washing, with or without colon decompression (separate procedure), discontinued procedure

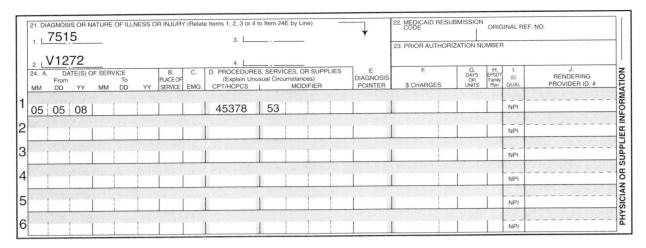

Figure 7-15 The use of -53 to show a discontinued procedure (Delmar/Cengage Learning)

Modifier -54 or 09954

The following describes using modifier -54 to show different physicians performing surgery and preoperative or postoperative management.

Definition of -54

Surgical care only: When one physician performs a surgical procedure and another provides a preoperative and/or postoperative management, surgical services may be identified by adding a modifier -54.

Scenario

The patient presents with a retinal tear and is referred to a retinologist. However, the patient's ophthalmologist did not relinquish the patient and did the postoperative visits and vision testing.

Explanation of Why the Modifier Is Used

Sometimes, the patient's physician will not relinquish preoperative or postoperative services. Sometimes this may be due to an obligation to an HMO or PPO for the contracted provider. Such a stipulation shows a recognition of postoperative service not being included in the global because the patient received his services from a physician other than the surgeon. The surgeon would bill a modifier -54. Figure 7-16 shows the use of modifier -54.

DIAGNOSIS

361.00   Retinal detachment with retinal defect, unspecified

PROCEDURE

67107-54   Repair of retinal detachment; scleral buckling, such as lamellar scleral dissection, imbrications or encircling procedure, with or without implant, with or without cryotherapy, photocoagulation and drainage or subretinal fluid – surgical care only

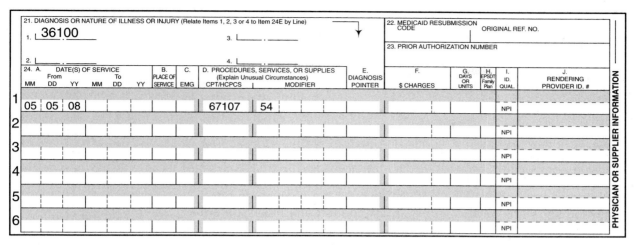

Figure 7-16 The use of -54 to show physicians performing different parts of a patient's care (Delmar/Cengage Learning)

Modifier -55 or 09955

The following describes using the -55 modifier to describe postoperative care.

Definition of -55

Postoperative management only: When one physician performs the postoperative management and another physician has performed the surgical procedure.

Scenario

In the same case as described earlier, the ophthalmologist would bill for the postmanagement only.

Explanation of Why the Modifier Is Used

Sometimes, the patient's physician will not relinquish preoperative or postoperative services. Sometimes this may be due to an obligation to an HMO or PPO for the contracted provider. Such a stipulation shows a recognition of postoperative service not being included in the global because the patient received his services from a physician other than the surgeon. The ophthalmologist would bill the -55 modifier. Figure 7-17 shows the use of modifier -55.

DIAGNOSIS

V67.09   Follow-up examination, following other surgery

PROCEDURE

67107-55   Repair of retinal detachment; scleral buckling (such as lamellar scleral dissection, imbrication or encircling procedure), with or without implant, with or without cryotherapy, photocoagulation and drainage of subretinal fluid – postoperative management only

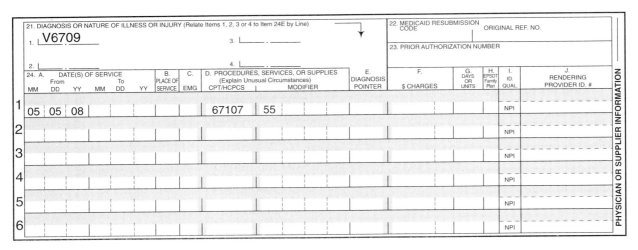

Figure 7-17 The use of -55 in coding (Delmar/Cengage Learning)

Modifier -56 or 09956

The following shows the use of -56 when coding different stages of surgical care.

Definition of -56

Preoperative management only: When one physician performs the preoperative care and evaluation and another physician performs the surgical procedure, the preoperative component may be identified with a modifier -56.

Scenario

In the same case, the patient's general practitioner did the preop due to comorbidity of hypertension and diabetes mellitus.

Explanation of Why the Modifier Is Used

The general practitioner is justified in doing the preoperative management because of the patient's illnesses and the GP's knowledge of them. Another physician may not understand the nuances of this patient's care as much as the physician who has been historically caring for the patient. Figure 7-18 shows the use of modifier -56.

DIAGNOSIS

361.00	Retinal detachment with retinal defect; retinal detachment with retinal defect, unspecified
401.9	Essential hypertension, unspecified
250.00	Diabetes mellitus without mention of complication, type two or unspecified type, not stated as uncontrolled

PROCEDURE

67107-56	Repair of retinal detachment; scleral buckling (such as lamellar scleral dissection, imbrication or encircling procedure), with or without implant, with or without cryotherapy, photocoagulation, and drainage of subretinal fluid, preoperative management only

21. DIAGNOSIS OR NATURE OF ILLNESS OR INJURY (Relate Items 1, 2, 3 or 4 to Item 24E by Line)
1. 361.00 3. 250.00
2. 401.9 4. .

22. MEDICAID RESUBMISSION CODE | ORIGINAL REF. NO.
23. PRIOR AUTHORIZATION NUMBER

	24. A. DATE(S) OF SERVICE From MM DD YY	To MM DD YY	B. PLACE OF SERVICE	C. EMG	D. PROCEDURES, SERVICES, OR SUPPLIES (Explain Unusual Circumstances) CPT/HCPCS	MODIFIER	E. DIAGNOSIS POINTER	F. $ CHARGES	G. DAYS OR UNITS	H. EPSDT Family Plan	I. ID. QUAL.	J. RENDERING PROVIDER ID. #
1	05 05 08				67107	56					NPI	
2											NPI	
3											NPI	
4											NPI	
5											NPI	
6											NPI	

PHYSICIAN OR SUPPLIER INFORMATION

Figure 7-18 The correct use of -56 when coding preoperative management (Delmar/Cengage Learning)

Modifier -57 or 09957

The following demonstrates the correct use of -57 when coding.

Definition of -57

Decision for surgery: An E/M service that resulted in the initial decision to perform the surgery may be identified by adding modifier -57 to the appropriate level of E/M service.

Scenario

The patient presents to the ophthalmologist for a routine eye exam when the physician diagnoses a retinal tear and decides surgery is necessary. The patient is referred to a retinologist for emergency repair.

Explanation of Why the Modifier Is Used

The ophthalmologist diagnoses a problem that is obvious and must be taken care of. Referring the patient is the initial decision. The retinologist may decide the approach and time frames needed for surgery. Figure 7-19 shows the use of modifier -57.

21. DIAGNOSIS OR NATURE OF ILLNESS OR INJURY (Relate Items 1, 2, 3 or 4 to Item 24E by Line)
1. 361.00 3. .
2. V72.0 4. .

22. MEDICAID RESUBMISSION CODE | ORIGINAL REF. NO.
23. PRIOR AUTHORIZATION NUMBER

	24. A. DATE(S) OF SERVICE From MM DD YY	To MM DD YY	B. PLACE OF SERVICE	C. EMG	D. PROCEDURES, SERVICES, OR SUPPLIES (Explain Unusual Circumstances) CPT/HCPCS	MODIFIER	E. DIAGNOSIS POINTER	F. $ CHARGES	G. DAYS OR UNITS	H. EPSDT Family Plan	I. ID. QUAL.	J. RENDERING PROVIDER ID. #
1	05 05 08				92012	57					NPI	
2											NPI	
3											NPI	
4											NPI	
5											NPI	
6											NPI	

PHYSICIAN OR SUPPLIER INFORMATION

Figure 7-19 The correct use of -57 when coding for an ophthalmic procedure (Delmar/Cengage Learning)

DIAGNOSIS

361.00   Retinal detachment with retinal defect;
              retinal detachment with retinal defect,
              unspecified
V72.0   Special investigation and examinations,
              examination of the eyes and vision

PROCEDURE

92012-57   Ophthalmological services: medical
              examination and evaluation with initiating
              or continuation of diagnostic and treatment
              program; intermediate, established
              patient – decision for surgery

Modifier -58 or 09958

The following describes using -58 when coding related procedures.

Definition of -58

Staged or related procedure or service by the same physician during the postoperative period; the physician may need to indicate that the performance of a procedure or service during the postoperative period was: a) planned prospectively at the time of the original procedure (staged), b) more extensive than the original procedure, or c) for therapy following a diagnostic surgical procedure.

Scenario

The patient had Mohs surgery on the bridge of the nose due to a melanoma. The plastic surgeon will treat the patient with a pedicle graft from the glabellar area to the nose to fill in the defect. **Mohs surgery** is used for the removal of skin cancer. It is famous for only removing the cancerous tissue and leaving the healthy tissue.

> **Mohs surgery** Used for the removal of skin cancer. It is famous for only removing the cancerous tissue and leaving the healthy tissue.

Explanation of Why the Modifier Is Used

This procedure is more extensive than the original planned procedure and is performed during the postoperative period. Figure 7-20 shows the use of modifier -58.

Figure 7-20 The correct use of -58 when coding staged procedures (Delmar/Cengage Learning)

DIAGNOSIS

V10.82	Personal history of malignant neoplasm of other sites, malignant melanoma of skin
V51	Aftercare involving the use of plastic surgery

PROCEDURE

15576-58	Formation of direct or tubed pedicle with or without transfer; eyelids, nose, ears, lips, or intraoral - staged or related procedure or service by the same physician during the postoperative period

Modifier -59 or 09959

The following describes how a coder would distinguish between different services by using a -59 modifier.

Definition of -59

Distinct procedural service: Under certain circumstances, the physician may need to indicate that a procedure or service was distinct or independent from other service performed on the same day. Modifier -59 is used to identify procedure(s) that are not normally reported together but are appropriate under the circumstances.

Scenario

The patient presents at the hospital for surgery on her right knee, arthroplasty, and her left shoulder, adhesive capsulitis, manipulation.

Explanation of Why the Modifier Is Used

There are two procedures that need to be done, the arthroplasty and the shoulder manipulation. The -59 recognizes the procedures are to occur at very different sites and that they are separate procedures. Figure 7-21 shows the use of modifier -59.

21. DIAGNOSIS OR NATURE OF ILLNESS OR INJURY (Relate Items 1, 2, 3 or 4 to Item 24E by Line)
1. 71536
2. 7260
3.
4.

22. MEDICAID RESUBMISSION CODE | ORIGINAL REF. NO.

23. PRIOR AUTHORIZATION NUMBER

	24. A. DATE(S) OF SERVICE From MM	DD	YY	To MM	DD	YY	B. PLACE OF SERVICE	C. EMG	D. PROCEDURES, SERVICES, OR SUPPLIES (Explain Unusual Circumstances) CPT/HCPCS	MODIFIER				E. DIAGNOSIS POINTER	F. $ CHARGES	G. DAYS OR UNITS	H. EPSDT Family Plan	I. ID. QUAL.	J. RENDERING PROVIDER ID. #
1	05	05	08						27442	RT								NPI	
2	05	05	08						23700	59	LT							NPI	
3																		NPI	
4																		NPI	
5																		NPI	
6																		NPI	

PHYSICIAN OR SUPPLIER INFORMATION

Figure 7-21 An example of how -59 modifier describes two distinct procedures (Delmar/Cengage Learning)

DIAGNOSIS

715.36	Osteoarthrosis, localized, not specified whether primary or secondary – lower leg
726.0	Adhesive capsulitis of shoulder

PROCEDURE

27442-RT	Arthroplasty, femoral condyles or tibial plateau(s) knee, right
23700-59-LT	Manipulation under anesthesia, shoulder joint, including application or fixation apparatus (dislocation excluded), distinct procedural service, left

Modifier -62 or 09962

The following describes how modifier -62 is used to describe work done by two surgeons, each performing a discrete portion of one procedure.

Definition of -62

Two surgeons: When two surgeons work together as primary surgeons performing discrete parts of a procedure, each surgeon should report his or her distinct operative work by each adding a -62 and any associated add-on codes for that procedure, as long as both surgeons continue to work together as primary surgeons.

Scenario

Patient is admitted to the hospital for a vertebral corpectomy T3/T4 through an anterior approach. Due to the complexity, a thoracic surgeon will open the patient for the orthopedic surgeon and close after the spine surgery is complete.

Explanation of Why the Modifier Is Used

Here, the opening and closing is too complex to be an assist. Figure 7-22 shows the use of modifier -62.

Figure 7-22 An example of how -62 describes two surgeons' parts of a single procedure (Delmar/Cengage Learning)

DIAGNOSIS

733.95   Stress fracture of other bone

724.4   Thoracic or lumbosacral neuritis or radiculitis, unspecified

733.00   Other disorders of bone and cartilage, osteoporosis, unspecified

PROCEDURE

Dr. Spine: 63085-62 – Vertebral corpectomy (vertebral body resection), partial or complete, transthoracic approach with decompression of spinal cord and/or nerve root(s); thoracic, single segment, two surgeons

Dr. Thoracic: 63085-62 – Vertebral corpectomy (vertebral body resection), partial or complete, transthoracic approach with decompression of spinal cord and/or nerve root(s); thoracic, single segment, two surgeons. Dr. Thoracic stays in the operating room and does not leave.

Note that cosurgeons usually bill a separate claim with a -62 CPT modifier. A processor would have to audit the claim. A payer may manually separate these claims based on an operative report to verify that the cosurgeon's claims are correctly stated. However, most of the time, cosurgeons do bill on two separate claims according to their specialty codes and use CCI.

Modifier -63 or 09963

The following describes the use of -63 for an infant's surgery due to low birth weight.

Definition of -63

Procedure performed on infants less than 4 kg. Procedures performed on neonates and infants up to a present body weight of 4 kg may involve significantly increased complexity and physician work commonly associated with these patients.

Scenario

Full-term newborn of low birth weight, due to the mother's tobacco use, presents with a congenital inguinal hernia on the left side.

Explanation of Why the Modifier Is Used

The physician takes more liability in treating the patient and may receive greater compensation because of it. The patient is of low birth weight because of the mother's tobacco use. Figure 7-23 shows the use of modifier -63.

DIAGNOSIS

550.90   Inguinal hernia, without mention of obstruction or gangrene, unilateral or unspecified

V21.30   Low-birth-weight status, unspecified

PROCEDURE

49495-63-LT   Repair, initial inguinal hernia, full-term infant under age six months, or preterm infant over 50 weeks postconception age and under age six months at the time of surgery, with or without hydrocelectomy; reducible

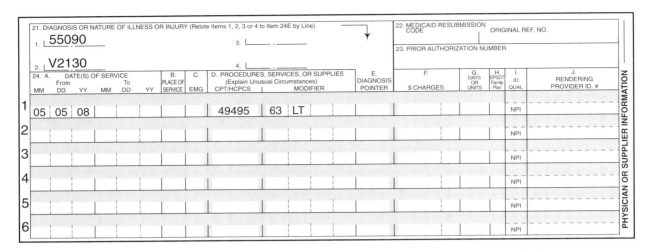

Figure 7-23 An example of using -63 to indicate greater risk (Delmar/Cengage Learning)

Modifier -66 or 09966

The following depicts the correct use of -66 to indicate the presence of a surgical team for a procedure.

Definition of -66

Surgical team: Under some circumstances, highly complex procedures that require concomitant services of several physicians, often of different specialties, plus other highly skilled specially trained personnel and various types of equipment are carried out under the "surgical team" concept.

Scenario

Patient has a diseased lung and qualifies for a lung transplant.

Explanation of Why the Modifier Is Used

Generally, the physicians bill their own claims using a modifier -66 to show they were a part of the team and to show the correct procedure(s) codes performed on an individual basis. Most physicians are paid on a by-report basis. Some payers want to see verification of medical necessity, such as operative reports, before payment.

Some payers want only one claim per surgical team. This stipulation may be found in some states' Medicaid programs. Figure 7-24 shows the use of modifier -66.

DIAGNOSIS

V42.6   Organ or tissue replaced by transplant – lung

PROCEDURE

32851   Lung transplant, single; without cardiopulmonary bypass

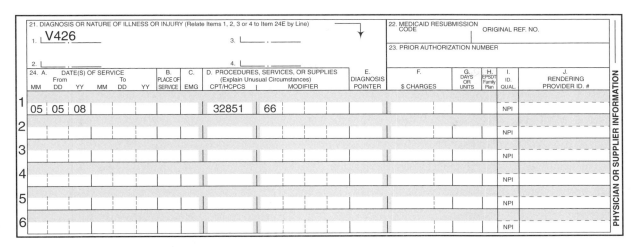

Figure 7-24 An example of a -66 modifier to indicate a surgical team (Delmar/Cengage Learning)

Modifier -76 or 09976

The -76 modifier is used when a physician repeats a procedure.

Definition of -76

Repeat procedure by the same physician: The physician may need to indicate that a procedure or service was repeated subsequent to the original procedure or service.

Scenario

The patient had breast augmentation on September 12. On September 20 the patient was involved in a rear-end motor vehicle accident, thrusting the patient forward into the steering wheel. The force of the impact ruptured one of the implants and ripped open the healing suture lines of both breasts. The surgeon readmits the patient for replacement of the ruptured implant, performs precautionary replacement of the intact implant, and resutures the open wounds.

Explanation of Why the Modifier Is Used

In this procedure, the physician had no choice but to perform the procedure again because of the accident suffered by the patient. Figure 7-25 shows the use of modifier -76.

DIAGNOSIS

996.54	Complication peculiar to specified procedures, due to breast prosthesis
879.1	Open wound of other and unspecified sites, except limb, breast complicated
V52.4	Fitting and adjustment of prosthetic device, breast prosthesis and implant
E819.0	Motor vehicle traffic accident of unspecified nature, driver

PROCEDURE

19328-76-LT	Removal of intact mammary implant, repeat procedure by the same physician, left side

21. DIAGNOSIS OR NATURE OF ILLNESS OR INJURY (Relate Items 1, 2, 3 or 4 to Item 24E by Line)								22. MEDICAID RESUBMISSION CODE	ORIGINAL REF. NO.			
1. 99654				3. V524				23. PRIOR AUTHORIZATION NUMBER				
2. 8791				4. E8190								

24. A. DATE(S) OF SERVICE						B. PLACE OF SERVICE	C. EMG	D. PROCEDURES, SERVICES, OR SUPPLIES (Explain Unusual Circumstances)		E. DIAGNOSIS POINTER	F. $ CHARGES	G. DAYS OR UNITS	H. EPSDT Family Plan	I. ID. QUAL.	J. RENDERING PROVIDER ID. #
From			To					CPT/HCPCS	MODIFIER						
MM	DD	YY	MM	DD	YY										
1 05	05	08						19328	76 LT					NPI	
2 05	05	08						19330	76 RT					NPI	
3														NPI	
4														NPI	
5														NPI	
6														NPI	

Figure 7-25 An example of using -76 for a repeated procedure (Delmar/Cengage Learning)

19330-76-RT   Removal of mammary implant material, repeat procedure by the same physician, right side

Modifier -77 or 09977

The following demonstrates the use of -77 to indicate a repeated procedure by a different physician.

Definition of -77

Repeat procedure by another physician: The physician may need to indicate that a basic procedure or service performed by another physician had to be repeated.

Scenario

A patient who injured, by an open wound, a tendon in his right pointer finger had a repair on January 10. On January 14, the patient hyperextended the finger, felt a pop, and immediately knew he had reinjured the finger. The patient presented to the emergency room, where he was sent immediately to the operating room for a second repair.

Explanation of Why the Modifier Is Used

Here, because the patient reinjured his finger, the same procedure was necessary. This injury occurred during the postop period. Double billing will not be suspected if a modifier -77 is used. Figure 7-26 shows the use of modifier -77.

DIAGNOSIS

883.2   Open wound of fingers with tendon involvement

PROCEDURE

26418-77-F6   Repair, extensor tendon, finger, primary or secondary; without free graft, each tendon – repeat procedure by another physician, right hand, second digit

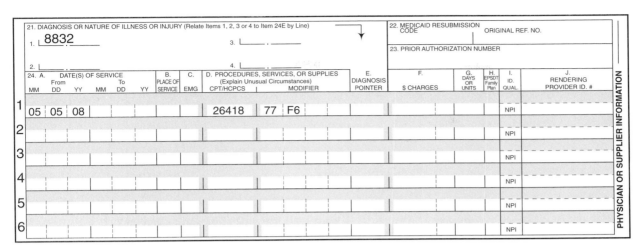

Figure 7-26 An example of a -77 to indicate a repeated procedure by another physician (Delmar/Cengage Learning)

Modifier -78 or 09978

The following describes how -78 is used to indicate a return to the operating room for a related procedure.

Definition of -78

Return to the operating room for a related procedure during the postoperative period: The physician may need to indicate that another procedure was performed during the postoperative period of the initial procedure. When this subsequent procedure is related to the first, and requires the use of the operating room, it may be reported by adding a modifier -78.

Scenario

A patient who injured, by open wound, a tendon in his right pointer finger had a repair on January 10. On January 14, the patient hyperextended the finger, felt a pop, and immediately knew he had reinjured the finger. The patient was taken to the operating room, where the primary surgeon decided to use a graft because the reinjury did not leave enough good tendon to resuture. Figure 7-27 shows the use of modifier -78.

DIAGNOSIS

883.2   Open wound of fingers with tendon involvement

PROCEDURE

26428-78-F6   Repair of extensor tendon, central slip, secondary (for example, boutonniere deformity), with free graft; includes obtaining graft, each finger

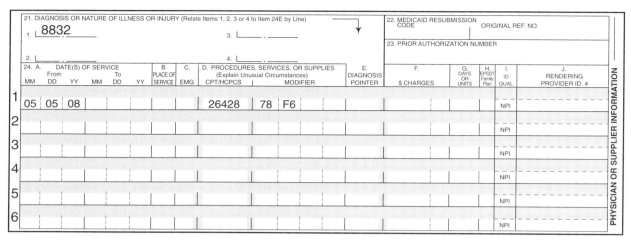

Figure 7-27 An example of a related surgery, using modifier -78, during a postoperative period (Delmar/Cengage Learning)

Modifier -79 or 09979

The following illustrates the use of -79 for an unrelated procedure during a postoperative period.

Definition of -79

Unrelated procedure or service by the same physician during the postoperative period: The physician may need to indicate that the performance of a procedure or service during the postoperative period was unrelated to the original procedure.

Scenario

Seventy-nine-year-old female had a bunionectomy, 28296, of the right hallux, on June 2. On June 15, she tripped and fractured the third metatarsal bone of the right foot. The doctor admitted her to the outpatient surgery department of the hospital for manipulation and percutaneous pinning.

Explanation of Why the Modifier Is Used

Here, the patient was still in the postoperative period of a global service. The insurance is expecting all service during the postoperative period to be related to its surgery; when it is not, there needs to be this modifier so the insurance company will consider this procedure for payment. Figure 7-28 shows the use of modifier -79.

DIAGNOSIS

825.25	Fracture of other and metatarsal bones, closed, metatarsal bone(s)
E928.9	Other and unspecified environment and accidental causes, unspecified accident
E849.9	Place of occurrence, unspecified place

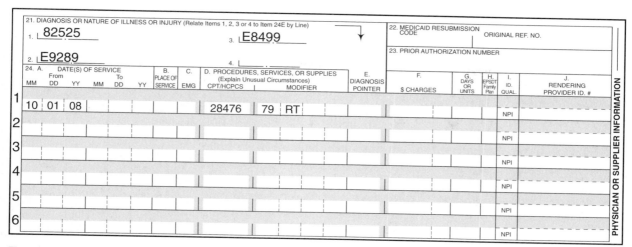

Figure 7-28 An example of -79 modifier distinguishing different procedures, by the same surgeon, during postoperative period (Delmar/Cengage Learning)

PROCEDURE

28476-79-RT   Percutaneous skeletal fixation of metatarsal fracture, with manipulation, each, unrelated procedure or service by the same physician during the postoperative period, right

Modifier -80 or 09980

The following illustrates how a -80 is used for an assistant surgeon's services.

Definition of -80

Assistant surgeon: Surgical assistant services may be identified by using a modifier -80.

Scenario

The patient is a 32-year-old semipro football player who tore/ruptured his left ACL and collateral ligaments in a game. No grafts required.

Explanation of Why the Modifier Is Used

Because of the extent of the repair and the patient's physical fitness, it is absolutely necessary to have another physician present during surgery to assist. Figure 7-29 shows the use of modifier -80.

DIAGNOSIS

844.2   Sprains and strains of knee and leg, cruciate ligament of knee

844.0   Sprains and strains of knee and leg, lateral collateral ligament of knee

E886.0   Fall on same level from collision, pushing, or shoving, by or with another person

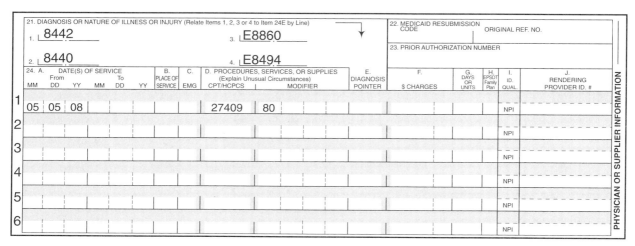

Figure 7-29 An example of -80 to identify an assistant surgeon's participation in a procedure (Delmar/Cengage Learning)

Nurse Practitioners and Physician's Assistants and the Modifier -80

When physicians and a nurse practitioner or a physician's assistant bill on the same claim, it is usually done under the physician's Medicare and tax identification number. The CCI indicates whether an assist is allowable for the procedure. Sometimes, practices bill a nurse practitioner's services as an assistant surgeon, and bill under the physician's name. The payer denies these claims. CCI usually does not edit them out, but the software denies the claims as duplicate services. Two physicians' names may not be entered into the system as dual payees.

Figure 7-30 Nurse practitioners and physician assistants and modifier -80 (Delmar/Cengage Learning)

E849.4   Place of occurrence, place for recreation
              and sport

PROCEDURE

27409-80   Repair primary, torn ligament and/or
              capsule, knee – assistant surgeon

Figure 7-30 discusses the use of nurse practitioners and physician assistants and modifier -80.

Modifier -81 or 09981

The following demonstrates using -81 for minimal assistance by a surgeon.

Definition of -81

Minimum assist surgeon: Minimum surgical assist services are identified by adding modifier -81.

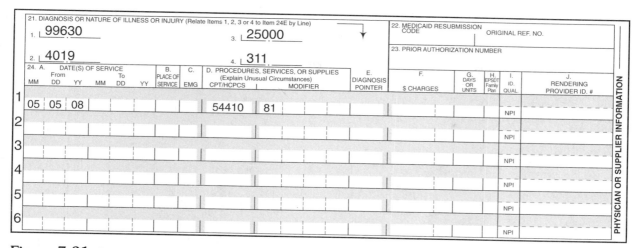

Figure 7-31 An example of -81 modifier to code removal of all prosthetic components (Delmar/Cengage Learning)

Scenario

Patient is a 58-year-old male, hypertensive, diabetic, with chronic depression on Wellbutrin®. Patient has a penile implant that is no longer functioning properly and needs replacement.

Explanation of Why the Modifier Is Used

The procedure takes only minimal assistance as urinary structures will not be compromised during this procedure. Figure 7-31 shows the use of modifier -81.

DIAGNOSIS

996.30	Mechanical complication of genitourinary device, implant, and graft, unspecified device, implant and graft
401.9	Essential hypertension, unspecified
250.00	Diabetes mellitus without mention of complication, type two, or unspecified type, not stated as uncontrolled
311	Depressive disorder, not otherwise classified

PROCEDURE

| 54410-81 | Removal and replacement of all component(s) of a multicomponent, inflatable penile prosthesis at the same operative session |

Modifier -82 or 09982

The following demonstrates the use of -82 to indicate use of different, but qualified, surgeons.

Definition of -82

Assistant surgeon when qualified resident surgeon is not available.

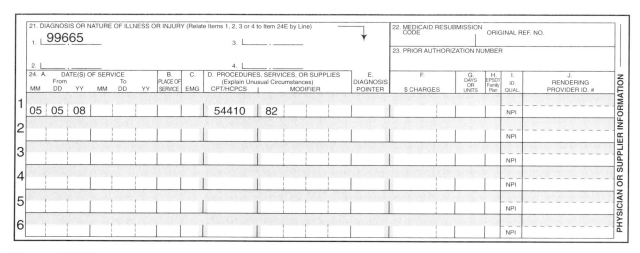

Figure 7-32 An example of -82 to show an assistant surgeon as a substitute (Delmar/Cengage Learning)

Scenario

At a military hospital that is also a teaching hospital, all possible troops are deployed and no resident in urology is available. Patient is a 58-year-old male, hypertensive, diabetic, with chronic depression and on Wellbutrin®. Patient has a penile implant that is no longer functioning properly and needs replacement.

Explanation of Why the Modifier Is Used

The procedure takes only minimal assistance as urinary structures will not be compromised during this procedure. Here, the qualified resident is not available. Figure 7-32 shows the use of modifier -82.

DIAGNOSIS

996.65   Infection and inflammatory reaction due to internal prosthetic device implant and graft

PROCEDURE

54410-82   Removal and replacement of all component(s) of a multicomponent, inflatable penile prosthesis at the same operative session; assistant surgeon when qualified resident surgeon is not available

Modifier -90 or 09990

The following demonstrates the use of -90 to indicate the use of an outside laboratory.

Definition of -90

Reference/outside laboratory: indicates when laboratory procedures are performed by a party other than the treating or reporting physician

Scenario

A single OB/GYN practice office has all nonurine tests drawn in the office by the back office staff. The physician sends all blood out to the lab in the same building. Cost of equipment and calibration is not cost effective.

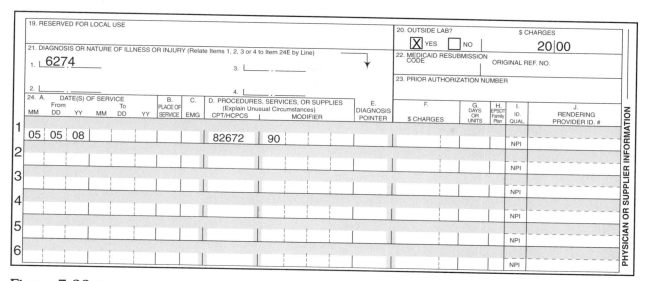

Figure 7-33 An example of -90 to indicate use of a reference/outside laboratory (Delmar/Cengage Learning)

Explanation of Why the Modifier Is Used

The coder knows to add the modifier, and the insurance carrier knows the physician paid the lab. The patient's insurance reimburses the physician. There is no billing from the lab to patient or insurance payer. Figure 7-33 shows the use of modifier -90.

DIAGNOSIS

627.4   States associated with artificial menopause

PROCEDURE

82672-90   Estrogens, total; reference/outside laboratory; when laboratory procedures are performed by a party other than the treating or reporting physician

Modifier -91 or 09991

The following is an example of using -91 for repeating diagnostic tests.

Definition of -91

Repeat clinical diagnostic test: In the course of treatment of the patient, it may be necessary to repeat the same laboratory test on the same day to obtain subsequent, or multiple, test results. Under these circumstances, the laboratory test performed can be identified by its usual procedure number and the addition of modifier -91. Note this modifier may not be used when tests are rerun to confirm initial results, due to testing problems with specimens or equipment, or for any other reason when a normal, one-time, reportable result is all that is required. This code may not be used when another code(s) describes a series of test results, for example, glucose tolerance tests or evocative/suppression testing. This modifier may only be used for a laboratory test(s) performed more than once on the same day on the same patient.

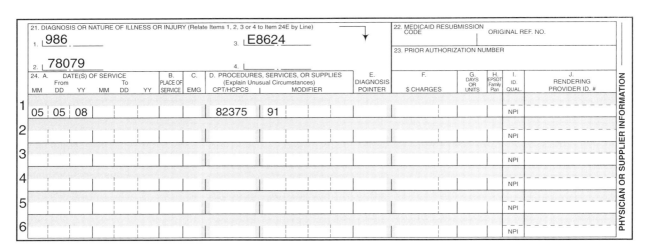

Figure 7-34 An example of -91 to indicate repeat of a clinical diagnostic test.

Scenario

A child suffering from lethargy is taken to the emergency room for possible carbon monoxide poisoning. The first test confirms high levels of CO_2. The patient is immediately put on oxygen therapy with a respiratory therapist. After eight hours of therapy, the patient is tested again. The levels are dramatically lower, but the patient is still critical and remains in the hospital for continuous care.

Explanation of Why the Modifier Is Used

This test is run to confirm changes in the levels of CO_2, not to confirm the CO_2 exists. Figure 7-34 shows the use of modifier -91.

DIAGNOSIS

986	Toxic effect of carbon monoxide
780.79	Other malaise and fatigue
E862.4	Accidental poisoning by petroleum products, other solvents, and their vapors, not elsewhere classifiable, other specified solvents

PROCEDURE

82375-91	Carbon monoxide (carboxyhemoglobin); quantitative

Modifier -99 or 09999

The following demonstrates the use of -99 to indicate multiple modifiers.

Definition of -99

Multiple modifiers: Under certain circumstances two or more modifiers may be necessary to completely delineate a service. In such situations, modifier -99 should be added to the basic procedure, and other applicable modifiers may be listed as part of the description of the service.

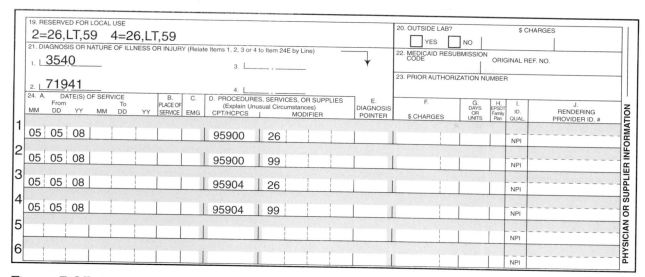

Figure 7-35 An example of modifier -99 to show multiple modifiers (Delmar/Cengage Learning)

Scenario

The patient has experienced years of neck pain, arm pain, and numbness C1-3, and the patient has experienced months of similar symptoms on the right, predominantly affecting C1-2.

Motor nerve study is done on median nerve, abductor pollicis brevis APB, stim site wrist and ulnar nerve, stim site wrist (left).

Sensory nerve study is done also, on median-palm nerve, stim site, wrist and ulnar-palm nerve, stim site palm (left).

Explanation of Why the Modifier Is Used

The multiple modifiers explain what is happening with the ulnar nerve:

26 = Professional component
LT = Left
59 = Distinct procedural service

The modifiers are needed to explain what the CPT manual could not. Figure 7-35 shows the use of modifier -99.

DIAGNOSIS

354.0	Mononeuritis of upper limb and mononeuritis multiplex, carpal tunnel syndrome
719.41	Other and unspecified disorder of joint, pain in joint, site unspecified

PROCEDURE

95900-26	Nerve conduction, amplitude and latency/velocity study, each nerve; motor, without F-wave study
95900-99	Nerve conduction, amplitude and latency/velocity study, each nerve; motor, without F-wave study

Table 7-1 Chart of modifiers used with specialties (Current Procedural Terminology, American Medical Association)

Modifiers used with					
Anesthesia	E/M	Medicine	Pathology and lab codes	Radiology	Surgery
22	21	22	22	22	22
23	24	26	26	26	26
32	25	32	32	32	32
47	32	47	52	50	50
51	62	50	53	51	51
53	57	51	59	52	53
59		52	90	53	55
		53	91	58	56
		54		59	58
		56		62	59
		58		76	76
		62		77	77
		66		78	78
		76		79	79
		77		80	99
		78		99	
		79			
		80			
		81			
		82			
		99			

```
95904-26   Nerve conduction, amplitude and latency/
           velocity study, each nerve; sensory
95904-99   Nerve conduction, amplitude and latency/
           velocity study, each nerve; sensory
```

Groupings of Modifiers for CPT Sections

Table 7-1 groups modifiers by sections for CPT codes. Check the CPT manual for yearly additions or deletions.

E-mail Addresses for Modifiers

Many insurance companies and state insurance programs like Medicaid have various rules and requirements regarding the use of modifiers. When looking for specific rules, do a search on the internet with the modifier number, title of what it does, state in which the coding is for, and the insurance company involved. You may find that there are universal rules and specific provider requirements that need to be met when submitting a claim with modifier(s).

Summary

Coders need to understand and be able to convey procedures in code form. Sometimes the circumstances of a procedure are altered, adjusted, amended, revised, or modulated, but not enough to choose separate or different codes. The modifier explains what needs to be recognized about the procedure it sits next to on the claim form. These modifications need to be recognized in order to tell the whole story accurately. The use of modifiers is a tool to be mastered by the coder. Understanding the nuances of just the right amount of information needed and when to report it is an art. Modifiers give predefined outcome reporting as it relates to how a service is modified; they state what happened completely and accurately. We have been given a set of possibilities of how some procedures change through the definitions of modifiers in the current procedural terminology manual.

Web Sites

The following Web sites contain more information regarding CPT modifiers:

http://www.asha.org

http://www.ut.regence.com/physician/billing/modifiers

Review

Fill in the Blank

1. Modifier codes are added to _____ _____ _____ codes already selected by the coder.

2. Modifiers help code definitions stay _____ sound.

3. Many payers' _____ _____ do not have the capability of reading modifiers.

4. Many times, claims with modifiers need to be _____ _____ for staff review.

5. _____ edits will tell a payer if the modifier can be used with a particular code.

6. Sometimes, the circumstances of a procedure is _____, _____, _____, revised, or modulated but not enough to choose a separate or different code.

7. Modifiers need to be recognized in order to tell the whole _____ _____.

8. Modifiers are tools to be mastered by a _____.

9. Modifiers give us _____ _____ reporting as it relates to how a service is changed.

10. Modifiers give us a set of possibilities of how some procedures _____ through the definitions of modifiers in the CPT.

Review Questions

1. Modifiers help define special circumstances of the code they appear next to on the claim form. _____ yes _____ no

2. Modifiers tell the story of how the procedure was changed but not enough to choose a separate or different code altogether. _____ yes _____ no

3. Modifiers have their own definitions, to be used along with the original code, to tell the rest of the story. _____ yes _____ no

4. Many payers' computer systems are capable of reading modifiers. _____ yes _____ no

5. Many payers consider the use of a modifier by the provider a cause for review of the claim. _____ yes _____ no

6. CCI cannot tell if the modifier can or cannot be used with the CPT code. _____ yes _____ no

7. A coder can assign HCPCS modifiers to CPT codes. _____ yes _____ no

8. A coder cannot assign CPT modifiers to HCPCS codes. _____ yes _____ no

9. Modifier -21 is not used in cases of evaluation and management. _____ yes _____ no

10. Modifier -22 can be used in regard to time. _____ yes _____ no

11. Modifier -23 needs unusual circumstances to cover the anesthesia. _____ yes _____ no

12. Modifier -24 should only be used during the postoperative period. _____ yes _____ no

13. The procedure and the evaluation and management of that procedure go hand in hand when using a modifier -25. _____ yes _____ no

14. Modifier -26 is used for the technical component only. _____ yes _____ no

15. Modifier -32 services can be ordered by a peer review organization, PRO, third-party payers, and government entities. _____ yes _____ no

16. Modifier -47 indicates the surgeon himself needs to administer the anesthesia. _____ yes _____ no

17. If the procedure code itself states two sides, a modifier -50 does not need to be used to recognize both sides. _____ yes _____ no

18. Modifier -51 indicates the procedures need to be for something other than E/M services. _____ yes _____ no

19. Modifier -52 indicates the procedure never takes place, even partially. _____ yes _____ no

20. To use modifier -53 there need to be extenuating circumstances or circumstances that are life threatening to the patient. _____ yes _____ no

21. Modifier -54 is not for surgical care only but is also for evaluation and management services. _____ yes _____ no

22. Modifier -55 indicates that physicians with this modifier do not perform the surgical procedure. _____ yes _____ no

23. Modifier -56 indicates that the preoperative care and the operation are performed together. _____ yes _____ no

24. Modifier -57 is used for the first decision that the patient needs surgery. _____ yes _____ no

25. Modifier -58 indicates the patient and the physician should agree ahead of time to the need of the procedure. _____ yes _____ no

26. Modifier -59 indicates the procedures must be dependent on one another. _____ yes _____ no

27. Modifier -62 indicates the surgeons have separate specialties. _____ yes _____ no

28. The birth weight of the baby must be considered to use modifier -63. _____ yes _____ no

29. Modifier -66 is for surgeries needing more than one surgeon. _____ yes _____ no

30. Modifier -76 indicates the physician is repeating the same service, not just a repeat visit. _____ yes _____ no

31. If modifier -77 is not used properly, double billing may be suspected. _____ yes _____ no

32. The coder needs to know that the patient is in the postoperative period before assigning modifier -78. _____ yes _____ no

33. If modifier -79 is not used for an unrelated procedure, the insurance company assumes this unrelated procedure is a postoperative visit. _____ yes _____ no

34. Modifier -80 is used in an extensive repair where an assistant surgeon may be needed. _____ yes _____ no

35. Modifier -81 is used when a provider simply needs another pair of hands during the procedure. _____ yes _____ no

36. Modifier -82 indicates the provider needs to prove no qualified physician was available at that time. _____ yes _____ no

Critical Thinking Exercise

Many states, municipalities, and insurance companies define their acceptable use of modifier -51 on the Web.

In this lesson, find two examples on the Internet. Compare and highlight what is the same or similar about both, and compare with the CPT Appendix to verify that the information for the year you are researching matches what is found online.

Materials Needed

2 different-colored highlighters
1 blue pen
2 examples of rules, definitions of use, payment provisions

Directions

1. Use your Web browser and search engine and type in phrases such as
    Modifier -51 _____ (your state)
    Modifier -51 _____ (your county)
    Modifier -51 _____ (Medicare)

2. Print the examples.

3. Use one color highlighter for generalized information, use the other for specified information, for example, dates, lists, schedules, and so on. Answer the following questions:
    a. What is similar and what is different?
    b. Are government entity and private insurances discussing their uses for or meanings of the modifier?
    c. Do they state what would constitute payment?
    d. Are there any requests you would deem out of the ordinary, such as paperwork or time requests?

4. Discuss the differences and similarities in the examples with your professor.

Professional Corner

1. Note what modifiers are used most often in your office. This can be seen through a report generated by the billing software that keeps track of the number of procedures performed by the practice.
    a. Are the modifiers assigned to the same procedure on a consistent basis? (This will usually depend upon the specialty.)
    b. Is there a trend of modifier use by patient?
    c. Do certain physicians in your practice take on patients with special circumstances needing regular modifier use?
2. Does your office use of modifier(s) increase when the provider performs experimental or research-type procedures on patients with special health problems?
3. Are modifiers most often used for patients with two or more chronic illnesses?

Your provider may perform services with the need of a modifier on patients who have a much more complex set of problems than the usual patients. Or, you may see a random variety of modifiers without a pattern. Most modifiers require a report be sent in with the claim.

References

Grinder, D. J. (2006). *Coding with Modifiers*. Chicago, IL: American Medical Association.

Ingenix Learning. (2008). *Understanding Modifiers*. Eden Prairie, MN: Ingenix Learning. U.S. Department of Health and Human Services. (2008).

National Correct Coding Initiative Edits. Washington, D.C.: U.S. Department of Health and Human Services.

U.S. Department of Health and Human Services. (2008). *Modifiers*. Washington D.C.: US Department of Health and Human Services.

Usual, Customary, and Reasonable

Chapter Objectives

Upon completion of this chapter, you should be able to

- Understand the meaning of usual, customary, and reasonable, or UCR
- Recognize how UCR can be used as a fee-based structure
- Describe how geographic area plays into UCR
- Understand charging the patient the difference between the provider rate and the UCR rate and when they cannot
- Identify how UCR may be used in managing an office
- Define the meaning of any willing provider regulation
- Distinguish how freedom of choice (or FOC) regulation may help the provider be reimbursed at a higher percentage
- Understand when an IPA may pay a portion of the claim
- Recognize what an outcome is, and how UCR in a geographic area plays into this

Key Terms

any willing provider (AWP)

freedom of choice (FOC)

geographic area

independent practice association (IPA)

point of service (POS)

usual, customary, and reasonable (UCR)

Introduction to Usual, Customary, and Reasonable Rates

This chapter will introduce the role of UCR in the establishment of fees and how it is considered in geographic area, recognized as a fee-based structure, used as a base for any willing provider (AWP) and freedom of choice (FOC) regulation, and considered in point-of-service plans.

usual, customary, and reasonable (UCR) Is a calculation of what a medical procedure is worth in a geographic area.

Usual, customary, and reasonable fees, or **UCR**s, are based on what providers in a geographic area charge for their services. This could be an averaging of services by CPT codes, or similar services in the same geographic area based on what the providers usually bill for that service, or what providers in a particular area have historically billed for the service, and/or what would be a reasonable charge for that service. A geographic area is a specified land area.

Usual and customary fees are determined by actuarial figures and insurance statistics. See Figure 8-1 for a definition of usual, customary, and reasonable.

Medicare publishes a participating provider fee schedule and a nonparticipating fee schedule or limiting charge. To set basic fees, a provider may multiply 125 percent to 150 percent of Medicare. Many providers use such formulas as a basic structure for setting fees. Figure 8-2 is an example of a basic fee structure many providers use.

Each word in *usual, customary, and reasonable* has a meaning, and each may have a high, low, or medium range of charges for one procedure

Usual – is based on what the provider usually charges the patient for a specific code or service.

Customary – is based on what providers in a particular geographic area customarily charge for their code.

Reasonable – is based on what the physician would reasonably charge for a code when that procedure may require additional expertise or skill. Many times medical records may need to be submitted with the bill for this fee to be paid. Many payers will not consider UCR in their fee negotiation for contracted rates. The payer may begin there at a percentage of Medicare rates (see the next example for an explanation – or RVS, relative valuescale – to calculate payment).

Figure 8-1 Definition of usual, customary, and reasonable (Delmar/Cengage Learning)

Limiting fee	$200
Multiplied by 150%	$300
This basic fee structure can be used for any CPT code.	

Figure 8-2 Basic fee structure (Delmar/Cengage Learning)

or service performed. For example, UCR fees might be broken down as follows:

Usual = $60

Customary = $57

Reasonable = $65

Many times, the approved or allowed amount is based on usual and customary but most payers will pay the lower average amount, not a medium or higher-end amount, for a service.

Providers can charge what they believe their services are worth. However, getting those rates fully reimbursed from the payer may not be so easy because of the UCR rates for the area. Providers who belong to a network have already negotiated discounted fees for their services, and many times those services are below usual and customary rates. The payer may state it will pay a percentage of the usual and customary; this example uses 80 percent. The theory is if the provider charges a rate below UCR, the claim payment will not be reduced to below 80 percent. Most insurance coverage is written to cover benefits up to usual, customary, and reasonable pricing for the area. Many insurance companies use an averaging over a three- to five-year period and Medicare ranges to set their examples. Figure 8-3 illustrates a payer complying with UCR rates per procedure.

Most plans define what UCR is and explain how claims will be paid and at what percentage of UCR, but not many explain the calculation of how UCR was reached. If asked, some payers may base their calculations of UCR on Medicare rates, relative value scale, worker's compensation, or RBRVS rates. One factor to notice is whether the UCR is based on what providers usually charge in a geographic area, or whether it is based on what providers usually receive in a geographic area. The difference in reimbursement could be huge for the provider. There are no regulatory guidelines for determining the calculation, so understanding the calculation the payer uses is critical.

Most states have laws that require carriers to disclose their methods of calculating UCR rates, but most carriers will not offer this information unless requested. Usually state law prohibits confidentiality agreements from overriding the disclosure of such formulas when requested. If the provider asks for the formula calculation, the payer needs to comply.

93000 – Electrocardiogram, routine ECG with at least 12 leads; with interpretation and report

A lower range UCR may be	$40.36
80% of UCR is	$31.93
The provider charged below UCR	$21.50

Some states have regulations stating that no payer can pay below UCR rates for a single procedure. In these cases, the payers will still need to pay their percentage of UCR, which in this case would be $31.93.

Figure 8-3 Complying with UCR rates per procedure (Delmar/Cengage Learning)

If the provider is a network provider or contracted, it may be willing to accept the percentage of UCR as payment in full, not charging the patient the balance. In these cases, the difference between the charged and the approved amount may be the same dollar amount or balance. If the provider is noncontracted, the payer may still only pay usual and customary rates for that service, and the provider may be able to bill the patient the difference between the UCR rate and its regular rate.

The Health Insurance Association of America, or HIAA, has a database profile set up that analyzes statistics from a national study of fees charged in various geographic areas. The association sends out fee surveys to keep track of UCR rates. However, insurance companies are not legally required to use HIAA rates. Many insurers use their own statistics to quote a range of UCR fees in their areas; then the payers look at the claims submitted and base their payment on the UCR from their studies. (See Web sites listed at the end of this chapter.)

Determining a Geographic Area

geographic area A specified land area.

One **geographic area** may be determined by ZIP code while another may be determined by a state, county, or city area. Geographic difference may not be taken into account fairly because payers may define boundaries differently. This may lead to variations in fees considered usual, customary, and reasonable for an area.

The Patient and UCR Rates

Coinsurance amounts for patients are usually calculated after the payer determines the UCR rate for a procedure code or service. However, most plans will not apply the difference between the full amount and the UCR to the deductible or out-of-pocket maximums set forth in the plan. Those usually begin at the UCR rate.

In this example the difference between the provider's rate and UCR might not be credited to the patient's deductible for the year, and the patient may be responsible for paying the difference between the provider's regular rate and the UCR rate through a statement generated by a noncontracted provider. However, this occurs only if the patient is responsible for this payment in a noncontracted situation. The payer will let the patient know. Figure 8-4 demonstrates the difference between the UCR, regular rates, and patient responsibility.

Provider's regular rate may be $100 for a 99213	
Usual, customary, and reasonable may be $75 for the same 99213	
The difference for the full fee, $25, not written off; the patient may be responsible	
CPT Code 99213	
Provider's regular rate	$100
Usual, customary, and reasonable	$ 75
Difference, may be payable by patient	$ 25

Figure 8-4 The difference between UCR, regular rates, and patient responsibility (Delmar/Cengage Learning)

A provider may be able to bill the patient participating in a PPO or indemnity plan the difference between the provider rate and the UCR rate in cases when

- The patient may reside in an area where there is no network available for the plan he participates in (for example, a New York resident moves to Florida for 5 months)

- The patient may travel to an area not within the UCR area; this is usually 50 miles away from the provider area

- The patient may see a provider out-of-network in the immediate area

A provider usually cannot charge the difference when

- The provider participates in the network and sees the patient in area

- The provider participates in contracted rates

- The provider agrees not to bill the patient the difference between its regular rates and the UCR rates

- An agreement is met between provider and carrier by contract per individual case

Not all areas are the same. Providers who practice in a higher rent district could reasonably charge higher fees because of the cost of doing business in the area; sometimes these are based on fees in the county or fees in various cities in the same county.

The Importance of UCR Rates by Specialty for Geographic Area

The following are occasions and explanations of why a practice would benefit from understanding geographic UCR in its specialty. It is important to note that not all of the examples will apply to every practice, but most will apply on some level. These levels may benefit provider, management, coders, and/or billers in their daily responsibilities to the practice.

Favorable Reimbursement and Fewer Disputes with Payers

Some providers charge exorbitant rates and then expect their staff to fight for the difference when no other providers in the area charge those rates nor are reimbursed at those rates. Understanding UCR keeps the range of fees understandable, and staff members challenging realistic disputes.

Managing Operation of the Office and Understanding What Is Expected

Understanding what will be realistically paid in an area helps with the cost of doing business in that area, including the cost for overhead, medical malpractice insurance, and performing the service itself.

In some offices, this may be known as reserves, which means the provider makes an educated guess as to what percentage of return or payment it will receive on its gross billing, before any discounts, and so on. The manager may base the practice's annual budget/operating expenses on this projected figure. In such cases, when write-offs and contractual agreements are considered, the figure may be 49 percent. If this is the case, the practice may be receiving an average of 51 percent to 55 percent of charges in most states. The following example illustrates this.

Gross billing $1,000,000

Expected write-off $490,000

Projected return $510,000

Developing a Review System for Procedures Performed and Reimbursed

Most billing software will generate monthly reports of

- Number of procedures performed by code
- Timeliness of payment per payer
- Write-off per procedure and payer
- Comparison of rates to reimbursement
- Monies owed per patient

When the software understands the rate expected, other calculations can be made by the software program, making the process of billing and payment more efficient. A provider can enter its contracted rates into the system and even bill the expected rate, but this is not advisable since this may lead to an automatic write-off in the system.

Case Study 8-1 – Reported Diagnosis Justifies Reported Services

If a provider takes more risk in treating a patient, it may be reasonable to charge more monies. This would have to be supported by the diagnosis on the claim and medical records reported with a modifier -22 for justification of the reasonable amount. The -22 modifier lets the payer know to look at the documentation and justifies the services. Knowing the UCR rate could help the provider's office understand what is reasonable. Case study 8-1 is an example of a procedure needing a modifier -22.

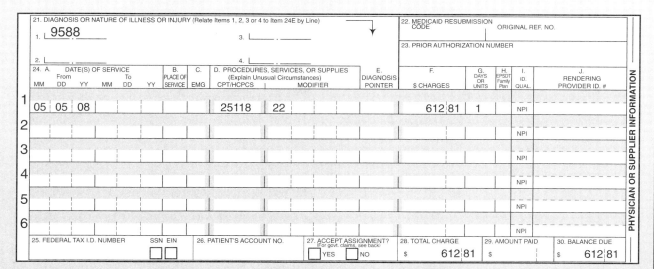

Figure 8-5 Case study 8-1 – an example of a procedure needing modifier -22 (Delmar/Cengage Learning)

```
DIAGNOSIS
     958.8        Other early complication of trauma

PROCEDURE

     25118-22     Synovectomy, exterior tendon sheath, wrist, single
                  compartment

     In this example, the patient has a congenital anomaly, two tendons in
     one compartment. This requires extra time due to the complication.
```

Note:

Every carrier has a team of medical advisors from each specialty. It would be appropriate to request a review by such an advisor in the event of a poor UCR determination. It would be advantageous to request a medical advisor in the same specialty as the provider requesting the review.

any willing provider (AWP) These laws do not let the health plan discriminate against providers who are willing to accept and meet the rules of participation in its plan. The AWP laws tell the networks they must let the providers participate.

point of service (POS) Point-of-service plans work like PPOs and HMOs, but the patient does not decide how she wants to use her benefit until she receives services/treatment.

Any Willing Provider Regulations from Various States

Most states have variations of what they term **any willing provider**, or **AWP**. These are rules of how a managed care plan lets providers become participants in its system or panel of doctors. Most regulations state that any provider who is willing to accept the rules of participation can join the plan, but usually the provider must pass a set criteria or credentialing process beforehand. Some states vary these rules for self-insured companies and worker's compensation. AWP rules are more commonly used for HMOs and **point of service**, or **POS** tier groups. Any willing provider (AWP) laws do not let the health plan discriminate against providers who are willing to accept and meet the rules of participation in the plan. The AWP laws tell the networks they must let the providers participate. Point-of-service plans work like a PPO and an HMO, but the patient does not decide how she wants to use her benefit until she receives services/treatment.

Figure 8-6 illustrates rules that may be used.

	Carrier	Charge
34201 =	Medicare	$638.95
	Medicaid	$638.95
	Cash Account	$520.00
	Private Insurer	$975.00
	Worker's Comp	$1,300.00

It is best not to charge less than what Medicare approves. Some providers get around this by rounding off the Medicare rate and giving the patient a discount of maybe 20 percent. The discount of 20 percent may be applied after the charge of $650 is entered into the computer (which is our example of a cash account with a 20 percent cash discount of $130, equaling $520). Most states do not allow multitiered pricing, meaning one fee to government carriers, one fee to private carriers, and one fee to cash and worker's compensation.

Figure 8-6 Various charges (Delmar/Cengage Learning)

Tier 1 = The patient must be seen on all HMO levels, from the provider to the facility, to ancillary services, and so on.

Tier 2 = The patient will still need a referral, as in an HMO, but the patient can see a non-HMO provider. The patient may have a deductible and co-pay. The patient may want to get a referral and stay in network, or go with an IPA. In these cases, the patient may have a small deductible. The plan may pay 80 percent or 90 percent. Here the patient is seeing a participating provider, but this treatment is on the level of point of service (POS).

Tier 3 = The HMO patient sees a provider outside of the network, a nonparticipating provider. The patient does not have to have a referral, and the patient will pay PPO rates. The insurance carrier will calculate UCR rates. The deductible and coinsurance may be due from the patient.

The patient usually has an HMO in this situation and enjoys being in this tier because he has choices.

Figure 8-7 An example of multitiered pricing with an insurance company (Delmar/Cengage Learning)

The following is an example of multitiered groups that give patients choices in the use of their plans. Figure 8-7 demonstrates multitiered groups.

Freedom of Choice Regulation

freedom of choice (FOC)
These laws allow patients to be reimbursed for services by a qualified provider that does not participate in their plan.

Freedom of choice, or **FOC,** laws work like basic indemnity plans. The patient can choose any provider he wants, in or out of the network. The plan pays a percentage of the fee, usually 75 percent to 80 percent, and the patient pays what is left over up to the billed rate. If the patient is in a managed care plan, the patient pays a co-pay plus what is left between the billed charges and what is approved by the managed care plan. What is paid by the plan may be UCR rates or the contracted rates of the plan.

This may be a good deal for the patient because many FOC laws require the plan to pay at least 75 percent of its contracted fees to the noncontracted provider of the patient's choice. The patient may have to pay the difference between the billed amount and what the plan pays. In some states, the 75 percent is mandatory, but in others it is not. Depending on the plan, some PPOs only pay 50 percent if the patient decides to go out of network. Depending on the state, this could be 50 percent of the billed charges or UCR rates.

Point-of-Service Plans and UCR

The FOC regulations may be hiding in point-of-service plans, POS, which basically work the same as FOC but in these cases, it is the employer who decides if the employee will have this option. Additionally, point-of-service plans usually come with a higher premium price tag that some employers are not willing to pay for or offer. The state may not have FOC rules that require an employer to offer such an option.

The benefit of FOC is that the provider still is paid a percentage of billed charges, regardless of whether the patient is in or out of network. Additionally, if the biller/collector knows the rules for the state in which the practice resides, this can be something the practice can use to negotiate payment. The provider knows that no matter how it is treated by the plan, it can survive, keep its practice open, and not be vulnerable in reimbursement to a plan that may or may not treat the practice favorably.

Whether there is an FOC regulation in place in the provider's state or not, sometimes the plans themselves offer FOC-type options. However, such offerings usually are limited to plans that have huge market share or population. It will be worth finding out if the patient belongs to such a plan. However, just by billing the claim the office would receive an answer in the EOB, or explanation of benefits. These may surface in tier plans. These are plans that give the patient options to stay in or go out of network; the patient is fully advised of the cost of his decision, which is his to make.

Not All Is Fair

The participating provider agreement may not allow the referring participating provider to send the patient to a nonparticipating provider. The referring participating provider may receive a cut in reimbursement as a penalty for that referral in that instance. In these cases, there is no use in disputing such a cut in fee reimbursement if the provider is following a course of action that the provider agreement specifically states will result in a reduction in reimbursement.

Usually the patient pays out of pocket for noncontracted services and is reimbursed at the predetermined out-of-network level. However, the biller or coder should check with the state; some rules require a payer to pay noncontracted providers directly for outpatient services. Providers should inquire if FOC laws exist in their states. The patient should agree to assign the reimbursement to the noncontracted provider so it can be reimbursed directly from the plan, but this is not a factor with some plans.

A student has school sports insurance and a private individual plan, which has a $1,000 deductible. The student has an injury to the knee that requires surgery. In this case, the school sports insurance will pay $500 per injury, to the physician. The provider would bill the school insurance first, then the plan. The plan will figure how much it will pay under any circumstance. The plan will also take its deductible. The plan will deduct that $500 from what it pays after the deductible is met. See how the process works via the following scenario.

Case Study 8-2 – Sports Billing Scenario

The following steps are taken to bill in a sports scenario. First the office bills the intramural sports plan, next it bills the individual plan, and last it bills the patient for his share. The following chart shows how the arithmetic works for this billing.

(Continued)

1. Billing the intramural sports plan	\$4,000 −500 \$3,500	Surgeon's original fee Plan pays \$500 to the surgeon Remainder
2. Billing the individual plan	\$4,000 −1,000 3,000	Billed to private insurance Deductible - patient responsibility Amount after deductible
	\$2,400 −\$500 \$1,900	80% of \$3,000, which insurance will pay The intramural sports insurance paid Will be paid to the surgeon
3. Billing the patient	\$1,000 +600 \$1,600	Deductible patient will pay Coinsurance - the difference between \$3,000 and \$2,400 The patient will pay

Figure 8-8 shows the claim in case study 8-2, the sports scenario.

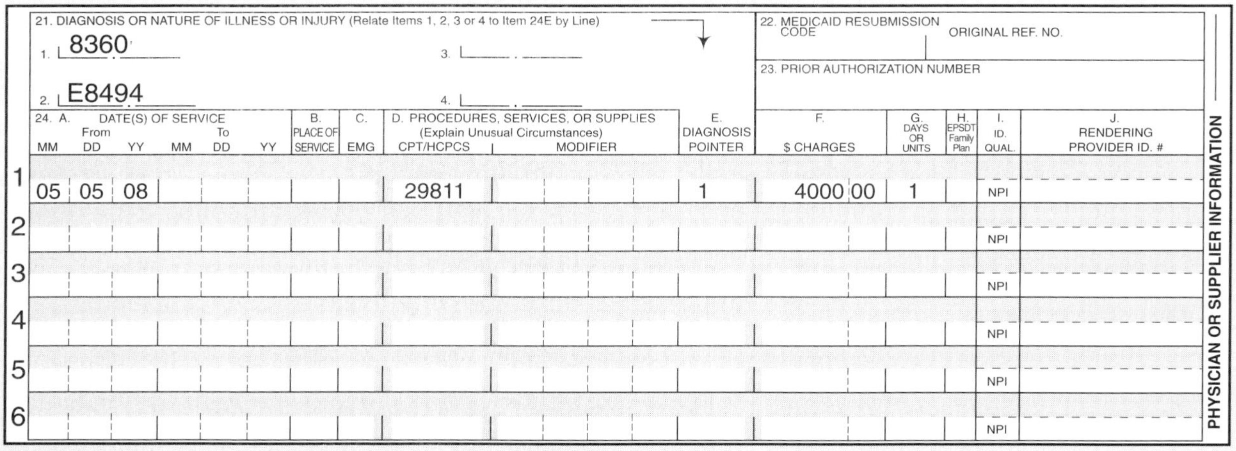
21. DIAGNOSIS OR NATURE OF ILLNESS OR INJURY (Relate Items 1, 2, 3 or 4 to Item 24E by Line)
1. 8360 3.
2. E8494 4.
22. MEDICAID RESUBMISSION CODE ORIGINAL REF. NO.
23. PRIOR AUTHORIZATION NUMBER

	24. A. DATE(S) OF SERVICE From MM DD YY	To MM DD YY	B. PLACE OF SERVICE	C. EMG	D. PROCEDURES, SERVICES, OR SUPPLIES (Explain Unusual Circumstances) CPT/HCPCS	MODIFIER	E. DIAGNOSIS POINTER	F. $ CHARGES	G. DAYS OR UNITS	H. EPSDT Family Plan	I. ID. QUAL.	J. RENDERING PROVIDER ID. #
1	05 05 08				29811		1	4000 00	1		NPI	
2											NPI	
3											NPI	
4											NPI	
5											NPI	
6											NPI	

PHYSICIAN OR SUPPLIER INFORMATION

Figure 8-8 Case study 8-2 (Delmar/Cengage Learning)

DIAGNOSIS

836.0 Dislocation of knee, tear of medial cartilage or meniscus of knee, current

E849.4 Place of recreation and sport

PROCEDURE

29881 Arthroscopy with meniscectomy (medial or lateral, including any medical shaving)

The Plan and the IPA

independent practice association (IPA)
Independent physicians who together negotiate fees and rates with a plan or an HMO.

A provider may have a UCR rate. If an HMO patient is involved, the plan and/or **independent practice association**, or **IPA,** will usually pay the remainder of HMO charges. Independent practice associations are independent physicians who together negotiate fees and rates with a plan or an HMO.

If the provider is not contracted, it will pay the billed charge just to keep the patient out of the loop. The following is an example of the plan and the IPA sharing the cost of treating the patient. Figure 8-9 shows an example of cost sharing between the plan and the IPA by procedure.

Indemnity and PPOs will pay their portions of the claim, and the patient may have a higher deductible or coinsurance. Some providers will pay UCR as payment in full. However, many times they do not. There are new laws in this regard that lean toward defining what is meant by gouging patients, protecting patients, and what constitutes this. Patients need to understand who the providers are in their network, read their policies, and ask any questions up front. Patients do need to take some responsibility for their health care, and they need to know what their out-of-pocket expenses will be.

Procedure	IPA	Insurance
UGI	Diagnostic	Biopsy
Colonoscopy	Diagnostic	Biopsy
Ear lavage	Cerumen impaction	FB removal, anesthesia required

Figure 8-9 Cost sharing between the plan and the IPA by procedure (Delmar/Cengage Learning)

Summary

Usual, customary, and reasonable rates are something your office should be aware of. Payment, fee negotiation, noncontracted rates, percentage payment, and practice management calculations all cross paths with UCR rates. A provider can use these to its advantage when billing a procedure and should understand what percentage of its fee it should receive. Payers are aware of UCR rates and use them when offering a fee schedule or percentage payment to the provider. If a provider does not understand UCR rates for its area, it may be negotiating for fees much less than those of its counterparts in a geographic area.

Web Sites

The following are suggested Web sites to peruse after reading this chapter. We also suggest a Web search of interest.

Health Insurance Association of America *www.hiaa.org*

Federal Registrar code *http://www.gpoaccess.gov/cfr/index.html*

Special payment for professional services in a health professional shortage area *http://bhpr.hrsa.gov/shortage*

Centers for Medicare and Medicaid *http://www.cms.hhs.gov*

National practitioner database *http://www.npdb-hipdb.com/*

Medical Group Management Association *http://www.mgma.com*

Review

Fill in the Blank

1. Coinsurance amounts for _____ are usually calculated after the _____ determines the _____ rate for a procedure code or service.

2. If a provider takes more _____ in treating a patient, it may be reasonable to charge more _____.

3. AWP are rules of how a _____ _____ plan lets providers become _____ in its _____.

4. AWP rules are more commonly used for _____ and _____ tier groups.

5. Many FOC laws require the _____ to pay at least 75 percent of its _____ fees to the noncontracted provider of the _____ choice.

6. The benefit of _____ is the _____ still are paid a percentage of billed charges regardless of whether the patient is in or _____ of network.

7. The participating provider agreement may not allow the _____ participating provider to send the _____ to nonparticipating providers.

8. Patients need to take some _____ for their health care, and they need to know what their _____ cost will be.

9. Payers are aware of _____ rates and use them when offering a _____ _____ or _____ _____ to the provider.

10. If a provider does not understand UCR rates for its area, it may be _____ for fees much less than those of its _____ in a geographic area.

Review Questions

1. In *usual, customary, and reasonable*, what is the definition of each word?

    Usual _____

    Customary _____

    Reasonable _____

2. What is an example of how a payer may calculate UCR rates?

    _____

    _____

3. What is HIAA and what does it do? _____

    _____

    _____

4. What are some examples of geographic area determination for fees?

    _____

    _____

5. Why should UCR rates be available to the billing/coding staff? _____

    _____

    _____

6. What are AWP or any willing provider rules? _____

    _____

    _____

7. In a freedom of choice, what portion of the bill, if any, does the patient pay? _____

    _____

    _____

8. What kind of penalty might a participating referring provider suffer if it sends the patient to a nonparticipating provider? _____

    _____

    _____

9. Why is it important for the patient to understand which providers participate in the network of the plan? _____

    _____

    _____

10. Why would a physician be a noncontracted provider? _____

    _____

    _____

Critical Thinking Exercise

Many geographic areas are within state lines because of the various laws set forth by each state's department of insurance. Usual, customary, and reasonable rates are established by geographic area. In this exercise, we will take note of rate variances/changes as they relate to geographic area.

Materials Needed

2 different-colored highlighters
1 blue pen
2 UCR rate schedules from two geographic areas

Directions

1. Use your Web browser and search engine and type in phrases such as

    UCR rates _____ (your state)

    UCR rates _____ (your county)

    UCR rates _____ (your city)

2. Print two rate schedules from different geographic areas.

3. Use one color highlighter to mark rates that are the same between the two. Use the other to highlight rates that vary in reimbursement. (Note: the fee schedule may appear only in coded form and not offer written procedure definitions.)

    Specifically look at procedures where the reimbursement is the same. Are these the most performed procedures in an office, such as E&M codes or lab? Also note how sharp the price differentials are for the same procedures that are awarded different reimbursements. Are the procedures more complicated or advanced?

    Discuss the differences and similarities with your teacher.

Professional Corner

The following are some questions to consider when you are working with UCR in your daily routine.

- *Who would you speak to, write to, or inquire of about UCR in your area?*
- *Is the UCR in your area based on what the provider usually bills, or is it based on what the provider usually receives?*
- *Give an example of the plan and an IPA sharing the cost of treating a patient in your practice.*
- *Does your state have FOC laws in place, and do these state a mandatory payment of a percentage of fees?*
- *In the office you reside in, do all providers participate in all plans? Or do some in your office not participate while others do?*
- *Does your office participate in the credentialing process for the providers who reside there? If so, are there different/various requirements per plan, per specialty the provider needs to participate in the same plan?*
- *Do providers in your office perform their services after hours? If so, does your office code for after-hour services?*
- *With noncontracted providers, denied claims are sent to the patient. Does your office get involved with these situations?*
- *Does your office participate in patient satisfaction surveys for the study of disease outcomes? If so, what is the process in which these are reported in your office? Does your office receive a fee for the survey?*

References

CareCounsel. (1997–2008). Usual, Customary and Reasonable Charges. San Rafael, CA: CareCounsel, LLC.

FamiliesUSA. Usual, Customary and Reasonable (UCR) Reimbursement Rates. Retrieved from FamiliesUSA website: www.familiesusa.org.

Prospect Medical Group. (June 11, 2008). Payment Issues, American Medical Association.

Max, Sarah. (August 30, 2005). The Fuzzy Math of Health Insurance. Retrieved from: Money.Com.

Threlkeld, Robert. (June 19, 2000). Court of Appeals Rules on Blue Cross Changes to Usual and Customary Reimbursement Formula. Atlanta, GA: Morris, Manning & Martin, LLP.

MedEquate. (2002–2007). Usual and Customary Fees.

CPT Conventions to Be Considered

Chapter Objectives

Upon completion of this chapter, you should be able to

- Recognize how E/Ms are considered for payment
- Understand E/M based on medical necessity of care
- Distinguish what payers dislike most about E/M reporting from physicians
- Identify what happens when a provider anesthetizes its own patients
- Acknowledge why some providers perform more procedures than authorized
- Categorize the importance of who reads the X-rays first and why
- Understand billing on a global for pathology and laboratory
- Apply medicine services as component parts of bundled procedures

Key Terms

chief complaint, history, examination, details, drugs and dosage, assessment of observations, return (CHEDDAR)

subjective, nature of illness, objective, counseling, assessment, medical decision making, plan (SNOCAMP)

subjective, objective, assessment, plan (SOAP)

wet read

Introduction to CPT Conventions

This chapter introduces various coding conventions, rules, and regulations and how they relate to reimbursement. It looks at how various groups of codes might be considered for payment in the medical report, various documentation needs, and what services the provider performs in different settings. This is not a complete guide but seeks to help the reader be aware of various factors that may change the reimbursement of the coding choice.

Current procedural terminology, or CPT, consists of service and procedure codes and their definitions most commonly reported on claim forms such as the CMS-1500 for professional medical procedures usually performed by a physician and ancillary staff. Also, CPT codes most commonly appear on the UB-04, formerly the UB-92, claim form, the uniform bill submitted to intermediaries and carriers by hospitals, nursing facilities, ASCs and home health agencies.

Although the American Medical Association owns the codes, various publishers distribute and interpret conventions and guidelines set forth every year. A provider may subscribe to such information, and the CPTs can be very helpful in the most current rules in the year they are published. Since the CPT is published every year, it adjusts to the changes in codes, additions, deletions, and revisions that are applicable for the current year. A coder/biller is expected to use the most up-to-date manual, as incorrect coding can be interpreted as abuse or fraud.

Many times, when a new coder begins his career, he begins a journey with a particular specialty, locked into understanding that specialty because it is his livelihood. Sometimes, coding businesses specialize in just one specialty and then go about recruiting as many clients as possible within that specialty. Theoretically, this would be simpler and more precise than recruiting as many kinds of specialties as possible and then keeping up with changes and rules in those specialties. But, there comes a time in the career of a coder, when he needs to decide if he wishes to expand his knowledge and move to, or also code, other specialties available to him. The basic coding rules of the CPT are an ideal place to begin an understanding of codes.

The Six Sections of the CPT

The book consists of six sections, evaluation and management, anesthesia, surgery, radiology, pathology and laboratory, and medicine. Each section consists of introductory pages with coding guidelines that apply only to that section; some include modifiers for that particular section. The beginning pages usually are of a different color, and may be gray, pink, or green to distinguish their importance. These pages should be read along with the appendices for modifiers, add-on codes, changes noted from the last year's book, and coding examples.

Evaluation and Management

In the evaluation and management, or E/M, section, the physician evaluates and manages the problem the patient presents at the time of the visit. The code is assigned based on how well the physician documented the file justifying the level of service and the setting in which the service took place. Various rules apply to chart a new or established patient, which adds to the selection process.

The system uses key components, such as history, examination, and medical decision making, at various levels; two or all three need to be on the same level before choosing the code on that level.

Payers know statistically the amount of time an evaluation and management service performed face to face should be, along with the type of code that should be used and at what level. This may be concluded by the payer from the individual physician's history of reporting E/M codes, geographic area reporting and/or national level reporting percentages of all specialties, and the need for diagnostic evaluation from symptoms and severity of illness.

Even from the beginning, when a physician receives her first license to practice in a state and begins reporting CPT codes for payment on claims, the insurance company captures, through the reporting of the codes, how that particular physician treats her patients on a diagnostic level and how thorough her reporting of the procedures are; then the company compares this with statistical norms.

A norm could be spending 15 minutes with a patient for a *level 3* office visit. But if when auditing the chart, the documentation does not justify such a level of service in a SOAP note, this could be considered fraud. The trigger for a payer to actually read individual charts of a provider (in other words, to audit) would be the physician consistently reporting codes above or below industry norms regarding symptoms and chronic illnesses present at the time of the visit. The provider is supposed to report what actually happened and not worry about staying in a range. The provider may have a disproportionately ill population that warrants higher level E/M visits, and if documenting the charts correctly, should not be concerned if this triggers an audit because the documentation will justify the level of service.

Some providers think that reporting E/M codes on an artificially low level will keep them out of potential audit range, which is not necessarily true. These providers do a disservice to their fellow practitioners because the statistical data can be skewed, which affects payment and the medical needs of the patient population or base.

Second-Opinion Claims

The patient may request a second opinion, but usually payers do not require second opinions to authorize procedures. The patient may want a second opinion for various reasons. Some of the reasons could be

- The patient may want a procedure the provider feels the symptoms do not warrant

- The patient may feel no need for the recommended procedure

- The patient may feel he needs an additional procedure or one that is not offered by the provider

- The patient may be in fear of the procedure recommended

If the patient wants a second opinion and wants his insurance to pay for it, he can appeal to the insurance company. Usually the patient will get the second opinion paid for by the payer because some states have laws to support such requests.

Second-Opinion Issues Not Authorized

A provider can refer a patient to a specialist for an office visit, but when the patient presents, the specialist sees a whole different set of problems that need to be addressed, discussed, or evaluated, and the provider performs a higher E/M level. The payer is not going to pay the claim based on what was previously authorized. In this case the payment would be based on the documentation in the medical records.

> **EXAMPLE:** A general practitioner wants to refer the patient to an ENT (ear, nose, and throat specialist). A prior authorization may be in order for such a visit. An authorization is obtained; the patient presents to the ENT, and the ENT finds the patient in need of tubes in her ears. This would be covered, as the management of the patient moves through the process of becoming well. This could be billed as a consult code, with a modifier indicating a medical decision for surgery. Usually, the payer's system has a referral that is an authorization for the patient to see the specialist. A referral would be the request from the physician, and the authorization would be the okay from the utilization review committee who give permission.

When a claim is denied as not having authorization, the denial can be appealed based on medical necessity. The claims department makes sure the procedure can be authorized and all paperwork necessary to pay that claim is appropriate. When the payer pays the claim, it is based on accurate information or else unauthorized dollars are being paid.

Consideration for Payment

E/M is coded from the history, exam, and medical-decision-making levels the physician notes/writes in the medical record or from what is in the chart. A trigger to audit may be a provider who consistently charges a 99215 or a 99214, very high-level E/M codes. This may be out of range for the provider's specialty. In other words, the average provider will not consistently bill a 99215, the highest level office visit.

To justify billing a level 5 office visit, a provider must have appropriate medical documentation. If the physician does not complete the necessary components to justify a *level 5,* a new or established patient designation will not matter.

If a patient presents as a new patient and the diagnosis, signs and symptoms, and medical record documentation justify the higher level, this can be billed and will stand up to audit scrutiny.

A neurosurgeon may constantly bill on a higher E/M level because of his specialty and the medical complexity of the medical condition of the patient. The payer understands this, and a red flag may not arise in such cases. But the billing of such a high code would be predicated on the correct amount of body systems being reviewed, chief complaint, history of present illness, past family and social history, physical examination, and medical decision making. In other words, coding on a Level 5 and

SOAP An acronym that stands for subjective, objective, assessment, plan.

CHEDDAR An acronym that stands for chief complaint, history, examination, details, drug and dosage, assessments of observations, return.

SNOCAMP An acronym that stands for subjective, nature of illness, objective, counseling, assessment, medical decision making, plan.

five lines of notes will not justify payment. The physician may have performed all services, but if the services are not documented correctly in a discernable order, such as **SOAP, CHEDDAR**, or **SNOCAMP**, then that will raise a red flag to the payer. Providers generally do not have to send the notes or reports for just E/M services, but the payer will look at patterns of reporting when the provider is audited. If there are inconsistencies, the payer will request medical records to be submitted for its review.

A consult is usually at the mid- to high-level range. The consult must clearly state why someone is being referred. Usually a patient is sent to a specialist when the care is beyond the scope of the primary physician or when the patient needs a service that involves another specialty. The example would be a patient who is referred to an ENT for an ear problem or to a neurologist for a neurological disease. A patient's reason for wanting to self-refer to a specialist for a treatment or opinion may be very different from why a provider would refer the patient to a specialist.

Payers run reports based on individual physicians/providers randomly. Some reports are generated regularly for certain physicians with a history of irregular reporting of E/M codes. The information is reviewed by the payer's medical director, who is a physician, if appropriateness and medical necessity warrant this. A coder would not perform this service nor would a utilization review nurse. A physician would need to make a decision for peer reasons or legal issues. Nurses, coders, and billers cannot deny E/Ms; doing so would be challenging a physician's opinion. Only a peer can do that. In these cases, the peer would be the payer's physician employee. The review may take place in a utilization management committee meeting that reviews all the requests for the referrals.

A physician can theoretically perform any procedure in the CPT book, but this is not what usually happens. For example, a payer does not want a family practice physician performing cardiology or gastroenterology services. Internal medicine providers may have a higher level of training, but they may not be performing higher level surgical procedures. If the payer receives such claims, it would probably question the claim and service billed. If an ENT is suddenly performing a colonoscopy, the payer would expect wrong coding, not that a physician would perform services outside of his specialty or license. A provider's license to practice and medical malpractice insurance would probably not cover such services outside the specialty. Usually in such cases, a biller or coder may have entered the wrong code or there may have been a data entry problem. Inappropriate care by the physician would not be routinely suspected.

Case Study 9-1 – E/M Based on Medical Necessity of Care

No payer can dictate on what level of E/M the provider can see a patient. One provider giving a level of service does not preclude another provider giving an additional E/M service. The service is based on what the patient presents with at the time of the visit and the medical necessity of care. Case study 9-1 is an example of this.

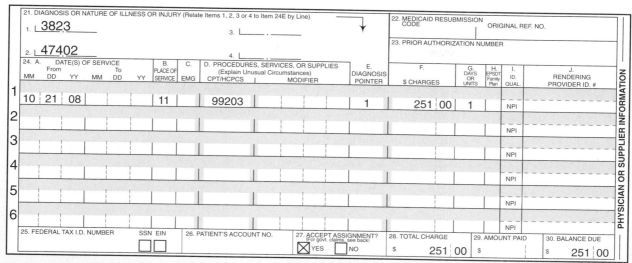

Figure 9-1 Case study 9-1 – an example of service based on medical necessity (Delmar/Cengage Learning)

A patient presents to a general practitioner, or GP, who concludes the patient has more than one chronic illness. The provider performs a higher level of service, including the necessary tests, blood work, and so on. If the GP decides to refer the patient to a cardiologist, usually the test results, blood work, and so on are given to the specialist for review.

At this point, the cardiologist can perform a higher level E/M. But the specialist is only going to perform services that are medically necessary. In other words, let us say the patient needs a thallium stress test. The cardiologist may need to obtain an authorization because the symptoms would need to justify this. Since this test is risky for the patient, the provider may order an EKG and assess the results, then order a stress treadmill test. Then if there is medical necessity, the provider orders the more risky test. This would constitute more than one office visit. Here the payer sees a progression of need for the patient and they advance in the E/M process.

If the patient walks in and his blood pressure is extremely high and his heart rate is very low, the provider can order testing on an emergency basis and refer the patient to the ED. There, the patient has emergency services in a hospital ED, and the insurance will cover these costs. In these cases, the ED physician has the oversight because this is his realm of expertise. The ED physicians also bill an E/M in these situations. The cardiologist is not necessarily going to give up care, though.

There may be a situation where both physicians are seeing the patient: the ED physician sees the patient for the emergency, and the cardiologist performs follow-up services in his specialty. The cardiologist may say, "I am here and assuming care of my patient." In such a case, the ED physician would step aside. The ED physician may be the one who brought the patient out of danger, and the cardiologist may be the physician who admits the patient to the hospital.

Case Study 9-2 – What Payers Dislike Most about Incorrect E/M Coding Reporting

We asked several payers what concerned them most about E/M coding guideline mistakes. Their response was almost always the same: coding a level of service that the provider felt applied but not actually held to the E/M guidelines regarding documentation of the chart.

(Continued)

In other words, the provider should document the appropriate history, exam, and decision making as performed in the visit and should include all elements of reporting levels stated in the claim. Case study 9-2 is an example of an appropriately documented E/M visit.

21. DIAGNOSIS OR NATURE OF ILLNESS OR INJURY (Relate Items 1, 2, 3 or 4 to Item 24E by Line)								22. MEDICAID RESUBMISSION CODE	ORIGINAL REF. NO.		
1. 8419				3. E8190							
2. 7020				4.				23. PRIOR AUTHORIZATION NUMBER			

	24. A. DATE(S) OF SERVICE From — To MM DD YY / MM DD YY	B. PLACE OF SERVICE	C. EMG	D. PROCEDURES, SERVICES, OR SUPPLIES (Explain Unusual Circumstances) CPT/HCPCS / MODIFIER	E. DIAGNOSIS POINTER	F. $ CHARGES	G. DAYS OR UNITS	H. EPSDT Family Plan	I. ID. QUAL.	J. RENDERING PROVIDER ID. #
1	10 21 08 10 21 08	11		99213 25	1.3	60 00	1		NPI	
2	10 21 08 10 21 08	11		17000	2	70 00	1		NPI	
3	10 21 08 10 21 08	11		17003	2	15 00	1		NPI	
4									NPI	
5									NPI	
6									NPI	

Figure 9-2 Case study 9-2 – an example of E/M; significant, separately identifiable evaluation and management service by the same physician on the same day of the procedure or other service (Delmar/Cengage Learning)

The patient presents with post-motor vehicle accident (MVA) three days ago, when he was hit broadside. The patient feels he strained or sprained his arms when he braced himself for the impact. The patient also has minor lacerations from the side window glass that shattered. At the time of the service, the patient is taking Flexeril® and Vicodin® as needed as prescribed by the ED provider. The patient is also concerned about some dry red spots on his arm and cheek. The patient reports no nausea or vomiting, no fatigue, no headache, and no other musculoskeletal complaints. The patient had squamous cell removed from his scalp in the past year.

Exam

W/D, W/N 47 YO male in NAD. Lungs are clear to percussion and auscultation. There are no limitations in the patient's ROM in both upper extremities. Cardio: no rubs, rales, pulse is good; pt has no evidence of the previously excised SQC on the scalp. Pt does have two seborrheic-type patches on his left cheek and right forearm.

Dx

Actinic keratoses, sprain R & L elbow, 2° to MVA

Plan

Continue meds as needed, rest, CO2 destruction AK cheek & forearm

E/M

99213-25   Office or other outpatient visit for the evaluation and management of an established patient, which requires at least two of these three components: an expanded-problem-focused history; an expanded-problem-focused exam; medical decision making of low complexity. Usually the presenting problem is of low to moderate severity. Physicians typically spend 15 minutes face to face with the patient and/or family.

PROCEDURE

    17000   Destruction (for example, laser surgery, electrosurgery, cryosurgery, chemosurgery, surgical curettement), premalignant lesions (for example, actinic kerotoses): First lesion

  +17003   Second through 14th lesions, each (list separately in addition to the first lesion)

EXPLANATION

The provider would need to give further documentation, such as consent, risks, benefits, follow-up care, anesthesia, if the procedure is performed in a doctor's office. This procedure would not be performed on an outpatient basis in a hospital or an ambulatory surgicenter.

Standardizing Physician Notes in the Medical Record

The following are various documentation styles the coder/biller may see a provider/practice use for patient visits.

Some practices may require specific documentation from the providers for various reasons (standardized notes in the record, cleaner audits, and so on); this may be written into the policy and procedures manual of the practice as SOAP, SNOCAMP, or CHEDDAR.

The detail given in each entry will determine the level of service performed at the time of the visit. The requirements for general multisystem examinations can be seen at www.cms.hhs.gov.

SOAP

Subjective	What the patient said, the problem(s) the patient presents with when he is at the exam
Objective	What the provider saw, what the provider observed
Assessment	The provider assesses the problem from the subjective and objective findings. The biller/coder may find a diagnosis or an impression
Plan	The plan to treat the patient. The biller/coder may see medications, instructions, tests, a plan to proceed

CHEDDAR

Chief complaint	The reason for the visit, statements of the patient, the problems the patient presents with
History	Past, family, and social history; and/or history of present illness, surgeries, or other illnesses contributing to the current problem
Examination	Body systems or organ systems may be examined and noted

Details	Pertinent details noted from problems or complaints
Drugs and dosage	Details of current dosage, lists of medications and how frequently they are used
Assessments of observations	Orders for tests, possible diagnosis, changes in medications, and so on
Return	When the patient needs to return

SNOCAMP

Subjective	What the patient said, the problem(s) the patient presents with when he is at the exam
Nature of illness	(high/medium or low severity) The provider will state
Objective	What the provider examines, what the provider observed
Counseling	What the provider discussed
Assessment	The provider assesses the problem from the subjective and objective findings. The biller/coder may find a diagnosis or an impression
Medical decision making	The provider may state high, medium, low severity, straightforward, and so on
Plan	Plan of care/treatment for the patient

Anesthesia

In the anesthesia section, the standard formula should apply when a physician specializes in anesthesia. A physician who is not a specialist in anesthesia should not use the standard formula but bill a flat fee agreed upon with the payer. The standard formula price varies because of the risk the anesthesiologist takes in anesthetizing the patient. The factors in the standard formula that may change reimbursement are time, physical status, and qualifying circumstances, with all adding extra units to the total. But if none of these apply, there is always a base unit that begins the price or is the price, depending on what is documented. A unit is worth a dollar amount, maybe $55 per unit depending on the payer. When all units that apply are added, they are multiplied by the dollar amount to make up the fee for that patient on the date of service. In these cases, the formula is added on an individual basis each time the specialist anesthetizes a patient as shown in the example.

Example of Standard Formula	**Units**
Basic value	3
Time units	3 (1 unit each 15 minutes)
Physical status	1
Qualifying circumstances	1
Total units	8 × $55 = $440
Total fee or reimbursement	**$440**

Explanation: The basic units, time units, physical status, and qualifying circumstances can be found in the ASA Guide published by the American Anesthesiology Association. Many times the unit value is a provider-specific contracted rate.

Position of a Patient Changes the Base Value

An anesthesiologist wants to see the patient's airway access. A patient lying in the supine position (on the back, face up) or lithotomy position (on the back, feet in the stirrups) will let the anesthesiologist easily see his face, and the base value will be quoted in the ASA guide. If a patient is lying on his stomach, or to the side where the face is not accessible to the anesthesiologist (such as the Sim's, Prone, or knee-chest position), then many times the base value is bumped up to five. Some software will change this automatically, but check with the payer.

Payment and Reporting

Few carriers will take surgical CPT codes with anesthesia modifiers in consideration for payment. Some software will have crossover capabilities and automatically change the surgical code(s) to the proper anesthesia code(s).

Some payers, such as Medicare, prefer the AA (HCPCS) modifiers to the CPT modifiers. The HCPCS modifiers can be reported with CPT codes but not vice versa.

Many payers do not pay extra units for physical status codes P1 through P6. Also, medical necessity codes, such as 99100, might not be paid any extra units, even though the standard formula may say to add units. Some providers do not include these when reporting because they will not be considered for payment. Yet other providers feel not reporting such elements would be incorrect.

Many coders complain of anesthesiologists not documenting time properly so this can be added to the standard formula.

A Surgeon Who Anesthetizes His Own Patient

Generally speaking, a surgeon will not anesthetize his own patient in a hospital, outpatient surgery department, or ambulatory surgical center (ASC). However, this may happen with an oral surgeon who is doing dental implants or removing wisdom teeth. In these cases, the oral surgeon will bill a flat rate. This would be incorporated in the rate for the surgeon's surgical suite in addition to his surgical fee. Or this flat rate may be added to the fee for the surgical procedure.

Some physicians put the patient under in a twilight sleep or light sedation. This is done by IV, usually an injection procedure that sedates the patient. The topical anesthesia used to initially numb the arm, if necessary, is included and not billed separately, as is administration of the agent, maintenance, monitoring, and recovery. Some think of this as a sedative type of situation rather than anesthesia. The surgical procedure dictates the anesthesia needs of the patient as well as the patient's personal medical status.

Case Study 9-3 – Anesthesiologists and RVGs

Anesthesiologists use the ASA codes from the American Society of Anesthesiologists Relative Value Guide in coordination with the CPT. This is helpful for anesthesia service provided by the anesthesiologist that appears in other sections of the CPT and for codes that can be used to supplement the CPT codes. The patient has the right to the best possible outcome of anesthesia care for the procedure; options may include general anesthesia, regional anesthesia, and supplemented local anesthesia, which could include pain control. The anesthesiologist should be reimbursed for providing appropriate care to the patient, as illustrated in case study 9-3.

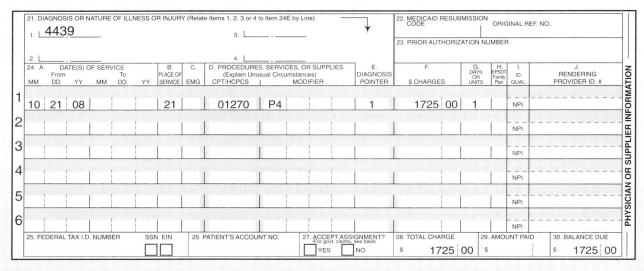

Figure 9-3 Case study 9-3 – An example of the anesthesia claim (Delmar/Cengage Learning)

DIAGNOSIS

443.9 Peripheral vascular disease, unspecified

PROCEDURE

01270 Anesthesia for procedures involving arteries of upper leg, including bypass graft; not otherwise specified

Basic value 5

P4 3 Peripheral vascular disease patient with severe systemic disease that is a constant threat to life

Time
1030 — 1411 3 hours 41 minutes, or 221 minutes altogether divided by 15 (15 is one unit) = 14.733

Total units 23 @ $75/unit = $1,725

EXPLANATION

Here the base units equal 5, the P4 equals 3; the minutes are rounded up to 15, and added together make a total of 23 units, which are then multiplied by the per-price unit of $75

Surgery Section

Most providers perform services documented in the surgery section of the CPT during the course of patient care. A provider may perform any procedure in the surgery section determined to be medically necessary and based on its area of expertise. Most of the time, a provider performs the same services for its patients again and again because it see patients for the same illnesses or injuries, for example, fractures and lacerations.

Sometimes, the provider is limited in the procedures it is able to choose. When becoming a participating provider of the insurance, the provider may agree to a certain section of codes it would bill the insurance company based on its specialty or medical area of expertise. This is also addressed during the credentialing process with an ASC.

The payer studies disease cost information gathered from insurance claims submitted through billing and coding. In this way, frequently performed, cost-effective procedures with successful outcomes can be performed so often that the cost per procedure is driven down, and the patient's health improves. The payer can anticipate future needs of a patient, leading to investment in managing a disease by way of patient care and equipment.

The payer may successfully exclude procedures with a higher cost that achieve the same potential results. A procedure may have approval potential if the outcome raises a patient's health above the outcomes of the frequently performed procedure using the cost-effective method. With this, the payer may be willing to develop its own outcomes through limited geographic approval and study of procedures already approved for treatment to the public.

In the following report, Figure 9-4, we see a procedure that traditionally was performed in a hospital setting moved to a physician's surgical suite. The procedure is a colposcopy with biopsy.

In the surgery section, coding conventions and guidelines apply that may affect codes in other sections, such as E/M and anesthesia. The surgery code being reported and sequenced correctly as it applies to the diagnosis is of the utmost importance, and the reporting and sequencing are noted by the payer in its decision to pay a claim.

When a surgery is performed on an elective basis (that is, not an emergency), most insurance companies require that the procedure be preapproved or preauthorized. The payer will determine medical necessity based on the medical records submitted and the anticipated procedure being authorized. With the authorization, the provider is able to bill those services. However, if the surgeon, once in surgery, finds the procedure needs to be much more extensive or there are extenuating circumstances, the surgeon will submit the operative report of what happened, and additional medical records, to have the service paid beyond the original medical authorization.

A surgeon sees a patient in the ED. Whatever the emergency situation, the ED visit will usually be covered by the health plan. Even if the provider is not a part of the plan, the payer cannot deny the service because the provider does not participate in the plan.

If the procedure is a scheduled or elective surgery, there is a process that needs to be followed for that service to be covered. If not done

---

NAME
PT#
SEX: F
DOB:
DOS:

PROCEDURE: COLPOSCOPY WITH BIOPSY

This is a 37YO who presents today for colposcopy with biopsy. The patient's questions were answered. Risks and complications were reviewed including bleeding, pelvic pain, irregular menses, perforation. The patient is status post cytology in December 2007 which was positive for intraepithelial lesion. She is GC and Chlamydia negative in March 2008.

DESCRIPTION: the patient was placed in the supine position, in stirrups. Bimanual performed and palpable adnexa. Uterus in midline, aneverted, speculum inserted, ectocervix and vaginal vault cleansed with betadine solution. Using sterile technique a tenaculum was placed in anterior cervix and using sound, uterus was sounded to 7.5 cm. Sterile package was opened. A vinegar solution to the cervix and vagina was applied with swab. Abnormal tissue was identified and three samples were taken for biopsy. Tissue samples were prepped and will be sent to pathology for analysis. Minimal bleeding was noted and the patient was advised to remain in the procedure room for 30 minutes or until discharge to home.

The patient is advised OTC motrin for pain. Patient is advised of possible dark colored vaginal discharge and/or spotting after the colposcopy. Patient was advised against the use of tampons or sexual intercourse for 7 days after the date of this procedure. Patient was advised to call me right away if she experiences any acute lower abdominal pain, bleeding that requires use of more than one sanitary pad per hour, fever, chills, or a bad smelling vaginal odor. Patient will return to the office in two weeks for follow up on pathology report.

_____
Physician signature

Figure 9-4 Example of a letter explaining a colposcopy with biopsy performed in a physician's office (Delmar/Cengage Learning)

properly, the plan can deny the service. For example, a patient cannot just walk in and say, "Please take my gallbladder out today." The procedure would not happen unless there is a medical necessity for it.

If the physician had an authorization for an anticipated surgery or procedure, but performed a different service or procedure, the payer would ask for the operative report and have it reviewed for medical necessity. Sometimes the procedure authorized and what is done are two different things. The physician may begin an authorized procedure and find a completely different problem once the preauthorized procedure begins. The provider will perform the services medically appropriate and explain this in the operative report, as illustrated in the example.

EXAMPLE: The patient is authorized to have an appendectomy, and then when the surgeon examines the patient, through the incision he sees a strangulated colon. The surgery would not be denied based on the authorization for the appendectomy. The claim will be paid based on medical necessity and what is documented in the medical record. This is what the payment is based on.

Radiology

Most radiology is standard films, two views, and not based on a global service. When the services are billed separately between the professional component (the interpretation and the report) and the technical component (the equipment, supplies, and performance by the service personnel, not the provider), the breakdown of percentage of payment is usually 40 percent reimbursement for the professional component and 60 percent for the technical component.

In radiology, there are a limited number of codes that can be billed; so, many times a payer sees these claims as very clean and precise in their reporting.

In the radiology section, there are four distinct sections:

- Diagnostic radiology
- Diagnostic ultrasound
- Radiation oncology
- Nuclear medicine

In this section, we will discuss three ways radiology is performed and reported.

Case Study 9-4 – Films Not Coded or Billed Separately for an E/M

In the first example, films are taken by a technician and read by a treating physician, GP, or family practitioner. The orthopedic specialist who is treating the patient used the films in her assessment to treat or diagnose the patient. These become a part of the evaluation and management visit, and the reading by the physician is not billed separately, as seen in case study 9-4.

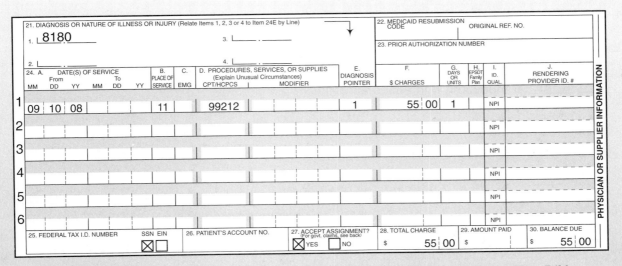

Figure 9-5 Case study 9-4 – an example of films not coded or billed separately from the E/M (Delmar/Cengage Learning)

(Continued)

A child broke his arm a week ago. The mother is concerned about the child because of complaints of pain and takes the child to a pediatrician. The mother brings the X-rays and wants the pediatrician to look at them during the visit. This is not a postoperative visit because the pediatrician has nothing to do with the global postoperative service. The pediatrician looks at the films and the report but only reports an E/M service

Case Study 9-5 – Billing for a Component Separately

There are circumstances when a physician can get paid for giving a separate report in a diagnostic radiology or ultrasound situation. This report would not be part of the E/M. The physician would write the report with the same requirements expected of a radiologist. The physician would need to document how many views were read and describe the nature and manifestation of disease visualized, if present. The physician would need to include soft tissues and bony structures along with the entire organ system on the film.

Films are taken by a technician, modifier -TC, and read by a physician, modifier -26. The physician gives his professional opinion, that is, a report, to the treating physician. Case study 9-5 is an example of billing for the physician component.

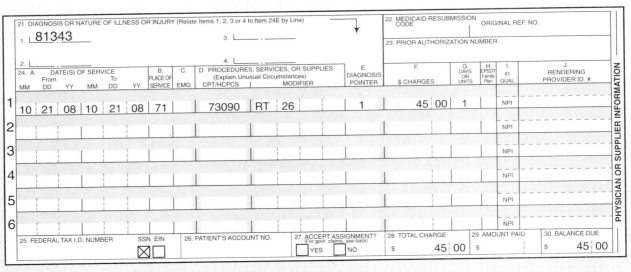

Figure 9-6 Case study 9-5 – an example of billing for a physician read and report (Delmar/Cengage Learning)

Case Study 9-6 – A Radiologist Performing Technical and Professional Components

Some procedures are complex and require the radiologist to perform the service, diagnostic or therapeutic, and generate a report. This would be based on the requested procedure, complexity of the procedure, and the needs of the patient. Of course, a radiologist may step in at any time and perform the technical component, if what she is looking for needs more specific care and examination. In these cases, the patient would be prepped by the nurse or a technician, and the radiologist would provide the professional and technical component. Case study 9-6 is an example of when a radiologist may perform a professional and technical component.

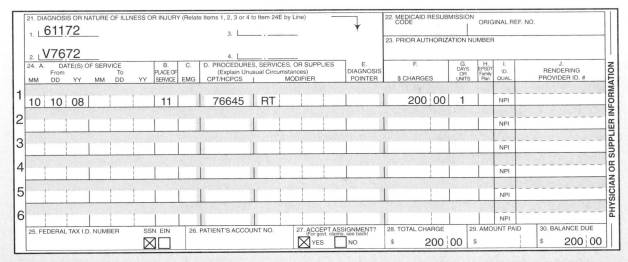

Figure 9-7 Case study 9-6 – an example of when a radiologist may perform a professional and technical component, global ultrasound (Delmar/Cengage Learning)

A patient has a routine mammography. The provider sights/notes a suspicious lump in the RUQ of the right breast. The patient has an ultrasound performed one day later by a radiologist who performs a global service, the technical and professional component together. The example is for the global ultrasound.

Who Reads the X-rays First?

The following cases are scenarios of coding reported by the specialist who reads the X-rays first.

Rural Hospital Scenario

If a patient has a broken arm at 3:00 a.m., the radiologist is not standing around waiting to read the films. The ED providers are the ones that utilize those X-rays. Radiologists do not read many X-rays in the emergency realm unless they are called in, but a trauma center may have a radiologist on call and do something called a **wet read** to assist in diagnosing the problem and embarking on the right avenue of care for the patient. Frequently, the next day a radiologist may look more closely at the films and give his final opinion of the X-ray with a report, billing this with a modifier -26 (professional component).

A radiologist may read all X-rays taken the previous evening and generate reports for those films, sitting down with a stack of films, dictating reports on all of them.

Cosmopolitan/Big-City Scenario

Many hospitals have invested in state-of-the-art radiology equipment that gives the radiologist on call the images he needs to render an opinion or make a diagnosis without being present or in the hospital. These images can be seen on a screen or faxed to the radiologist.

wet read A wet read is when an ED physician reads the film(s) to examine the problem and embark on the right avenue of care for the patient during the time the patient is in the emergency room.

Case Study 9-7 – Interventional Radiology

More and more radiologists are moving into the area of interventional radiology, which can involve angiography, balloon angioplasty, and chemoembolization.

Some procedures such as CTs and MRIs are not read by physicians who do not have a specialty license in radiology. In these procedures, a radiologist is trained to specifically understand and diagnose for the images. The provider contract and/or LMRPs may heavily influence reimbursement in interventional radiology. Case study 9-7 is an example of interventional radiology.

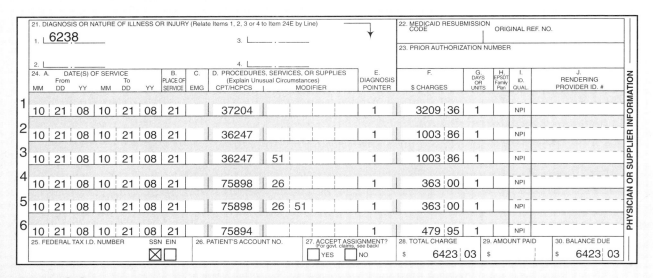

Figure 9-8 Case study 9-7 – an example of interventional radiology (Delmar/Cengage Learning)

DIAGNOSIS

623.8   Noninflammatory disorders of vagina. Other specified noninflammatory disorders of vagina

PROCEDURE

37204   Transcatheter occlusion or embolization (for example, for tumor destruction, to achieve homeostasis, to occlude a vascular malformation), percutaneous, any method, non-central nervous system, nonhead or neck

36247   Selective catheter placement arterial stem: initial third order or more selective abdominal, pelvic, or lower extremity artery branch, within the vascular family

36247-51   Selective catheter placement arterial stem: initial third order or more selective abdominal, pelvic, or lower extremity artery branch, within the vascular family — multiple procedures

75898-26   Angiography through existing catheter for follow-up study and for transcatheter therapy, embolization, or infusion — professional component

```
75898-26-51   Angiography through existing catheter for follow-up study
              and for transcatheter therapy, embolization, or infusion -
              professional component - multiple procedures
75894         Transcatheter therapy, embolization, any method, radical
              supervision and interpretation
```

EXPLANATION

This is an interventional radiology example. The radiologist performed all services listed on the claim. The procedure was performed in a facility. The facility billed for the supplies used, the room, tubes, drugs, and so on, but none of those are billed on the CMS-1500 claim form in this example. Only the services performed by the radiologist are billed. Notice the modifier -26 for the interpretations and the -51 modifier emphasizing the multiple procedures performed. Although there are two codes (75898-26, 51), the payer explains there is no need to add a modifier -51 because these procedures will not be reduced in payment. This claim was paid.

Pathology and Laboratory

Pathology and laboratory testing and procedures will become easier to understand when taking into account the following considerations before choosing a code.

First, many clinical tests are not reimbursable for the professional component unless written into the provider's contract. Many clinical tests are included in the payment of diagnostic related groups, or DRGs, and are reimbursed to the facility. Many codes that pay a professional component need direct supervision by the physician or are overread by the physician.

Each pathology test has a technical and professional component. Usually, the facility bills the technical component, TC, and is reimbursed at 80 percent, and the physician bills the professional component -26 and is reimbursed at 20 percent. A physician will need to oversee the lab.

Second, are the services qualitative or quantitative? Qualitative measures look at the presence of a substance by identifying it (80100-80103). Quantitative measures look at the concentration of a substance, which can be found in the chemistry section or the therapeutic drug assay section.

A qualitative screen testing positive may require a second technique to absolutely confirm the findings. In these cases, how does the insurance pay for such requirements? A drug confirmation test may be listed, however many times the procedure was performed. An 80102 may be listed or units may be identified on the claim. A modifier may be required.

A quantitative test looks at the substance being tested. A good example of this is chemistry codes. A good code of this is 82947, but beware the semicolon, which changes the descriptor.

Third, are all services documented in the chart and medically necessary? Do all services together qualify for a panel? A panel includes a series of tests, but all tests need to be ordered by the provider and identified in the analysis. If a test is not needed or not included in the panel, the coder should list the test separately and bill accordingly. The OIG is focusing on unbundling of panels. CCI edits are very specific and explain how not to unbundle panels. We suggest you see the CCI Web site.

Where Do Pathologists Work?

Pathologists usually perform their services in a freestanding lab or a hospital. Pathologists rarely work in doctors' offices, but there are exceptions, such as those who work in dermatology or plastic surgeons' offices. The place of service code should be assigned where the pathologist examined the specimen.

Medicine Section

The medicine section specifies in its subsections specialty types for a physician's practicing expertise used frequently or on a regular basis, for example, psychiatry or ophthalmology. This may be recognized by specialty or services that pertain to a specialty like nutritional therapy or dialysis, also listed as subcategories.

If any of the subcategories apply to your specialty, it is important to understand the bundling concept of the provider performing services. Some of the services in the medicine section may be included in the physician's procedure or service, elsewhere in the CPT.

What is meant by *bundling* is certain services are included as integral component parts of a service. And, if the specialist performs those services, the payer will know if they are an integral part of the service or not included. If the provider only performs that component part, the code should be able to stand alone as a billable service as well. The medicine section will let us have that flexibility, but it is up to the coder to know the difference. Sometimes, a bundled code can be broken into components if the provider performs her services outside of her office setting, and the facility bills its portion of the procedure, that would be everything other than the provider procedure. For example 93000 would include an interpretation and report. The report only would be 93010.

An example of an administration code and a separate code for the product are the vaccine/toxoid codes. Here the administration is reported, and the vaccine product is reported by a separate code. Both are in the medicine section. For the product 90476-90479, the administration codes 90471-90474 will be coded together to report the full service.

Case Study 9-8 – Immunization Administration without Bundling

Also, immune globulins codes have a supply code and an administrative code reported separately, 90281-90399. Case study 9-8 is an example of an administration of immunization without bundling the procedures.

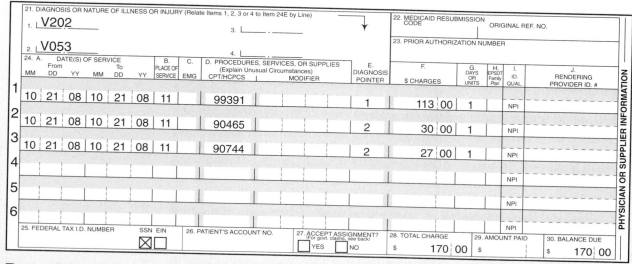

Figure 9-9 Case study 9-8 – an example of administration of immunization without bundling the procedures (Delmar/Cengage Learning)

DIAGNOSIS

V20.2	Routine infant or child health check
V05.3	Need for other prophylactic vaccination and inoculation against single diseases – viral hepatitis

PROCEDURE

99391	Periodic comprehensive preventive medicine reevaluation and management of an individual, including an age- and gender-appropriate history, examination, counseling/anticipatory guidance/risk factor reduction interventions, and the ordering of appropriate immunization(s), laboratory/diagnostic procedures, established patient; infant (age under 1 year)
90465	Immunization administration under 8 years of age when the physician counsels the family; first injection (single or combination vaccine/toxoid, per day)
90744	Hepatitis B vaccine, pediatric/adolescent dosage (3-dose schedule) for intramuscular use

EXPLANATION

In this example, the payer paid the claim and paid for the hepatitis B vaccine and the administration of the immunization without bundling the procedures.

(Continued)

If the drug is an injectable, the provider would have to note how it administered it to the patient and list the drug. It could be an IV push. The drugs would be on the claim form. These could be the HCPCS codes, J codes, if it is therapeutically (for example, antibiotic), given as an injectable, orally, or as a nasal spray. Does the physician give it or does the nurse? How is it administered?

Most of the injectables, like a B-12 shot, are given by nursing staff. But they would not bill for the nurse (99211); they would bill for the injection administration and injectable. Medicare and commercial insurance may pay.

HCPCS codes are used most of the time for the drug codes, or J codes.

Case Study 9-9 – Add-on Codes

Some codes reflect different types of service possibilities, such as dialysis, for which the coder chooses hemodialysis, or miscellaneous dialysis, procedures. Case study 9-9 is an example of add-on codes that apply in the procedure.

21. DIAGNOSIS OR NATURE OF ILLNESS OR INJURY (Relate Items 1, 2, 3 or 4 to Item 24E by Line)
1. 4259
2.
3.
4.

22. MEDICAID RESUBMISSION CODE ORIGINAL REF. NO.

23. PRIOR AUTHORIZATION NUMBER

	24. A. DATE(S) OF SERVICE From MM	DD	YY	To MM	DD	YY	B. PLACE OF SERVICE	C. EMG	D. PROCEDURES, SERVICES, OR SUPPLIES (Explain Unusual Circumstances) CPT/HCPCS	MODIFIER	E. DIAGNOSIS POINTER	F. $ CHARGES	G. DAYS OR UNITS	H. EPSDT Family Plan	I. ID. QUAL.	J. RENDERING PROVIDER ID. #
1	10	21	08	10	21	08	11		93307	26	1				NPI	
2	10	21	08	10	21	08	11		93320	26	1				NPI	
3	10	21	08	10	21	08	11		93325	26	1				NPI	
4															NPI	
5															NPI	
6															NPI	

PHYSICIAN OR SUPPLIER INFORMATION

Figure 9-10 Case study 9-9 – an example of add-on codes that apply in the procedure (Delmar/Cengage Learning)

DIAGNOSIS

425.9	Cardiomyopathy, secondary cardiomyopathy, unspecified

PROCEDURE

93307-26	Echocardiography, transthorasic, real time with image documentation (2D) with or without M-mode recording; complete - professional component
+93320-26	Doppler echocardiography, pulsed wave and/or continuous wave with spectral display (list separately in addition to codes for echocardiographic imaging); complete - professional component
+93325-26	Doppler echocardiography color flow velocity mapping (list separately in addition to codes for echocardiography)

EXPLANATION

Even though 99320 and 99325 are add-on codes, in this situation they are not used with a code choice directly above them; they still apply because they can be used with a variety of main codes in the category of echocardiography.

Case Study 9-10 – Chiropractic Modalities Not Paid

This case study reflects modalities not paid by Medicare, as illustrated in case study 9-10.

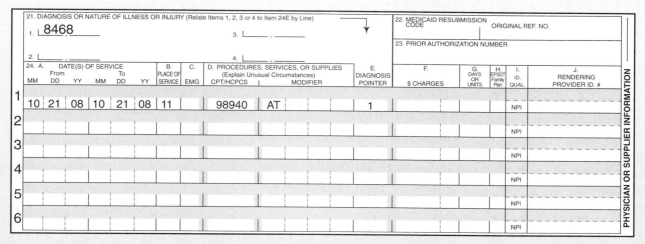

Figure 9-11 Case study 9-10 – an example of chiropractic care subluxation, modalities not paid (Delmar/Cengage Learning)

DIAGNOSIS

846.8   Sprains and strains of sacroiliac region; other specified sites of sacroiliac region

PROCEDURE

98940 AT   Chiropractic manipulative treatment (CMT); spinal, one to two regions

EXPLANATION

Medicare will pay for a subluxation of the spine, but it will not pay for modalities.

Note:

What is a modality? The CPT Manual describes it as, "any physical agent applied to produce therapeutic changes to biologic tissue, including but not limited to thermal acoustic, light, and mechanical or electrical energy.")

Summary

The CPT is used by all providers to report services and procedures performed to insurance companies and government agencies. The codes are also used in gathering statistical data needed to support clinical trials and funding for research. Payment is also equated to the codes in fee schedules, units of measure, and percentage billed. When reporting the codes, payers and their computer programs analyze their groupings and sequencing through coding conventions, guidelines, federal and state regulation, and law and contract agreement.

The responsibility of correct coding falls on the shoulders of the physician who reports what services or procedures were performed. The coder assigns a code from the written word, and the biller types the code onto the claim form. The three people are linked and must individually perform their duties correctly for an accurate/true outcome. One reward for correct coding is payment of services rendered in a timely manner, without needing to repeat any part of the processes. Another reward is understanding the reason for payment and how the codes are considered or measured by the payer.

Web Sites

Medical review, *www.cms.hhs.gov/xproviders/mr*

Coding Edge, *www.aapc.com/networking/coding_edge* (**Go to news and press.**)

Advance Magazine, *www.advanceweb.com*

Part B News, *www.partbnews.com/pbnweb/index.htm*

Review

Fill in the Blank

1. In evaluation and management the physician evaluates and _____ the _____ the patient presents with.

2. In a second-opinion claim, the payers usually do _____ require second opinions to authorize services.

3. One provider giving a level of service does not _____ another provider giving an additional E/M service.

4. In the anesthesia section, the _____ should apply to a physician who specializes in anesthesia.

5. When positioning a patient, the anesthesiologist wants to see the patient's _____.

6. When a surgery is performed on an _____ basis, the procedure needs to be preapproved.

7. In _____, standard films are two views.

8. ER physicians do a _____ _____ of X-rays to examine the problem.

9. A _____ screen testing positive may require a second technique.

10. A _____ test looks at the substance being tested.

Review Questions

1. The CPT codes are most commonly reported on

   _____ CMS-1500 claim forms

   _____ UB-04 (formerly UB-04) forms

   _____ both the CMS-1500 and the UB-04

   _____ none of the above

2. Who owns the CPT codes?

   _____ American Medical Association

   _____ Correct Coding Initiative

   _____ Medicare

3. The CPT is published

   _____ once a year

   _____ once every two years

   _____ once; the codes do not change

4. How many sections are there in the CPT Manual?

   _____ five sections

   _____ six sections

   _____ eight sections

5. In evaluation and management, the code is assigned based on

   _____ how well the provider documents the file

   _____ whether the patient is new or established

   _____ the key component – history exam and medical decision making

   _____ all of the above

   _____ none of the above

6. Most payers ask for a second opinion

   _____ before authorizing a surgery

   _____ before the patient presents with a new illness

   _____ at the family member's request

7. If the patient wants a second opinion,

   _____ most payers pay for one

   _____ most payers deny this

   _____ he doesn't ask for a second opinion

8. A specialist can trigger an audit for medical records when he statistically bills on a higher level of service and

   _____ the payer sees this in its system

   _____ the payer has no ability to see this

   _____ the specialist sends in his notes

9. A standard formula for anesthesia should be used

    _____ by all providers

    _____ by anesthesiologists only

    _____ sometimes by both

10. If the payer authorized a service but the surgeon performed a different service than what was authorized, the payer would

    _____ deny the service outright

    _____ request the operative report to decide payment

    _____ pay the claim unconditionally

11. Most radiology services are

    _____ billed on a global service

    _____ not billed on a global service

    _____ billed at 100 percent

12. In a lab panel, all services

    _____ must be ordered in the panel to code the panel

    _____ don't need to be in the panel

    _____ not included in the panel can be included

13. Many pathologists

    _____ are hospital based

    _____ are from a freestanding facility

    _____ have their own offices

14. Injections need two codes,

    _____ one for the administration of the code and one for the drug

    _____ one for the facility and one for the nurse

    _____ one for the needle and one for the syringe

Critical Thinking Exercise

In this exercise, the student will be looking for base units values. These can be differences between payers or the differences from state to state.

On the Web, search for comparisons between the ASA RVG – American Society of Anesthesiologists and the base unit value of the anesthesia codes for CMS.

1. Compare. If using the ASA RVG, give the base unit higher value.

2. Note if the description changes with the codes staying the same.

3. If you can, find quoted prices in published fee schedules; who has the higher dollar amount?

4. Note your findings and opinions, along with examples, in a two-page report, and give it to your professor.

Professional Corner

Consider the following questions and items, and reflect on how they might affect your professional development or growth. In addition, consider how not having them might affect your performance for your provider.

1. *Do you have access to any of the coding newsletters and magazines, such as Coding Edge, Part B News, Coding Clinic, or Advance Magazine?*
2. *Will your employer pay for such information?*
3. *Do you receive a yearly educational budget for continuing education?*
4. *How is your office informed of coding guideline changes and how often?*
5. *Does your office keep at least one copy of the CPT manual for every year the office has been reporting codes?*

References

American Medical Association. (2008). *Current Procedural Terminology.* Eden Prairie, MN: Ingenix, 2008.

Centers for Medicaid and Medicare. (2008). Retrieved from: HHS.gov. "Regulations and guidance".

Bierstein, Karen, J.D., MPH. (January 7, 2008). "Medicare Conversion Factors and Coding Changes for 2007". ASA *Practice Management,* Volume 71, Page 34.

Centers for Medicare and Medicaid. (May 30, 2008). *Conversion Factors by Geographic Locality.* Warren, MI: South Oakland Services.

Centers for Medicare and Medicaid. (May 30, 2008). *Looking Ahead in 2008, CPT Changes.* Warren, MI: South Oakland Services.

10 Provider Disputes and Balance Billing

Chapter Objectives

Upon completion of this chapter, you should be able to

- Gather patient information needed for a dispute
- Comprehend backing out overpayments from claims payable
- Apply time lines involved in resolving a disputed claim
- Comprehend tracking claims through the dispute process
- Understand where to find the payer's criteria for payment
- Comprehend the appeals process in audits of the health plan
- Understand settling disputed claims with noncontracted providers
- Identify when to balance bill for contracted and noncontracted providers
- Identify when to balance bill for primary and secondary insurances
- Recognize Medicaid percentage penalties for late filings

Key Terms

good faith

Introduction to Provider Disputes and Balance Billing

This chapter introduces the concept of provider disputes and helps the reader understand the process that may be used when handling a dispute by identifying basic information, how to track a dispute, time limits and interest on claims, the appeals process, and audited disputes. The balance billing portion of the chapter looks at how contracted and noncontracted providers may handle what is left after the insurance has paid their portions of the claim.

Every state has various laws to address a provider dispute for resolving claims that are cost- effective for all parties. A dispute may include claims issues, timeliness issues, and payment issues for contracted and noncontracted physicians and facilities. When submitting a provider dispute resolution request, the provider agrees not to bill the patient. Unfortunately the provider sometimes does bill the patient, leaving the patient billed for services that are not necessarily his responsibility.

A state or provider may call a dispute resolution something different, such as payment disputes, provider disputes, or contract disputes. But no matter what the name, there is basic information needed to be exchanged by both parties to resolve the disagreement regarding claims payments or lack of payment. Both the payer and the provider must communicate the process in which they will explain to each other their views and rulings. Most disputes will revolve around a single claim. Or the provider may have the same procedure performed on several patients from the same insurance/payer and want them all to be taken care of together as a batch or group of *like* claims rather than individually. These are the issues we will explore in this chapter.

Basic Identifying Information Needed for Both the Provider and Payer

Basic data set information needed to complete a dispute between the payer and the provider are

- Provider name
- Taxpayer identification number
- Provider address
- Provider type
  - Mental health
  - Ambulance
  - Skilled nursing facility, or SNF
  - Home health
- Patient's name
- Patient's date of birth
- Original claim number

Single or Multiple Claims

If the provider has multiple claims in the dispute, there may be an extra pages of paperwork to fill out, but in many cases, multiple or *like* claims are more cost-effective to send together in the same envelope certified with return receipt. Disputes may include an appeal for medical necessity and utilization management service denials. The referral number(s) is needed when the provider is appealing a service's denial of claims payment.

Seeking Resolution of a Billing Determination

Timeliness issues of when a claim is submitted for procedure eligibility and contract disputes are all reasons for providers to seek resolution determination. An example of timeliness of claim submission for an initial claim by provider is an average of 90 days, and 180 days for noncontracted providers. *This means if a biller has submitted a claim and needs to resolve a dispute regarding that claim, he has 90 days and/or 180 days in which to do it.* Supplemental paperwork enables a claim to be paid, and should be submitted when a material or service is above and beyond what is usually paid for.

The provider needs to be prepared to give a description of the dispute and the expected outcome. The provider should also include the following when seeking resolution:

- Proof of what happened
- The claim
- An internal letter
- The name of a contact
- The expected outcome

Usually there is only one dispute for one claim. There usually are not group/batch disputes. A follow-up regarding a claim is not a *provider dispute* nor are *patient eligibility* inquiries.

Tracking Form

A dispute needs to be tracked through the system both by the payer and the provider because it must be taken care of within a required time frame. This is for payment status, time frames, and where the dispute is in the system. The entity processing the claim should track the claim internally.

The age of a claim also counts; there is a timeliness of submitting the payment dispute in how old the claim is. Usually, if the claim is one or two years old, the claim is too old to submit a dispute, but a biller should check with his state and payer to make sure.

This means contracted and noncontracted providers, even though the payer may establish separate rules, both must still be fair and not linger to the point of claims' cost-effectiveness being lost waiting for a resolution.

Internal Tracking of Disputes by the Provider

Figure 10-1 is an example of a form the provider can use in-house to track submitted disputes between the provider's office and the payer. Since there are time limits regarding responses to continue to dispute a claim,

Disputes Submitted Tracking Form

Insurance Company	Patient Name	Date of Service	Date of Dispute	Date of Expected Resolution	Dollar Amount	Amount Disputed	Tracking Number	Response

Figure 10-1 An example of a provider tracking form (Delmar/Cengage Learning)

an untimely response could carry the loss of monies. The provider's office will need to track disputed claims.

How a Payer Is Paying Claims and the Criteria

The payer will need to, on request by the provider, acknowledge the fee schedule used to pay the claim. Medicare fee schedules, worker's compensation, capitation, and so on are all various methods of payment. Many providers can have access to a Web site set up by the payer that states the criteria for payment.

Payers need to make their best efforts, in writing, for the provider to understand and work with the dispute process. This begins with agreed-upon tracking numbers and information the payer and provider will use when identifying and discussing a claim. They could be any combination of the following:

- Name
- Social Security number
- Date of service
- Services provided
- Diagnosis
- Why the provider feels there is a dispute

When contesting a claim, the provider should follow the formal dispute of claims process explained in writing by the payer. Since some providers only dispute certain procedures on claims and are okay with other procedures paid on the same claim, the provider should specifically identify the item and not just the claim number, and explain very plainly the basis of its dispute. If the provider needs additional information to explain the dispute logic, the process of gaining access to that information from the payer should be provided.

The provider will need to understand why this dispute is happening, to prevent future delays in payment and develop a process that prevents this from happening again, especially if the procedures are going to be performed often and/or carry a high dollar amount reimbursement.

A payer may feel they have overpaid a claim and request a return of overpaid portion of the claim. This may be a code that holds a lower dollar amount than what was reported. In this case, the biller should be prepared to justify coding statements with SOAP notes, operative reports, and entries of special circumstances of the patient.

Also, the provider may need to answer a patient complaint sent to the payer. This could be anything from the patient claiming he did not receive services, to the patient not understanding what the services entailed. Sometimes, if a patient is responsible for a portion of the payment he feels is too much or does not want to pay, they may claim this. In this case, it is best to have the patient sign an acknowledgment of his financial responsibility before he receives any elective surgery.

Then the acknowledgement will become a part of the appeal to the payer.

Miscellaneous Reasons for a Dispute

The following could be some reasons a dispute takes place. These may result in an outright denial of the claim or causes for rebundling and the payer reimbursing for the rebundle.

- The diagnosis codes were too general, using the .9s (__ __ __ . 9), from the ICD-9–CM, in the fourth digit when the procedure demands a more specific code in order to be paid.

- The procedure is not included in the list of procedures the payer will pay for that specific diagnosis. In other words, some insurances will only pay for traditional procedures with a specific diagnosis. These may be procedures used by so many physicians in the industry that the cost to perform them is lower. Or maybe, the agreed-upon procedures have a proven track record and the payer has an idea of their effective rate and the overall cost to make the patient well. Medicare is very specific in this regard.

- Some procedures were paid on a claim and some were not paid. The payer may say the code is bundled with other codes or the codes are mutually exclusive based on CCI guidelines. If either of these is the case, the payer considers these codes paid and to bill the patient would be double billing or billing for a procedure the payer considers already paid.

A Time Limit on Claim Disputes

A time limit should be established by the payer. This should comply with state or federal laws and be consistent with all specialties providing services to the patients. But, of course, if the provider does not submit the paperwork for the dispute in a timely manner, the dispute will not be considered or recognized and will be rejected by the payer for the timeliness issues.

The payer must develop a uniform procedure of providing acknowledgement of receipt of the disputed claim. A written procedure for all to follow should be in place and consistently followed by all who participate in the process; this is for consideration of the claim.

But, what if the dispute has incomplete information? A short period of time should be established to submit missing or fragmented information. This time period also needs to be in writing and followed by both the payer and the provider of service. The average time incomplete information can be submitted is from 30 to 60 days in some states.

Once a dispute is complete, from that time, the payer will need to establish its own time frame for reviewing the validity and ability to make a reasonable decision. If a provider is still not satisfied with the payer's decision regarding the dispute, the provider should have the ability to appeal the decision. Time frames are needed for this. The decision of the appeal will need to be in writing by the provider. And if the appeal is not timely, the dispute would be rejected by the health plan.

A contracted provider dispute, which does not include complete documentation for a resolution, can be returned for completion. The amended dispute needs to be submitted within 30 working days of the provider receipt of the dispute, or else the payer is not obligated to make a decision on the claim.

At this point in the dispute, the biller may be wondering if it is worth the hassle. Well . . . yes it is. Consider the situation a learning experience, and, above all, find out what must be done to submit the claim right the first time (what attachments are needed, coding issues and changes, precertification, prequalification, and so on). Eliminate the factors that brought about the claims dispute and make a list of what must be done. Missing proper steps/documentation in the first submission could lead to the payer retrieving the monies deserving payment.

Interest on Claims

If the payer goes beyond its allotted decision making time to decide whether to pay a claim or not, there should be a penalty of a percentage of the claim (interest) calculated in a preestablished time for all to know and adhere to. This helps the payer to make a decision regarding a claim and not just "sit" on the claim until it is ready to do something about it. The amount of interest paid would be after the 45th day. Interest is only on the portion that is the adjusted payment from the 45th day, not from the date the claim was originally paid.

Is The Appeal Process Included in Annual Audits of the Health Plan?

If yes, there should be a sample audit a provider can follow comfortably, explained on every level of the process. These audits usually track timeliness in the communication between the provider and the payer.

Audits for timeliness apply to commercial claims, HMO, and Medicare HMO claims, CMS, which are reported monthly to the health plan. Disputes are reported quarterly, and the provider must state the resolution of those disputes. The provider should track resolutions as well. The provider should check their own policy and procedures when an audit is performed for compliance and all parties are involved.

Audits of Provider Disputes

There may be a law in your state that requires the payer to report a separate audit just on the disputes. When health plan auditors come to your office and audit the payer, they may be doing a separate audit just to see that those provider disputes are looked at and resolved in a timely manner. This would be an audit apart from the paid claims and the denied claims. Each health plan will only audit their subscribers' claims.

Acknowledgment of Disputes

Usually a payer will acknowledge the receipt of a dispute received electronically within 2 working days, and the receipt of a paper claim within 15 working days.

Retention and accessibility is the key when future questions arise in such cases.

How will the files be stored? Will they be electronic or paper? How soon can the record be accessed? Is it in hours or days? And, for how long are the files to be stored or accessible? Is it months or years? Answers to these questions should also be in written policy form by the payer.

Laws tend to regulate when interest must be given to the provider, without the provider needing to request the interest. In some states the interest must be given in as few as five days. However, the provider should be sure the interest is self-imposed and paid in the final payment. Payers may "conveniently" forget to pay it.

The payer can pay low-interest amounts together with other low-interest amounts, as long as the payer clearly identifies each specific interest payment on a statement. Usually there is a flat rate for commercial claims, for example, $15.00 for ER claims. Interest on commercial claims may be as low as $2.00 and under in some states.

If the claim needs to be forwarded to another payer, the health plans have the option of denying the claim or forwarding it on to the correct payer themselves, but the provider should know ahead of time what the payer's policy is on this.

Information the Adjuster Needs

An adjuster must be able to understand the billed services for processing the claim. The claim needs to have very specific information included, such as:

- Cost of services

- Liability of plan

- Ability to understand all information given to consider payment and comply with the state and federal laws applicable

- The processor needs at least the minimal amount of data necessary to pay the claim and establish liability, if any

There is a timeliness issue here, and it is stated in the regulations. The provider must understand what applies to its timeliness issues based on being a contracted or noncontracted provider.

Acknowledgement of Claims

Acknowledgment of receipt of claims is very specific to either electronic or paper claims. The provider needs to be able to know if its claim was received, and it has a right to know within 2 working days of receipt of electronic claims; on paper claims that rises to 15 working days.

Reimbursement time lines commence from the date of receipt. That is why knowing when a payer has received the clean claim/complete claim becomes important. Payment of a clean claim should happen within 45 working days, and the state's regulation should back this up. Denied claims need to be denied within 30 calendar days according to some plans.

A Request for Reimbursement of Overpayment by the Payer

The payer overpaid the claim, and the payer is requesting that the money be taken back or refunded. Some providers are very diligent about refunding overpayment. Some providers just go ahead and keep the money, which is not correct. If a provider does not refund the money and does not dispute that the payment is correct, the payer, after giving the provider the correct amount of time to explain its side, will take the overpayment back. This could be through retracting payments from other claims that are payable at the time. Here is an example of the process.

If the payer finds it has overpaid the claim, it must notify the provider in writing and the provider must have a chance to contest the notice and explain why there is no overpayment in its opinion. But if the provider does not respond or challenge the overpayment claim within a specified number of days, a retraction to the payer would be performed and specified on future EOBs. In some states, this would be performed in 30 calendar days.

When a Payer Backs Out Overpayment from Other Claims

If a payer receives a nonresponse from a request for overpayment, the provider will have a period of time either to pay back the monies or explain why it believes the claim was paid correctly. Such requests by a payer should be responded to within the time frame given by the payer. The payer will take the nonresponse to its request as an admission of overpayment and may take back the disputed amount from other claim monies. The following example is a case of monies being withheld due to overpayment of other claims.

EXAMPLE: The payer overpaid claim (A) by $200.

The payer wrote the provider a letter stating claim (A) was overpaid and the provider has 45 days from the date of the letter or notice (not postal date or date of provider receipt) to write back if it disagrees.

The provider does not write back at all!

The payer takes $200 out of the following claims: $50 out of claim (B), $100 out of claim (C), and $50 out of claim (D).

The EOBs from claims (B), (C), and (D) will explain that, yes, the provider was paid in theory for those claims, but no monies are included with the EOB because the funds were taken back from disputed claim (A).

The claim would be entered, and the money would be subtracted from whatever the dollar amount value of the total number of claims would be. If the money amount is more than what is being reimbursed, then this would show as a negative claim.

This can be a mess for the biller posting the payments, but good billing software has a mechanism for which to do this. If the biller does not understand how this works with his billing software, he should call the company and ask and then make sure to always use the same procedure when this type of situation arises.

Settling Claims with Noncontracted Providers

For noncontracted providers, *usual and customary* seems to be the payment value. Usual and customary are calculated from the prevailing rates taken from a geographic area in which other providers of the same specialty practice. Some practices may base their rates on usual and customary or even develop their own rates.

In settling a claim, the provider should be able to justify additional amounts of money requested regarding the special circumstances on the case, and the physician's special expertise should reflect this justification for more money; if it does not, then no more or extra monies will probably be paid.

> **good faith** Working with a desire not to defraud.

The payer should make a **good faith** effort to settle claims, whether they are new or disputed claims by the provider. A good faith effort is not always a negotiated effort between the payer and the provider. Good faith is very simply working with a desire not to defraud.

The payer will need to notify the provider in writing of any issues to track the written documentation as proof of what the payer intended to do. If either party wants to keep track of this by phone, it will need to document the name of the person spoken to, title, date the conversation took place, and if it has the authority to accept a negotiated settlement on a claim.

In a settlement where the provider receives money, the written notice, adjustment, and interest should be issued within the time set forth by state regulation. In some states this is within five working days of the decision.

Sometimes the payer needs more information to make a decision on a claim; this holds a time limit also. The provider needs to stay within submittal guidelines and realize that the payer counts its days of *need to pay* from the time it receives the requested information. In the state of California, this is 45 working days of the receipt of the requested/needed information.

Balance Billing

Balance billing is when the provider bills the patient for the balance of what is left after the payer has paid what it considers its responsible/negotiated/agreed-upon fee. Many providers have in their contracts that they will not balance bill the patient what is left over, or the balance. But some providers, if they are in dispute with the payer say, "If this is not paid by the payer, we will bill the patient." The provider needs to read its participating contract to be sure it can do this. If not, it is in violation of its participating contract. Managed care plans, such as HMOs or PPOs, usually have a provision in them that the provider will not balance bill the patient.

Contracted and Noncontracted Providers

If the provider is contracted, the payer has more leverage; this could be a group or a health plan. Sometimes payments are based on diagnosis codes, but they are usually paid for procedure codes. Some providers contract for Medicare rates, others contract for flat rates for procedures and this is negotiated in their contracts. The payer's computer system needs to be very sophisticated to deny based on diagnosis codes.

Many systems are set up to look at procedure codes for denial purposes. The majority that are denied through medical procedure or diagnosis codes are done so by the computer system recognizing this and setting the claim aside to be looked at manually by a claims processor.

Rebundling Based on Claim Check Edit Systems

If the provider is disputing a rebundle, it will need to provide documentation based on CPT guidelines or any other viable guidelines, such as CCI, included in its contract. If it is a noncontracted provider, it will need to base its argument on a viable methodology like CPT, HCPCS, ICD Volume 3, or CCI.

In balance billing, the payer has paid some portion of the claim, whether it be a percentage of the total or specific procedures. The explanation of benefits, or EOB, will tell the provider what to do with the balance of the monies from the claim. This may be a write-off, bill the secondary insurance, or bill the patient.

If the EOB states the provider needs to write off the balance, then this pertains to the participating provider agreement and the provider agreed to do this when the contract was signed.

Case Studies – Where the Primary and Secondary Insurance Rates Are Different

In secondary billing, the primary insurance has paid its responsible portion of the claim and there is a balance. The provider should bill the secondary insurance and be paid the secondary's responsibility of the claim before billing the patient for the balance, if there is a balance. If the provider is not contracted, this is a courtesy. Case study 10-1 is an example of when the PPO is primary and the HMO is secondary. Notice how the secondary HMO pays its capitated rate and not the regular rate of the claim.

The PPO is primary and the HMO is secondary; the provider would send the HMO the EOB from the PPO. The PPO would only pay up to its own contracted rate. If the first insurance said the bill was $500 and the allowed/contracted rate was $300, the primary would only pay its portion of that, which is about $200 (the other $100 was the coinsurance or the deductible); then the provider of service would send the claim to the secondary for payment; the HMO would look at the contracted rate. Let us say the HMO rate was $250; then the HMO would pay $50 to come up to what its contracted rate was. The rest would need to be written off, and the provider could not balance bill the patient for what was left, leaving a write-off of $200 ($500 − $300 = $200).

Regular rate	$500
Primary insurance contracted rate	$300
Contracted rate percentage responsibility	$200
Billing the secondary	$100
Secondary capitated rate	$250
Secondary pays the difference	$50
Written off or billed the patient	$50
Difference between the contracted and regular rates	$200

Figure 10-2 Case Study 10-1 When the PPO is the primary and the HMO is secondary (Delmar/Cengage Learning)

Case study 10-2 is an example of patient responsibility in an HMO/PPO. Notice the PPO had a higher approved rate and percentage paid. Notice what the patient paid in each example.

Case Study of One Insurance

	PPO as the primary	HMO as the secondary
Service	$100	$100
Approved	$80	$64
Percentage paid	$60	$44
Percentage patient paid	$20	Co-pay $20
Write-off	$20	See PPO figure

Since the primary PPO approved and paid a higher amount than the HMO contract rate, there is no supplemental payment. The patient is responsible for the $20 balance.

Figure 10-3 Case Study 10-2 (Delmar/Cengage Learning)

Regarding the Write-off

The disposition codes used show up in a certain column of the EOB that tells the biller what to do with the monies. One example is a code 315, which is usually a contract adjustment. This means the provider has to write that entry off. Or another may be a coinsurance deductible column or adjustment so the biller knows what to do with the balance monies. Some billing systems are set up to do this manually, but others are not. Many providers do not look at their EOBs right away, hence leaving large balances due on their aging reports, and leaving other managers to think there are collectable balances due, when really there are not.

Medicaid

Each state has developed its own way of delivering services to those participating in its Medicaid system. Each state personalizes the name of its program, for example, Medi-Cal, Tenn Care, and so on, just as it personalizes the system(s) for which service is provided and paid. The state may manage their system in various ways, depending on high populations, to capture all participating members, and offer a mix of plans. Here are a few examples:

Countywide: If there is a high population in particular counties, the state may feel countywide management is a more effective way to manage the Medicaid population.

Regionally: The state may divide by region, contracting with commercial plan(s) to capture all participating members. The most cost-effective may be a managed care capitated model.

Patient choice: The patients may have choices of plans. Choices could be a mixture of county plans, regional plans, and commercial plans.

The state Medicaid systems will usually contract with medical groups or health plans in their perspective areas and with specific physicians or physician groups as participating providers for state Medicaid programs. Even though the state contracts with the health plan, *every physician who belongs to the plan is not required to participate in Medicaid.* If a medical group participates, not every provider is subject to participation. Many times the reimbursement is extremely low because the money is divided up through a pool of monies that may be all that is available. This will affect both plan and provider decision to participate.

Reimbursement

Medicaid reimbursement is likely to be low compared to that of other payers. Many times a provider's billing office may give top priority to high-dollar reimbursement claims of the same procedure. Since those claims go out first, those with lower potential reimbursement for the same work may be given low priority in the daily routine of the biller.

To counter this, some states make claim filing time lines much shorter – sometimes less than a year, with potential penalty to the reimbursement if filed after the time limit.

For example, if the filing period is 9 months,

- The 10th month may be 75 percent of full payment consideration
- The 11th month may be 50 percent of full payment consideration
- The 12th month may be denied altogether and not considered for payment at all

> **Note:**
>
> *What is meant by* full payment consideration *is the negotiated fee, not the full fee or physician's regular fees.*

This puts the provider of services in the position of making the low-reimbursement claims just as important as the high-dollar reimbursement claims. If the claims can be sent electronically, this is even better. But unfortunately, many providers who have a high volume of Medicaid patients are not of a mindset to invest large volumes of monies in their billing systems. This potentially sets a cycle of even lower reimbursement to the provider and its staff, which in turn equates to higher overhead and lower payment potential.

Cost-Effectiveness in Billing

Some providers feel that on a low-level office visit, the time it takes to do the service and file the claim is not worth their time to even bill the service. But under Medicaid they must bill the service or else they are providing services free, which the provider cannot do. This is against regulation.

Noncontracted Providers

Sometimes a noncontracted provider will not receive from a patient all the information needed to get claims paid (for example, no identification is presented at the time of service or there is no way to check eligibility through the Medicaid system). A noncontracted provider still has timeliness issues. Most payers will only consider a claim up to one year.

Sometimes the payer will still only pay its contracted rate to the noncontracted provider. The provider bills the patient the difference between its regular rates and what was paid, stating the payer did not pay the whole bill. (It is not in either party's best interest to pursue this situation. A patient who qualifies for Medicaid does not have the financial capability to make the payment to a noncontracted provider.)

Some payers pay noncontracted providers at usual and customary rates. The payers may use a code that states they are paying a claim in good faith to keep the patient from having to pay out of pocket. The code gives the payer a way to track these claims. Some noncontracted payers may get paid 100 percent because they say they will bill the patient if they do not.

Submission of claims for noncontracted providers is 180 days. Sometimes noncontracted providers do not get the correct information from the patient himself, or, if their information is secondary and they have billed the health plan, the claim should have gone to the provider group. The health plan is bound by law to forward the claim to the group within a reasonable amount of time.

Retention of Files

Many times a payer will keep files active for about five years, then purge to an archive. Many payers divide their files by paid and nonpaid claims. Provider disputes are active usually at least 365 days during the active period of the dispute and keep them active beyond six months. Financial records may be retained at the discretion of the payer yet archived as well.

Forwarding the Claim to Another Payer

If the patient is not a member of the medical group, the group would ask for instruction from the health plan, and if the patient is still eligible, the claim would be forwarded to the correct payer. If the medical group cannot ascertain that information, the claim would be forwarded on to the health plan and the plan would forward it on to the correct payer. The claim would not be denied as ineligible unless the patient is no longer eligible with the health plan it was submitted to. In these cases, the claim would be denied and forwarded to the proper health plan, and the respective health plan would decide if the claim has merit.

Some payers want names of employees who verbally state a patient is ineligible. This is for auditing purposes and/or potential appeal.

Claim Overpayment Written Notice

If the payer determines there is an overpayment, it must provide a written notice to the provider that clearly identifies the name, claim, dates, and so on and any amount that was paid on the claim was in excess of the amount due including interest and penalties. Plus they would have to do this within 30 days of overpayment of a claim and they have to provide the plan with a written notice based on their belief of why they feel it is not overpaid. The written notice would be looked at in accordance with the payer's provider resolution process.

If there is no contest of the overpayment, the provider has to pay within 30 working days of its receipt of the overpay notice. If there are current claims submissions, and the provider fails to reimburse within the time frames, the contract specifically authorizes the payer to offset any uncontested notice of overpayment from claims in process. The payer may do this because it can otherwise be confusing to the provider. If there is an overpayment of claims, and it is offset by other claims, the payer will notify the provider with a detailed written explanation of the specific overpayment and what it was offset against. If it was offset, the payer would back out the claims for the dollar amount needed, and that would show up as a negative on the claim amount in the EOB.

> **EXAMPLE:** There are 10 claims batched. Of these, 9 are paid, 1 is not; the EOB and the check would be offset by this amount. This is very different from all 10 claims being paid and posted. Some billing software and billers are not sophisticated enough to post these payments correctly. To do this, the payer would back out the payment and adjust it to reflect the overpayment amount.

Summary

Both payers and providers hope for a correct flow of paperwork, information, and payable claims with little dispute. But at times a dispute is unavoidable. To help resolve these problems, many states have laws that hold payers and providers to guidelines and time lines cost-effective to both parties, holding both to penalties for nondecisions, nondisclosure, and nonpayment. The process to resolve such disagreements can be time consuming, but for many, the ground rules for handling such disputes have become understood in a process of what both are to expect from their inquiries. Check with your state's insurance commissioner or on the Web for dispute resolution processes in your state.

Web Sites

The best Web sites in these cases are found through the search mode and specified by agency, state or county, name of insurance company, government ruling, the current year to date, and so on. By searching in this way, you can get the most current information/rules that would apply in your area.

Type in search phrases such as

- provider dispute billing 2007
- provider dispute coding 2007
- balance billing _____ (state or county you live in)
- balance billing Medicare

Review

Fill in the Blank

1. When submitting a provider dispute resolution request, the provider agrees _____ to _____ the patient.

2. Most disputes will resolve around a _____ claim.

3. A _____ _____ is needed when the provider is appealing a service denial of claims payment.

4. When contesting a claim, the provider should follow the formal _____ _____ _____ process in writing by the payer.

5. Usually, a payer who receives disputes electronically will acknowledge the receipt of a dispute within _____ working days, a paper claim within _____ working days of receipt of the claim.

6. The provider should specifically identify the _____ and not just the _____, and explain very plainly the basis for the _____.

7. If a provider is not satisfied with the payer's decision, the provider should be able to _____ the decision.

8. If the claim needs to be forwarded to another payer, the _____ _____ have the option of denying the _____ or forwarding it on to the correct payer themselves.

9. _____ _____ is when the provider bills the patient for the balance of what is left after the payer has paid.

10. What is meant by full payment consideration is the _____ fee, not the _____ fee of the _____ regular fees.

Review Questions

1. What are some of the various names a provider may call a dispute?

   _____

   _____

2. If the provider is nonresponsive to a request for overpayment, what might the payer do to recoup its monies? _____

   _____

   _____

3. When submitting a claim for dispute, how old is too old for claims to be submitted to begin the dispute process? _____

   _____

   _____

4. How may a provider find out what payment schedule is used by a
    payer? _____

    _____

    _____

5. Name four reasons why a dispute happens. _____

    _____

    _____

6. If a dispute has incomplete information, what can the provider do?

    _____

    _____

7. When do payers pay interest on claims and why? _____

    _____

    _____

8. When appeals are included in annual audits of the health plan, what
    should the provider do? _____

    _____

    _____

9. What should the provider do if its dispute is based on rebundling? ___

    _____

    _____

10. In balance billing, explain "write-offs" and what should be done. _____

    _____

    _____

Critical Thinking Exercise

Many insurers post their provider dispute policies on the Web. The
policy could be posted from an insurance company, specified contract,
government payer, or state insurance commissioner. In this exercise, you
will be asked to review three dispute policies and the proper procedures
to resolve the claims in question.

Materials Needed

2 different-colored highlighters
1 blue pen
3 printed provider dispute information policies and procedures from
various payers

Directions

1. Use your Web browser and search engine and type in phrases such as
    • provider disputes – _____ (your state)
    • resolving provider disputes
    • policy and procedure regarding provider dispute

2. Print the policy information from three sources.

3. Use one color highlighter to mark information/instructions that are the same in each policy. Use the other to highlight policy that is different, such as extra steps in submitting information or requesting more for the same type of dispute.

4. Discuss the differences and similarities with your professor.

Professional Corner

Who is responsible for handling provider disputes in your office? The following are some questions to consider if this is a part of your job description:

- *Who in your office oversees disputes?*
- *What category does your office consider first when accessing disputed information (for example, date of service, payer/company, dollar amount)?*
- *Do the employees have access to training? Do outside providers offer training in-house or online?*
- *Do you have access to office policy regarding timeliness and procedure issues?*
- *What percentage of potential disputes generates activity?*
- *How successful is your office in arguing disputes?*
- *Is your office aware of state laws protecting providers in timely payment issues?*
- *Does your office cross-train the staff to handle functions essential to reimbursement?*
- *What are three common disputes, and can they be avoided by implementing procedures for the daily routines of employees?*

References

California Departmental of Managed Healthcare. (2004). "Assembly Bill 1455." San Diego, CA Rady's Children's Hospital.

Cigna Healthcare. (2008). "California Disputes Policy." Glendale, CA CIGNA.

Aetna California. (January 1, 2004). "Practitioner/Provider Dispute Policy." Fresno, CA, AETNA.

Industry Collaboration Effort, Health Plans, Providers Associations, Appeals and Grievance Form, Newport Beach, CA, Industry Collaboration Effort.

Industry Collaboration Effort, Health Plans, Providers Associations, Appeals, Newport Beach, CA, Industry Collaboration Effort.

Parra, Joe. (2/27/08). *Balance Billing — What is really going on?* Sacramento, CA: Republican State Senate.

CHAPTER 11

Compliance and Audits

Chapter Objectives

Upon completion of this chapter, you should be able to

- Understand general policy guidelines most compliance plans address and their corresponding policy and procedures
- Take steps if your practice wants to do its own audit
- Recognize postaudit findings
- Compare participation in Medicare and Medicaid
- Understand what to do if a government investigator wants to search the office but does not have a valid search warrant
- Identify superbills that do not support the medical record
- Recognize providers who ignore compliance
- Defend being a whistleblower
- Understand how to deal with noncompliance
- Identify Stark rules

Key Terms

compliance

Stark Rules

Introduction to Compliance and Audits

The chapter introduces the compliance process as it relates to in-house audits, general guidelines, preparing for an audit, and what to do with postaudit findings. The chapter also describes how to recognize a process that is illegal and what action can be taken to begin to become compliant.

Compliance should be a form of training, a mind-set, and a routine to detect and recognize practices that can, honestly and with integrity, monitor the paperwork exchanged, filed, and observed by employees, vendors, government agencies, and payers.

Companies develop compliance policies and procedures to uniform their employees' ability to identify when something is not right. The practice is obligated to train and/or *make its best documented effort* to train its employees and those it does business with. The goal is to have every employee able to identify noncompliance on a level appropriate to his job description.

Where do we look to find what is appropriate? A practice cannot be so overburdened with rules that work suffers or slows because of them. But, the practice cannot overlook critical steps all specialties are expected to perform on a routine basis to preserve the integrity of the documentation the provider is responsible for. Some good places to begin are

- Centers for Medicare and Medicaid Services (CMS)
- Health Care Compliance Association (HCCA)
- Health Information Portability and Accountability Act (HIPAA)
- The Office of the Inspector General (OIG)
- American Health Information Management Association (AHIMA)
- American Academy of Professional Coders (AAPC)

compliance A mentoring system of rules and regulations; laws that must be adhered to. This ensures consistency and fulfillment of expectations of the entity, business, or practice.

Compliance should be achieved in the daily routine of employees. Compliance is a mentoring system of rules and regulations, laws that must be adhered to. This ensures consistency and fulfillment of expectations of the entity, business, and the medical practice, Medicare, etc., and when audited, only minor to no infractions should be discovered. There should not be critical steps omitted routinely. For example, if one step is not complied with or performed that should be performed on a regular basis, let's say 5 times a day, within a week the provider will be out of compliance 25 times during the course of doing business. And if the noncompliance is not recognized quickly, the corrective measure could be very costly and time-consuming.

In compliance, there are steps that do not change but stay the same year after year. These steps should be recognized in policy and procedure and may be documented in the job descriptions of those who will routinely be responsible for their outcomes. An employee may not be expected to know how critical the steps to compliance are, but should be very aware of the importance of completing compliance tasks on a daily, weekly, monthly, and/or yearly basis.

Employees should also be aware of how a daily routine will keep them up-to-date and audit ready in compliance issues set forth by various agencies contracted with the provider. Awareness of changes in how a provider will comply with necessary oversight will be a factor in keeping compliant.

Some Considerations in an In-House Audit for Compliance

- Who is the compliance officer for the office, responsible for organizational duties being fulfilled and timely? What are her individual duties as the compliance officer, and what authority does she have to maintain policy guidelines, make changes, and give review reports? Is there a committee the compliance officer reports to, and when does it meet?

- What is the criterion for the evaluation? For example, if it is charts, then how many charts? And in a sampling, is it every 3rd chart or every 10th chart? What standard criteria should be used, and where should the practice focus its efforts?

- When will in-house compliance reviews take place? Are these quarterly, monthly, twice a year, etc.? How will this review be compiled?

  - An audit of advised changes: Are the changes implemented and being performed?

  - An audit to find problems: What should be done that is not being done?

  - An audit to assess current practices: Are they sufficient to the needs of the practice to stay compliant?

- When an in-house audit is performed, there will need to be a report prepared. The in-house report usually addresses the following findings:

  - Intentional misconduct

  - Unintentional misconduct

  - Training of new employees

  - Noncompliant conduct of employees

  - Disciplinary actions taken

  - A time frame to become compliant in the various areas

General Policy Guidelines Most Compliance Plans Address and Their Corresponding Policy and Procedures

Many practice compliance plans are about 10 pages in length and plainly state what is expected to stay in compliance. These documents might not, however, specify how the practice will go about these expectations in great detail, hence the need for a policy and procedure manual.

Most practices have policy and procedure manuals. The manuals explain procedures of doing business and the policy behind the decision to implement the procedure. These can be written to comply with an industry standard, an internal management decision, and/or an issue of compliance the practice must maintain to participate as a provider of service. For an employee, the practice might not distinguish which of these is the reason the task is necessary, nor is it the job of the employee to question a decided procedure. But, an employee should have some idea of the importance of his task and the weight of importance it represents.

Most compliance plans will have some mention of the following listed items, in great detail or in generalized statements of good faith representing their wish for correct documentation, programs, department structure, liaisons, chart organization, and so forth.

- Documentation rules
- Retention of records
- Chart organization
- Medical necessity
- Abbreviations the department will recognize
- Coding responsibilities
- Billing responsibilities
- Bad debt
- Credit balances and collection
- Difficulty areas of the practice
- Patterns of noncompliance

How Might Our Practice Be Considered for an Audit?

Take Medicare as an example. Medicare looks at claims for compliance through automated edits called prepayment screens. These decide if payment should be made on the claims. These edits look at the type of services and number of services given in a predefined period of time or date range. Also, they ask: Do the claims meet the criteria for the procedure to be covered? Is the coding appropriate for the guidelines used in the year the visit/service took place? Medicare may see patterns of inconsistency or dollar amount thresholds that surpass an amount appropriate for the disease.

The claims are profiled and comparisons made with peer groups of physicians in the same geographic areas, same specialty, and so on. Each physician is tracked and compared with peers through the claims history submitted by the billing/coding departments. CMS has an expectation of what should be appropriate and if the claims fall within the range of expectation. Is there a pattern of inconsistency? If there is, the claims could be reviewed. Approximately 10 percent of a physician's claims are being reviewed at any given time without her knowledge.

Carriers look at claims they pay out either from themselves or from acting as third-party administrators. In a third-party capacity, the carrier will follow appropriate billing and coding guidelines set forth by the payer. A carrier paying its own subscriber claims may have different criteria on which to base an internal review or audit. As a participating provider, the office should be advised of compliance requirements and notified of changes as they occur.

Do not be afraid to ask for an in-service or training from Medicare or other carriers. Request to hear about new requirements for the year; this will give the trainee a chance to ask questions that will be answered by the appropriate payer, eliminating speculation and doubt.

A patient may complain to the carrier about the provider. Some payers encourage complaints by offering money to the patient if the concern is legitimate. Any complaint by a patient should be dealt with immediately. Most patients will continue to complain to different sources if they feel their concerns are not being taken seriously and dealt with in a timely manner. But what kinds of complaints from patients raise concerns to the payer? Here are just a few:

- Inconsistencies in what the patient said he received and what was billed

- The provider waives co-payments and deductibles, not having permission to write them off

- The patient and payer are billed for the same service, with the patient's monthly statement stating "pay from this statement" and not "your insurance has been billed"

- The patient is billed for a covered service and/or the cost is more to the patient (that is, regular noninsurance fee, $100; negotiated carrier fee, $70)

My Practice Wants To Do Its Own Audit. What Should I Do?

The practice may have an idea of what it considers inconsistencies in documentation and paperwork. This may stem from old audit reports, employee findings, or regulations needing attention. If this is your responsibility, ask what the scope of the audit is about. Some facilities are mandated to have audits done once a year for funding purposes. Some practices may have this necessity written into their bylaws of incorporation, as a sound business practice or to prove sound business practices to stockholders. The following are some issues to consider:

- What questions are we looking to answer in the audit? Write them down to refer to them later on. What are the specific issues? Are they referrals dealing with Stark? Is it up-coding of certain procedures? Is the audit looking for consistency or specificity in its scope?

- What government carriers or insurance company patients will the audit be looking at? Medicare, Tricare, a commercial carrier? Pull their unique requirements, if any, and have them available. Certain practices and documentation may be required by one carrier and not by the other. Know the carrier's requirements.

- Take a sampling. A sampling is not all charts from a specific carrier but may be every 5th or 10th chart to be pulled. In this way, the office will get an idea of whether certain documentation requirements are being met. But if every chart from a carrier needs to be pulled, have a list of patients. Usually, lists like these can be provided easily from a billing software system or database.

- What are the dates or period of time our audit will consist of? Will it be June through December of this year? Will the time frame be three months or a year? Always have a date range to work with. If not, the audit may be peppered with requirement changes that make the audit inconsistent and unusable.

- When will the audit take place? Give your office a period of time, a beginning and an ending date. The audit should not drag on and on. You may wish to have a certain time of day when employees work on the audit. Daily scheduled tasks should not suffer too greatly or become unmanageable as a result.

- How will you tally the findings? Will they be in a one-page checklist with questions to answer? Will there be one page per chart audited?

Figure 11-1 is an example of a coding audit review in spreadsheet form.

The audit should answer the original questions necessitating its purpose. Never try to influence or guide an audit to achieve the outcomes of opinion. The findings should always be the truth, so that problems

				CODING AUDIT REVIEW RESULTS							
	Date of Service	Diagnosis Billed	Diagnosis Documented	Procedures Billed	Procedures Documented	Modifiers Billed	Modifiers Documented	Amount Billed	Amount Paid	Review Code	Financial Impact
1											
2											
3											
4											
5											
6											
7											
8											
9											
10											
11											
12											
13											
14											
15											
16											
17											
18											
19											

Figure 11-1 An example of a coding audit review results form (Delmar/Cengage Learning)

can be dealt with correctly and in a realistic manner appropriate to the information gathered and studied.

Postaudit Findings

Upon completion of an audit, the findings need to be documented and reported to the committee responsible for compliance. The committee will read the findings, which may be addressed in a formal meeting. The findings may also be complete with recommendations from the compliance officer or the auditing entity reporting the outcomes.

The following are questions many practices face after an audit has been completed. The committee should recognize the problems discovered, agree upon solutions, and give a time frame of when the needed changes should be concluded and when follow-up meetings will be held to discuss progress and implementation schedules.

What will the practice do if

- The practice has not implemented policy changes suggested in the previous audit?

- Documentation does not support coded and/or billed services?

- Multiple coding reaching into unbundling is discovered?

- Financial gain is found through inappropriate coding? Will the practice refund monies in these situations?

- A physician very simply does not comply? Is this a refusal or training problem?

- Nurse practitioners or physician's assistants are being presented on the billings as physicians?

- The audit shows noncompliance in areas not considered a part of the focus audit?

- Patients who cancel their appointments are still being billed as if the office visit happened?

Participation in Medicare and Medicaid

If a practice/provider participates and sees patients who participate in these plans, the office will be expected to comply with mandated rules and regulations set forth by Health and Human Services – Office of the Inspector General (OIG).

The government may begin with a limited audit, but remember, when an auditor has access to whole charts, it may not be so hard to find other problems of compliance existing there. These may trigger a more extensive audit because the auditors are duty bound to examine inconsistencies under the circumstances.

Office of the Inspector General Work Plan for the Year

Each year, the Office of the Inspector General publishes a work plan online (see Web sites at end of chapter) that targets its activities for the year. Here a biller will find specific coding and billing issues that will be studied for the year. The OIG accomplishes this task by performing program audits, program

Coding	• Review, evaluation, and management services during the global surgery period
Procedures	• Lasik and cataract surgeries
Claims	• Duplicate claims for physical therapy submitted by providers
Inappropriate payment	• Wound care
Medical necessity	• "Incident to" services

Figure 11-2 An example of an HHS/OIG work plan (Delmar/Cengage Learning)

inspections, investigative focus areas, and legal counsel focus areas. The plan divides facilities, equipment, drug, and physician/health professional areas. An audit of medical records are a verification of documents/records for correct information, whole information, requested information, and complete documentation. Audits sometimes look at exposure or risk.

The plan may target certain areas of coding, procedures, claims, inappropriate payments, medical necessity, and so on. Example 11-2 is an example for physician services in 2007.

Any office contemplating an in-house audit should include any OIG focus pertaining to its specialty along with identified compliance issues being corrected or needing change.

Billing Medicare or Medicaid Incorrectly . . . Occasionally

The Office of the Inspector General has stated that innocent errors are not subject to penalties. But, if there was actual knowledge of the falsity or recklessness, or the preparer went about deliberately not knowing of the falsification of claim(s), as stated in the False Claims Act, then they are subject to problems like criminal, civil, and administrative penalties. Both the Civil Monetary Penalties Law and the False Claims Act state the difference between "erroneous claims" and "fraudulent claims." Did the provider intend to defraud the government? If so, the evidence should prove this "beyond a reasonable doubt."

A Government Investigator Wants To Search My Office

A government investigator can search your office without a search warrant if you give valid consent to him. The office has the right to refuse the investigator if there is not a valid search warrant. What does your office say in this matter? If it does not want a search without a search warrant, *everyone* in the office should understand this.

If the investigator *does* have a valid search warrant, the investigator *does* have the right to search the premises. All employees should know the following:

- Should the employee notify anyone? The provider, lawyers, managers? The answer should be yes, as soon as possible.

- How does the employee handle questions from the investigators, directed to them verbally or in writing. The employee should understand that what he says will be noted by the investigators and may be used against the practice.

- Are the investigators allowed to see all the charts or just charts from patients participating in the program they represent? The answer should be: Only the charts of the patients from the programs they represent.

The Government Investigator Wants To Ask Me Questions

Usually the government agent will make an appointment. But, if the agent feels that this will hurt the investigation, he may ask for an interview on the spot. The employee must not be coerced and should feel free to answer or not answer a direct question. It may be a good idea to have a third person in the room. This is required in various degrees for minors, members of the opposite sex, a hostile interviewee, and if the person is under arrest or indictment.

If you find yourself being interviewed by a government investigator, tell the truth. If you mislead, obstruct, willfully prevent, or delay the communication of information, you could be charged with Obstruction of Criminal Investigations of Health Care Offenses. This holds penalties of fines and imprisonment.

The Carriers and Fiscal Intermediaries Are Requesting Records. Can They Do That?

The answer is yes. Private insurers who contract with CMS to process their claims have their own in-house fraud units who do investigations. They are expected to do a preliminary investigation if they suspect fraud involving Medicare or Medicaid patients. These intermediaries and carriers have the right to demand and recoup monies deemed as overpayments from payments due the provider from Medicare or Medicaid. They can also suspend payments for suspected fraud.

What Carriers and/or Fiscal Intermediaries Do When They Suspect Fraud

The carriers and fiscal intermediaries are supposed to refer fraud and abuse allegations to the OIG's Office of Investigations immediately. Those involved in fraud may be contractor employees, an informant who is an employee, a former employee, providers with prior convictions, providers who are part of a current investigation, a crime by a federal employee, organized crime, or a third party that is primary to Medicare.

These persons may be involved in indications of fraud, bribes, kickbacks, current program investigations, and/or cases involving an informant. In these kinds of situations, there is a need for OIG involvement because of the seriousness and potential criminal activity implied. These situations would need to be investigated to see if the claim of wrongdoing has merit; then, if the investigation proves the allegations, the OIG takes the case to the next level.

My Doctor Wants Me To Bill for the Services a Nurse, Not the Doctor Himself, Furnished. Is This Fraud?

Medicare has definite rules where these situations are concerned, and they are plainly stated in the Medicare Carrier's Manual section 2050.2. This may take some understanding of the procedure and disease the physician is treating because the treatment has to be provided under the "direct supervision" of the physician and should be something "ordinarily done" in the physician's office. This person needs to be a licensed employee of the physician. Billing for these services would be illegal if the physician was not licensed; the employees performing services were not trained, certified, or licensed to perform; or the physician misrepresented himself, by presenting himself as having a license, when really he did not, or by telling the patient he was certified in the medical specialty and in fact was not.

Producing a Claim from the Superbill but Found No Supporting Documentation in the Record

Bring this to the provider's attention. If there is no justification for the claim in the medical record, one should not be produced. The physician must document the file, sign, and date the encounter. This is also true from a coding standpoint. A code should be given at the level of service documented. Remember, you were not in the room at the time of the visit and only have the medical chart as an explanation of what took place. It is best to be exact.

My Provider Ignores Compliance Problems

In these cases, the provider is knowingly defrauding the government because he is not doing anything about the problem yet has knowledge of it. This can be seen as a conspiratorial act to defraud the U.S. government or armed forces. The provider needs to have procedures in place that address such problems as they appear and then needs to be sure the correctional measures are actually performed by management or staff. Not taking care of the situation(s) is a violation of the False Claims Act; if discovered by the payer, the provider could be charged fines of up to $5,500 to $11,000 per false claim (the dollar amounts may change) plus three times the amount of damages plus a prison sentence of up to five years in federal prison.

In Order To Make a Billing Quota, I Billed Services I Knew Would Not Be Paid

Medicare takes every claim seriously and may ask for more information to see if the claim(s) has merit.

It may ask for more information, and the provider is obligated to give it. The OIG will begin to notice lack of response to the requests for more information. The government will look for a pattern of how many times the information was not provided and payment amounts. These could be seen as a refusal to submit information needed to make payment decisions, and the provider could be taken out of the program or excluded from the program for a period of time. If you submit claims, you should also be willing to submit paperwork for justification of the claim. Also note the time frame in which to submit requested information; letting the time lapse is not a good idea either.

What if My Employer Retaliates for My Being a Whistleblower (Qui Tam)?

Deciding to come forward in such cases can be heartrending. Many employees do not come forward out of fear of retaliation and mistreatment by the employer. Employers are not allowed to engage in such behaviors. Some examples of what employers are not allowed to do are harass, threaten, demote, suspend, or discriminate against their employees because of the situation. If this happens, the employee is entitled compensation for damages incurred. If the employee suffers such loss, it is common for him to receive back pay and interest on the back pay, to be reinstated in his job at the seniority level he previously held, and/or to receive attorney's fees and compensation for the damage.

If My Provider Is Convicted of a Misdemeanor, Can the Provider Be Forced Not To Participate or Excluded from Medicare?

The answer is yes. Health and Human Services, or HHS, can decide if it will let a provider continue seeing patients even if the provider's offense is a misdemeanor. This is at its discretion, and the average length of exclusion is about three years. The kinds of offenses can be acts of omissions by a program that has been financed by federal, state, or local government and/or a non-health care program financed by federal, state, or local governments. The kinds of misconduct may be a misdemeanor fraud, theft, embezzlement, or breach of fiduciary responsibility.

My Provider Has Decided To Come Forward with the Compliance Problem

Document everything from the day of the discovery. This will need to include a time line of dates of when the corrective measures took place, because the provider should come forward within 30 days, be willing to cooperate with investigators, and do so before criminal or civil prosecution begins.

Steps To Clean Up Noncompliance

Have procedures in place that address noncompliance and corrective measures stated plainly to be followed and easily understood. Have a sign-off sheet and time frame of expectations of when the problem should be corrected. Who will do the follow-up to make sure the corrective measures are actually taking place? The provider may need to disclose the problem to the OIG, refund monies, and take disciplinary actions against employees.

Under what regulation is the provider in noncompliance, and how long has this regulation been in effect? This is usually stated in newsletters and Web sites maintained by the payer. Although ignorance is no excuse for noncompliance, the provider will get an idea of how long it has been out of compliance and maybe how far back the incident needs to be looked at to be cleaned up.

The Stark Rules

Stark Rules When a provider refers a patient to a facility that they or their families have a financial interest, this would be a violation. The Stark Act does not permit a provider to refer patients to a business they own or are financially involved. This only applies to Medicare and Medicaid patients.

Stark Rules discuss referrals and physicians making a profit through referrals from groups or labs they have a financial interest in. If a physician refers a patient to another medical group or lab that he has a financial interest in, this is an unfair advantage and is against the law. This includes things like an indirect financial interest, such as the loaning of monies with secured assets, or ownership or investment interests between family members. But there are exceptions. If a provider feels there is an exception, he can ask for an official ruling from the OIG.

Self-referral rules are far reaching and address things like overall profit sharing, productivity bonuses, subleasing office space, percentage-based compensation, hourly payments to a physician that is considered fair market value, and submitting information about a financial relationship. These are good places to start if you feel your practice falls under these circumstances.

What Is the Antikickback Statute About?

This statute looks at discounts that would encourage the purchase of a service or an item. These items or services are something that Medicare and Medicaid would pay for under their programs. As is the case with so many other compliance rules, there are exceptions. One exception to check into is the "safe harbors." Some of the 24 safe harbors worth checking out are referral services, warranties, discounts, investments in underserved areas, investments in group practices, referral agreements for specialty services, and so on.

Case Study 11-1 – Claims Coded Incorrectly and Correctly

When claims are coded incorrectly in bulk, a payer's computer system usually sets aside those claims for review. And, when the coding is also questionable, this may trigger a visit from the payer's office.

In this case, we see both claims reported in an unusually high number for the provider and incorrect coding due to a misinterpretation of coding guidelines.

The provider had an unusual amount of visits from construction workers with cerumen buildup or impaction. The normal procedure to care for cerumen impaction is lavage, unless there are symptoms such are hearing loss or unless the wax completely covers the eardrum. There would be obvious need for the provider to use curettes or forceps to remove the wax. Some symptoms that justify this that may be found in medical record are

- The wax is blocking the view of the provider
- The patient may be in pain or have hearing loss

(Continued)

- There may be an infection present
- The provider may need to use a microscope

The following are two very different cases, yet they are coded the same. One is correct, and the other may be red flagged by compliance. Case study 11-1 is an example of correct coding based on impaction.

21. DIAGNOSIS OR NATURE OF ILLNESS OR INJURY (Relate Items 1, 2, 3 or 4 to Item 24E by Line)							22. MEDICAID RESUBMISSION CODE	ORIGINAL REF. NO.
1. 3804			3.				23. PRIOR AUTHORIZATION NUMBER	
2.			4.					

	24. A. DATE(S) OF SERVICE From MM DD YY To MM DD YY	B. PLACE OF SERVICE	C. EMG	D. PROCEDURES, SERVICES, OR SUPPLIES (Explain Unusual Circumstances) CPT/HCPCS	MODIFIER	E. DIAGNOSIS POINTER	F. $ CHARGES	G. DAYS OR UNITS	H. EPSDT Family Plan	I. ID. QUAL.	J. RENDERING PROVIDER ID. #
1	10 21 08 10 21 08			99202	25	1	100 00	1		NPI	
2	10 21 08 10 21 08			69210		1	150 00	1		NPI	
3										NPI	
4										NPI	
5										NPI	
6										NPI	

25. FEDERAL TAX I.D. NUMBER SSN EIN ☒ ☐	26. PATIENT'S ACCOUNT NO.	27. ACCEPT ASSIGNMENT? (For govt. claims, see back) ☐ YES ☐ NO	28. TOTAL CHARGE $ 250 00	29. AMOUNT PAID $	30. BALANCE DUE $ 250 00

Figure 11-3 Case study 11-1 – an example of correct coding based on impaction (Delmar/Cengage Learning)

Case Study 11-1A – Incorrect Coding Based on Lavage Method

The patient presents for ear wax removal and has some irritation. The provider performs a Level 2 E/M and instructs the medical assistant to perform the lavage. Since the provider did not perform a curette, forceps, or suction for removal of the wax, the 69210 is not justified and the lavage is absorbed in the E/M.

Case Study 11-1B – Correct Coding Based on Impaction

The patient presents with ear pain, cerumen impaction, and a foul odor in the ears. The medical assistant sets up a surgical tray with various instruments for removal of the impaction. The provider uses wax curettes and forceps. This justifies coding the 69210 along with the 99202-25.

Summary

Being aware of practice policy and procedure as it relates to compliance becomes very important when an audit begins. Performing expected duties timely and completely will help build upon periodic changes expected from governmental and nongovernmental agencies.

Coders are keenly aware of how well a chart is documented because the assignment of codes is based on the written word. Codes are a snapshot of how proficient and detailed the medical chart is kept. Accurate and complete records are the foundation to build compliance regulation and periodic change needed in timely reporting to be used in payment consideration, statistical purposes, grants, and, finally, audit practices.

Many employees have an "idea" of what is wrong with practice documentation but are unaware of the time lines involved in change, how to change procedure for correct documentation, whose responsibility it is to bring about change, and what procedures can be changed to meet reporting needs. A compliance plan will help the practice live through an audit and catch problems before patterns become unmanageable and/or mistakenly adopted as acceptable because that is "how we have always done it."

Compliance can be defined in corporate bylaws, government regulations, participating provider agreements, fiscal intermediaries, third party administrators' rules of participation, and agency/association affiliation. When deciding and implementing a compliance plan, the practice should take into consideration specialty/facility type, the top-20 diagnoses and procedures performed for year-to-date changes. Education and training opportunities can help the entire staff on every level to stay compliant and not overlook the fundamental need for correct and timely documentation as it relates regulation requirements.

Web Sites

Centers for Medicare and Medicaid Services *http://www.cms.hhs.gov*

Department of Health and Human Services, Office of the Inspector General *www.oig.hhs.gov.*

Federal Bureau of Investigation *http://www.oig.hhs.gov, http://www.oig.hhs. gov/progorg/org*

U.S. Government Printing Office/Online Federal Register *http://www. gpoaccess.gov,* search: Federal Registrar; *http://www.archives.gov,* search: **Federal Registrar**

Medicare and Medicaid fraud *http://cms.hhs.gov,* search: **providers fraud**

Review

Fill in the Blank

1. Companies develop compliance _____ and _____ to uniform their employees' ability to identify when something is not right.

2. Compliance should be achieved in the _____ routine of employees.

3. An employee should be aware of the importance of completing _____ _____ on a daily, weekly, monthly, and yearly basis.

4. Policy and procedure manuals explain procedures of doing business and the policy behind the _____ to implement the _____.

5. A prepayment screen decides if payment should be made on a _____.

6. Claims are _____ and comparisons made with _____ _____ of physicians in the same geographic area, specialty, and so on.

7. A _____ is not all charts from a specific carrier, but may be every _____ or _____ chart to be pulled.

8. Upon completion of an audit, the _____ need to be _____ and reported to the committee responsible for _____.

9. Practices that participate in Medicare and Medicaid will be expected to _____ with mandated rules and regulations set forth by _____ and _____ _____.

10. A _____ _____ can search your office without a search warrant if you give valid _____ to him.

Review Questions

1. Describe the practice's obligation toward its employees in compliance issues. _____
   _____
   _____
   _____

2. Name agencies and associations that address compliance rules and regulations. _____
   _____
   _____
   _____

3. What is an in-house audit? _____
   _____
   _____
   _____

4. What will an in-house audit report usually address? _____
   _____
   _____

5. What do policy and procedure manuals usually comply with? _____
    _____
    _____

6. What are some items that compliance plans address? _____
    _____
    _____
    _____

7. How are claims profiled with peer groups of physicians? _____
    _____
    _____
    _____

8. What kinds of patient complaints to a payer will raise concern? _____
    _____
    _____
    _____

9. Write five possible questions to answer in an audit situation. _____
    _____
    _____
    _____

10. What are some challenges a practice may face after postaudit findings?
    _____
    _____
    _____
    _____

Critical Thinking Exercise

Identifying Audit and Compliance Issues from the OIG Work Plan

Materials Needed

A computer with Internet access
Ability to print information from the computer

Internet Sites

Go to your favorite search engine, for example, Google, Yahoo, or MSN. In the search window type in *Health and Human Services, Office of the Inspector General Work Plan* and the year of interest (for example: HHS OIG Work Plan 2007).

Directions

1. Look through the Work Plan and find the section for physicians and health care providers.

2. Choose a topic and read the OIG focus for that topic. Print just the pages you need on that topic, and answer the following questions.

   - Write what the OIG plans to do with your topic (for example, review, evaluate, assess, identify, and so on).

   - Write how the OIG plans to go about finding the answers it needs (for example, ordering dates, performing services, excluded codes, physician receiving reimbursement, types of arrangements, services furnished, and so on).

   - Write a one-page audit plan of how you would go about checking the data and bring your office into compliance.

3. Turn in to your professor the following:

   - The answers to questions 1 and 2

   - The one-page audit plan

   - The original information you printed from the work plan

Professional Corner

If you are a professional coder, here are some basic questions you should know the answers to. If you do not know the answers, you may wish to ask your employer about them or to consult the office policy and procedure manual.

1. *Do you know your office policy regarding search of the premises or your individual work space?*
2. *Do you know what to do when an investigator wants to question you?*
3. *When fraud is suspected, do you know at what point the OIG will get involved?*
4. *Is there a time line to be followed when discovering noncompliance?*
5. *Do you know your rights as a whistleblower?*
6. *What are some steps in cleaning up noncompliance that you have seen in your office?*
7. *Does your employer have training available for compliance? Is this mandatory for all employees? Or for just a few?*
8. *Is everyone in your office familiar with the Stark Rules? Have these ever been explained to the staff in a meeting?*

References

Madison, Gail. (4/27/04). Clinical Documentation & Compliance Manual. Denton, TX: University of North Texas.

Wolters Kluwer. (2008). The Healthcare Compliance Professional's Manual. Waltham, MA: Healthcare Compliance Association.

University of Alabama. (January, 2001). Laws that Limit Providers and Limit Patient Choice May have Limited Effects. Princeton, NJ: Robert Wood Johnson Foundations.

University of Alabama. (January 2001). AWP and FOC Law Findings, Princeton, NJ: Robert Wood Johnson Foundations.

Weber, Gil, MBA. (Fall, 2003). "Any Willing Provider Laws, Private Practice Optometry, Retail Chains, and VSP." Practice Management and Managed Care Consulting. Volume 4, Number 3.

HHS-OIG. Fraud and Prevention and Detection. Retrieved January 4, 2008 from http://oig.hhs.gov/fraud/cia/cia_list.asp

(Summer 2006). Health Industry Collaboration Effort. Blue Cross of California Foundation.

HHS-OIG. Fraud and Prevention and Detection. Retrieved from http://oig.hhs.gov/fraud/enforcement.

Testimony of Daniel R. Levinson, Inspector General. U.S. Department of Health and Human Services. "Integrity Provisions, OIG Investigative Fraud Priorities. Hearing March 28, 2006, Whistleblower Protection Act."

Statement for the Record, House Budget Committee Healthcare Task Force. (July 12, 2000). "OIG, Medicare Program, Reducing Improper Payment and Fraud."

Cassil, Alwyn. (November, 1999). OIG, Fact Sheet, Anti Kickback Law and Regulatory Safe Harbors. Washington DC: OIG, Office of Public Affairs.

Kenny, Thomas J. (April 1998). Healthcare Compliance, A Physician's Guide to Recent Enforcement Trends. Omaha, NE: Kutak Rock Law Firm.

CHAPTER

12

Noncontracted Providers

Chapter Objectives

Upon completion of this chapter, you should be able to

- Recognize the choices of a noncontracted provider
- Understand why some providers are unable to participate in the plan
- Describe why the plan can terminate the provider contract at any time
- Recognize why some plans limit patient options
- Understand why an employer may limit patient options
- Explain incentives for providers to participate in the plan
- Explain reciprocity and deciding not to participate
- Understand why providers choose not to participate
- Ascertain when a medical group is involved
- Understand denied claims sent to the patient
- Identify claims not meeting medical necessity

Key Terms

closed networks

full-risk claims

incentives

noncontracted
providers

reciprocity

Introduction to Noncontracted Providers

This chapter looks at some of the issues a provider must face when billing a payer whom it is not contracted with; issues discussed in the chapter are incentives to participate in the plans, claims not meeting medical necessity, any willing provider laws, reciprocity rates, and closed networks, **full-risk claims**, and denied claims sent to the patient.

A provider may choose to not contract with insurance companies in its area or may be unable to contract due to factors it has very little control over. Medical associations and state legislators become involved with studies that explain the marketplace in a specific geographic area and the reasoning for participation or nonparticipation of providers.

Various state rules and regulations come into play for **noncontracted providers** to legally be paid from the insurance claims submitted by the provider, and are considered by the payer when reconciling/recognizing its responsibility for payment. The nuances of participation may hinder a provider from signing with a specific carrier. The provider must understand what it gains or loses in an agreement and the options available if an agreement cannot be reached.

> **full-risk claims** The plan pays all the claims for all the patients; sometimes these claims must be in area.

> **noncontracted providers** Physicians or facilities with which the insurer does not have contractual agreements.

Providers Who Are Unable To Participate

Insurance companies have various rules of how a provider would qualify to participate in their plans. These may happen to a new physician just starting in the industry who has no history of these requirements or a physician who does not meet all requirements.

The physicians themselves may need to

- Be board certified
- Hold certain licenses
- Give practice histories
- Have or obtain hospital privileges
- Carry a certain amount of malpractice insurance

Some problems in becoming a participating provider may be

- A history of paid malpractice judgments
- Noneconomic performance history
- Disciplined by state boards
- Staff privileges taken away at hospitals
- Complaints against the provider

Disciplinary actions usually last for a specific period of time. Most providers will have a chance to apply for reinstatement. New providers may need to wait for an available opening to participate as many carriers have a limit on how many providers they will contract with for a specific specialty. Rural or inadequately serviced areas are usually always open or available.

The Plan Can Terminate the Provider Contract at Any Time

Some plans have written into their provider contracts their ability to terminate the relationship for specific/no reason, and the provider's length of time with the plan may not matter. Providers are usually wary of a plan that may give a large percentage of their patients to the provider only to terminate the contract and cripple the practice to the point of shutting it down. Notification periods for termination will be written into the contracts, and either side giving the notice would have to adhere to them. Most notification periods are 30, 60, 90 days, providing continuity of care for the patients. In most contracts, the provider should negotiate to have the right to terminate the contract for the same notification periods given to the plan.

Some Plans Limit Patient Options

Some insurance companies may limit the patient's choices of providers who participate in his plan or may limit the geographic area in which the patient can receive services. Patients may need to travel farther to see a provider who participates in the plan. Alternatively, a plan may write out coverage of certain disease(s) or treatment, for example, acupuncture or chiropractic. Some patients feel that if their plans do not cover a certain service or provider type, they cannot consider going out of network and/or this type of coverage would not be affordable.

Also, some patients feel that if they choose to go outside the plan, they may fall out of favor with the plan and not get the same kind of service. Although the latter simply would be a thought of the patient and not a reality, many patients feel the provider knows best about their health needs and the payer knows best about paying for the services. Many times a patient will not see how limited a plan is because he will simply take the treatment that the provider offers and the plan pays, no questions asked.

Some PPOs and indemnity plans may have written into the contract clauses for preexisting conditions, which the patient had knowledge of for a certain period of time before she signed up with the plan. If the plan knows of a preexisting condition before the patient purchases the plan, it will usually give a time frame of when it will cover the condition (bunions, tonsillectomy, hysterectomy, hernia repair, and so on.), for example, 6 months or a year. If the plan will never cover the preexisting condition (for example, cancer, neuromuscular disease, terminal illness), it is obligated to tell the patient before the patient purchases the coverage.

Employers May Limit Patient Options

An employer may only offer one plan to its employees, and if the provider of choice is not a member of the plan, the patients feel they cannot see that provider. Some providers want to compete for these kinds of patients with their quality of care, so maybe the patient will be willing to spend his money for services not covered or demand from his employer that services be covered. However, the addition of services for an employer could be added when the plan is scheduled for contract renewal. The employer may wish to offer a limited benefit package because of the cost of premiums. An employer may wish to only spend up to a certain amount on a monthly premium for its employees and tailor a plan that is within that range regardless of what may be written out of the plan itself (for example, maternity benefits). Companies that self-insure sometimes offer limited benefit packages. Of course, in an HMO setting if the patient wants to go out of network, she will pay out of pocket for those services unless her plan has a point of service option that will allow certain out-of-network coverage.

Any Willing Provider Laws and Closed Networks

closed networks These networks usually have a closed group of physicians the patients must choose from. The network does not accept new physicians so the patients are limited to those who participate. Some networks have limited providers, while others have a larger variety for the patient to choose from.

Closed networks restrict how many physicians can participate in the plan at any given time. These are used to control costs, to keep premiums low, and to have physicians follow strict policy and practice guidelines of the network. The problem is, the network does not let any other physicians participate in the network if it has reached the maximum number of physicians the network is willing to contract with.

Any willing provider, or AWP, laws do not let the health plan discriminate against providers that are willing to accept and meet the rules of participation in the plan. The AWP laws tell the networks they must let the providers participate. Since AWP laws have been around since the mid-1990s, it will be in your best interest to investigate current legislation in your state and see how it handles AWP. Some states participate, some do not.

Freedom of Choice and the Price to the Patient

Freedom of choice, or FOC, laws allow patients to be reimbursed for services by a qualified provider who does not participate in their plan. The managed care organization usually pays the same for out-of-network services as they would for in-network services. Out-of-network, noncontracted rates are usually higher than contracted ones, and the patient would be expected to pay the difference between the two.

Most patients do not know such laws exist, and not all states have them. Any provider who accepts out-of-network patients will need to understand its right to reimbursement in its state. Remember, not all states have adopted such laws.

Incentives for Providers To Participate in the Plan

Patients soon find they are penalized if they do not choose participating providers. FOC laws may protect them for a percentage of reimbursement, but who receives the reimbursement from the payer? Payers usually determine this. The provider usually bills the charge to the insurance as a courtesy – this may be mandatory depending on the state and type of insurance. The patient usually pays the whole fee out of pocket directly to the provider, and takes whatever the insurance pays as the acceptable reimbursement and determination.

In addition, if the patient pays out of pocket to a noncontracted provider, does this affect her deductible? Will the payment to the noncontracted provider be considered as part of her annual deductible payment requirements? In general, payers won't have noncontracted payments counted toward the deductible. The payments the patient makes to noncontracted providers are usually considered to be out of pocket. The idea is to have the patient not feel very good about it and to instead stay in the plan's participating provider network. This is an incentive for the patient to stay in network. An **incentive** is a motivator and could take the form of a reimbursement, something contributing to the success, or an "extra."

incentive A motivator, could take the form of a reimbursement or something contributing to the success or an "extra." The incentive may provide extra value.

Frequently, the carrier for hospital claims will have an in-network deductible that differs from the out-of-network deductible. A claim must be submitted to the payer for the deductible to be considered. An example would be

| In network | $250 |
| Out of network | $500, or $500 per occurrence in an ASC or hospital setting |

Reciprocity and Deciding Not To Participate

reciprocity Contractual agreement between insurance and providers regarding rates if a medical group or facility is paying a claim on behalf of its members.

In **reciprocity**, the plan can look for affiliates with whom the provider is contracted and ask for the affiliate-contracted rate to forego noncontracted rates. The plans have contractual reciprocity agreements between themselves and may look for these when a provider that is not contracted with their plan sees one of their patients. This may happen with managed care plans that are trying to control costs. The provider may wish to check its participating agreements for a reciprocity clause. In these cases, the biller trying to collect the full fee may have no choice but to accept the contracted fee-for-service rates from another plan.

Providers Who Choose Not To Participate

Certain specialties have the ability to not contract with any government or insurance entity and still be paid for their services. One example is the emergency room physician. Since an emergency is unforeseen, the ED physicians many times do not need to contract with insurance companies for clientele. In addition, since most illness is not planned, emergencies are the reason health insurance exists. All health insurance plans offer some sort of coverage for unforeseen emergencies. Insurance companies find themselves "on the hook" for these unforeseen emergencies because of their agreement with the patient. Moreover, payers are much less apt to question medically necessary procedures in an emergency.

Along this line, many coders itemize the bill for the ED visit with an E/M code, procedure and after-hours code, and sometimes holiday codes. Notice the cases that follow.

Case Study 12-1 – Payment of a Senior HMO Claim

Senior HMO claims are processed according to Medicare rules and regulations since the patient's Medicare benefit has been assigned to the HMO.

Case study 12-1 shows an example of a senior HMO member claim and how it was paid.

21. DIAGNOSIS OR NATURE OF ILLNESS OR INJURY		
1. 7802	3. E8889	
2. 8730	4.	

22. MEDICAID RESUBMISSION CODE / ORIGINAL REF. NO.

23. PRIOR AUTHORIZATION NUMBER

	DATE(S) OF SERVICE From / To	B. PLACE OF SERVICE	C. EMG	D. CPT/HCPCS	MODIFIER	E. DIAGNOSIS POINTER	F. $ CHARGES	G. DAYS OR UNITS	H.	I. ID QUAL	J. RENDERING PROVIDER ID. #
1	10 05 08	23		99284	25	1	245 53	1		NPI	
2	10 05 08	23		12034		2	179 00	1		NPI	
3	10 05 08	23		99053		1	103 00	1		NPI	
4										NPI	
5										NPI	
6										NPI	

| 25. FEDERAL TAX I.D. NUMBER | SSN EIN | 26. PATIENT'S ACCOUNT NO. | 27. ACCEPT ASSIGNMENT? YES NO | 28. TOTAL CHARGE $ 527 53 | 29. AMOUNT PAID $ | 30. BALANCE DUE $ 527 53 |

Figure 12-1 Senior HMO member claim (Delmar/Cengage Learning)

DIAGNOSIS

780.2	Syncope
873.0	Open wound, scalp
E888.9	Unspecified fall

PROCEDURES

99284-25 Emergency department visit for evaluation and management of a patient presenting problems of high severity and require urgent evaluation by the physician but do not pose an immediate significant threat to life or physiologic function

Modifier 25 Significant separately identifiable evaluation and management service by the same physician on the same day of the procedure or other service

12034 Intermediate repair: layer closure wounds of scalp 7.6–12.5 cm

99053 Services provided between 10 p.m. and 8 a.m. at 24-hour facility in addition to basic service

The claim is processed as a noncontracted claim, which means payment must be mailed out within 30 days (paper) of the first date stamp on the claim – no matter where the claim was first received.

Medicare now includes payment of the EKG with an ED department facility charge. However, this needs to be noted in the documentation as a separate report within the ED chart note. Medicare does not allow payment for after-hours, weekend, or holiday codes. Emergency departments are open 24 hours a day, seven days a week.

(Continued)

The Medicare fee schedule will not pay for the after-hours charges, and if the patient is a Medicare HMO patient, the provider cannot bill for after-hour charges.

The claim would be paid at the Medicare allowable rate for the area of service. If the provider is not contracted with Medicare, it will pay its noncontracted (nonparticipating) rate, not the area UCR and not the provider's regular rates.

Case Study 12-2 – Commercial HMO Claim

Plans will pay and deduct from capitation, or groups pay the full billed charges. There are a few health plans that do not have reciprocity language in their contracts, but some facilities will share the plan rate and accept reimbursement based on the plan rate. This may vary based on the geographic area and the individual contracts.

Full risk means under the HMO, the insurance company itself does not have risk for those payments. Contracted medical groups assume all the risk (full risk) for most services and are responsible to pay for all medically appropriate charges.

Figure 12-2 is an example of a commercial HMO claim and how it was paid. There are four scenarios in this example: commercial HMO claims, when a medical group is involved, denied claims sent to the patient, and claims not meeting medical necessity.

Figure 12-2 A commercial HMO claim (Delmar/Cengage Learning)

DIAGNOSIS

780.2	Syncope
873.0	Open wound, scalp
E888.9	Unspecified fall

PROCEDURES

99284-25   Emergency department visit for evaluation and management of a patient presenting problems of high severity and require urgent evaluation by the physician but do not pose an immediate significant threat to life or physiologic function

```
Modifier 25        Significant separately identifiable evaluation and
                   management service by the same physician on the same day
                   of the procedure or other service
12034              Intermediate repair: layer closure wounds of
                   scalp 7.6-12.5 cm
99053              Services provided between 10 p.m. and 8 a.m. at 24-hour
                   facility in addition to basic service
```

Commercial HMO Claims for Case Study 12-2

In the case of a commercial HMO, the ED physicians do bill with all codes for after hours, and other procedures provided. They expect to be paid for all charges billed if they are not contracted and will balance bill the patient for services that are not paid. Nevertheless, many HMOs do not let their patients get involved with payment beyond their contracted responsibility, which may mean the HMO pays the full amount of the claim or the responsible medical group if ED charges are its financial risk.

These claims may be paid at 100 percent of billed charges, but what are the criteria for this? Is the patient out of area? Was the nearest hospital a noncontracted hospital? Did the patient have a choice of where to go during the emergency? Most ambulances go to the nearest emergency department without regard to contract issues.

What Does EMTALA Have To Do with Billing Charges?

EMTALA stands for the Emergency Medical Treatment and Active Labor Act. The act basically states that patients needing emergency treatment have a right to it, regardless of their legal status or ability to pay for the services (see www.hhs.gov; type in the search prompt: EMTALA).

Hospitals that take Medicare patients or accept payments from CMS are obligated to take the patients. There are some exceptions but very few. EMTALA also applies to urgent care facilities owned/operated by the hospital if the billing is under the hospital's provider number (see www.aaem.org/emtala/emtalaeffect.php).

When a Medical Group Is Involved for Case Study 12-2

If the medical group does not pay the balance, an HMO health plan may pay the claim and do a capitation deduction for the charge.

If the medical group has an urgent care department, it needs to audit the ED claims for the time of service. Some plans expect the patient to use urgent care for non-life-threatening urgent needs after hours up to 10:00 p.m. or during whatever hours are designated. The urgent care decides if the patient is sick enough to go to emergency. The urgent care provider designates need and if the urgent care is incapable or not equipped to help the patient to the extent his illness necessitates. After hours' charges cannot be billed if the medical group's urgent care is open.

Denied Claims Sent to the Patient for Case Study 12-2

All denial letters must have language stating the patient has a right to appeal the denial of payment, also the address, phone number, and directions of how to submit an appeal if the patient decides to do so; the patient must be given a chance to do so since, at this point, the patient may be responsible for the entire bill. All senior HMO patients' comments have required CMS language that more completely describes appeal options.

(Continued)

When the patient appeals the payment denial of inappropriate billing to the health plan, the health plan will usually overturn the denial if the diagnosis met ED criteria. These may be defined in coded form, ICD-9 CM, at the provider's request or in written form, stated in the patient's member handbook from the carrier.

Frequently, the senior patient claims are overturned based on the layperson's definition of an emergency. The patient may have felt he was truly dying. That is why a physician review of the ED report is mandatory for a denial or overturn of a denial.

Claims Not Meeting Medical Necessity for Case Study 12-2

The claim would also need to be audited based on the diagnosis code. All health plans have a list of diagnosis codes that are approved, automatic approval, based on medical criteria. If the diagnosis code is not on the health plan list, it is subject to review for medical necessity.

Both commercial and senior ED claims that do not meet the ED criteria should be reviewed and may be denied as not meeting medical necessity. All denied claims must be reviewed by a physician and be denied only by a physician if they do not meet criteria standards.

Depending on the contract with the medical group/IPA, out-of-area urgent/emergency claims would usually be the financial responsibility of the health plan. If received by the medical group/IPA, all claims should be forwarded to the health plan within five days of receipt of claim.

A commercial HMO member can be charged for the after-hours charges, Sunday and holiday charges, and the provider is paid for those charges.

Case Study 12-3 – A Preferred Provider Organization and How It Was Paid

Case study 12-3 is information regarding a preferred provider organization claim and how it was paid. There are four scenarios: Medicare only, PPO only, both insurances, and senior HMO radiology/emergency scenario.

21. DIAGNOSIS OR NATURE OF ILLNESS OR INJURY (Relate Items 1, 2, 3 or 4 to Item 24E by Line)
1. 7802
2. 8730
3. E8889
4.

22. MEDICAID RESUBMISSION CODE ORIGINAL REF. NO.

23. PRIOR AUTHORIZATION NUMBER

	24. A. DATE(S) OF SERVICE From MM DD YY	To MM DD YY	B. PLACE OF SERVICE	C. EMG	D. PROCEDURES, SERVICES, OR SUPPLIES (Explain Unusual Circumstances) CPT/HCPCS	MODIFIER	E. DIAGNOSIS POINTER	F. $ CHARGES	G. DAYS OR UNITS	H. EPSDT Family Plan	I. ID. QUAL.	J. RENDERING PROVIDER ID. #
1	10 10 08		23		99284	25	1	245 53	1		NPI	
2	10 10 08		23		12034		2	179 00	1		NPI	
3	10 10 08		23		99053		1 2	103 00	1		NPI	
4											NPI	
5											NPI	
6											NPI	

PHYSICIAN OR SUPPLIER INFORMATION

25. FEDERAL TAX I.D. NUMBER SSN EIN	26. PATIENT'S ACCOUNT NO.	27. ACCEPT ASSIGNMENT? (For govt. claims, see back) YES NO	28. TOTAL CHARGE	29. AMOUNT PAID	30. BALANCE DUE
			$ 527 53	$	$ 527 53

Figure 12-3 A PPO claim (Delmar/Cengage Learning)

DIAGNOSIS

780.2	Syncope and collapse
873.0	Other open wound of head: Scalp, without mention of complication
E888.9	Unspecified fall, Fall NOS

PROCEDURES

99284-25	Emergency department visit for evaluation and management of a patient presenting problems of high severity and require urgent evaluation by the physician but do not pose an immediate significant threat to life or physiologic function
Modifier 25	Significant separately identifiable evaluation and management service by the same physician on the same day of the procedure or other service
12034	Intermediate repair: layer closure wounds of scalp 7.6–12.5 cm
99053	Service(s) provided between 10 p.m. and 8 a.m. at 24-hour facility, in addition to basic service

Medicare Only for Case Study 12-3

Medicare applies the same rules as the groups processing the senior HMO claims. The guidelines are the same for both. And a payer would run the claims through the traditional CCI edits for the codes and timeliness issues with electronic claims and paper claims as well.

PPO Only for Case Study 12-3

Traditional non-Medicare PPO claims are processed according to the individual PPO; however, they usually have the same standard for code review as Medicare and other commercial insurances have. And, the participating provider contract may come into play for such issues as percentage of payment in and out of network.

Both Insurances – Medicare and the PPO for Case Study 12-3

When a patient has both of these insurances, the patient would usually pay coinsurance on both the professional and facility claims. For the PPO or indemnity plans, the coinsurance would vary depending on the patient's plan and if the provider was considered a preferred provider in or out of network.

Usually the PPO/indemnity plan considers the ED physicians as out of network if they are not contracted with them. However, some hospitals have arrangements with the insurance that may include certain rates or reimbursement for the ED physicians in their contracts. These rates are usually not published or shared with a medical group, as the health plan would pay these claims.

The complete claim would be billed, and the PPO would pay its portion. The patient may have out-of-pocket expense for the balance billing.

Senior HMO Radiology/Emergency Scenario for Case Study 12-3

If the ED physician bills for the EKG or the X-ray and the ED physician does an actual interpretation, the EKG has to be a separate report to be paid. It does not have to be a physically

(Continued)

separate report but does need to be separately identifiable in the ED notes. The ED provider does a separate report and reads the same films.

The payer will need to check when the radiologist claims come in and make sure that the claim has not been paid to the ED physician for the interpretation. If this is not checked by the payer, the radiologist may inadvertently also be paid for the same service. The payer will more than likely not pay for the second reading by the radiologist. A payer will not pay for the same service twice.

Case Study 12-4 – Coding of Multiple Procedures – Sinus

Coding multiple bilateral procedures can be confusing. The following gives an example of bilateral procedures and how they are billed, with correct and incorrect examples.

21. DIAGNOSIS OR NATURE OF ILLNESS OR INJURY (Relate Items 1, 2, 3 or 4 to Item 24E by Line)			22. MEDICAID RESUBMISSION CODE / ORIGINAL REF. NO.					
1. 7540	3. 4718		23. PRIOR AUTHORIZATION NUMBER					
2. 4710	4. 4732							

	24. A. DATE(S) OF SERVICE From MM DD YY To MM DD YY	B. PLACE OF SERVICE	C. EMG	D. PROCEDURES, SERVICES, OR SUPPLIES (Explain Unusual Circumstances) CPT/HCPCS / MODIFIER	E. DIAGNOSIS POINTER	F. $ CHARGES	G. DAYS OR UNITS	H. EPSDT Family Plan	I. ID. QUAL.	J. RENDERING PROVIDER ID. #
1	10 21 08	24		30520	1	1601 18	1		NPI	
2	10 21 08	24		31237 50	2	1727 50	2		NPI	
3	10 21 08	24		31267 50	3	1528 10	2		NPI	
4	10 21 08	24		31254 50	4	1451 35	2		NPI	
5									NPI	
6									NPI	

Figure 12-4 Coding multiple procedures (Delmar/Cengage Learning)

```
Procedures Performed for Diagnosis
Septoplasty for deviated septum/congenital
Nasal polyps - nasal cavity and turbinates bilateral
Sinus polyps - maxillary bilateral
Chronic sinusitis - ethmoid bilateral/anterior
```

DIAGNOSIS

```
754.0       Certain congenital musculoskeletal deformities
471.0       Nasal polyps, polyps of nasal cavity
471.8       Other polyp of sinus
473.2       Chronic sinusitis ethmoidal
```

PROCEDURE

```
30520       Septoplasty or submucous resection, with or without cartilage
            scoring, contouring, or replacement with graft
31237-50    This will be bundled - nasal/sinus endoscopy with polypectomy
            - bilateral
```

```
31267-50   Nasal/sinus endoscopy, surgical with maxillary antrostomy
           with removal of tissue from maxillary sinus - bilateral
31254-50   Nasal sinus endoscopy, surgical with ethmoidectomy partial
           (anterior) - bilateral
```

In these cases, the provider should double the dollar amount and never discount multiple procedure lines. The insurance company will do that for you.

Unilateral one side = $100

Bilateral two sides = $200

It is common for a payer to consider a 150 percent approved amount on a bilateral procedure. It is common for a provider to double the amount for bilateral (-50) procedures.

	Correct	Incorrect
Line 1	$1,455.00	$727.50
Line 2	$1,056.20	$528.10
Line 3	$902.72	$451.35

Summary

A payer may see the same codes reported correctly, but as we see in the examples, consider them very differently in potential dollar amount payment if the patient is responsible for a portion or full payment. The more the insurance is responsible for payment, even out of network, it appears there are tighter controls in how the patients receive services and payment consideration.

Noncontracted providers may or may not wish to participate in the plan. How they qualify for participation in a plan may be economic, personal, or regulation driven. These providers may have patients who have insurance but they do not participate in those insurances. Understanding the options available with the plan can give the provider choices in how it will run its practice and not be potentially mistreated.

Web Sites

Any willing provider (AWP) and freedom of choice (FOC) laws *http://www.rwjf.org*; search FOC laws (The Robert Wood Johnson Foundation did a study on the effects of FOC and AWP law.)

http://www.cmanet.org, search dmhc, templates; then look for 083106 (This Web site gives proposed legislation to limit noncontracted providers in their ability to be reimbursed and describes the long-terms effects of such legislation.)

Review

Fill in the Blank

1. The provider must understand what he gains or loses in an
_____ and the options available if an _____ cannot
be reached.

2. A provider who is unable to participate in a plan may have no _____
of the requirements or does not meet all of the _____.

3. Some plans have written into their provider _____ their
ability to _____ the relationship for any/no reason.

4. Some insurance companies may limit the _____ choices of
_____ who participate in their plan.

5. An employer may wish to offer a limited benefit package because of
the cost of the _____.

6. In reciprocity, the _____ can look for affiliates with whom the
provider is _____ and ask for the affiliate-_____
rate to forego _____ rates.

7. All denial letters must have language stating the patient has the right
to _____ the denial of payment.

8. How a provider qualifies for participation in a plan may be
_____, _____, or _____ driven.

9. Companies that self-insure sometimes offer limited _____
_____.

10. Many times, a patient will not see how limited a plan is because he
will simply take the _____ the _____ offers.

Review Questions

1. Why are patients wary of going out of network?

_____

_____

_____

_____

2. Under what circumstances would the provider have a say in the
patient going to a provider in or out of network?

_____

_____

_____

3. When will an IPA and the plan share costs? Explain.

_____

_____

_____

4. Name two requirements physicians may need to follow to become participating providers in a plan.

   _____

   _____

   _____

5. Name three problems providers may face when attempting to become participating providers.

   _____

   _____

   _____

6. If the provider is terminated from the plan, where is the language and notification period written in how the insurance company will handle this?

   _____

   _____

   _____

7. In what ways may an employer limit a patient's options when participating in its plan/benefits?

   _____

   _____

   _____

8. Name one incentive for a provider to participate in the plan.

   _____

   _____

   _____

9. In reciprocity, when may the provider/biller have no choice but to accept the contracted fee for the service provided?

   _____

   _____

   _____

10. What are the various factors payers take into consideration before payment?

   _____

   _____

   _____

Critical Thinking Exercise

Since legislation began in the early 1990s, some states have embraced the idea of FOC and AWP. Others have refined the rules in which payers are obligated in such cases, and yet still other states have chosen not to participate. Where does your state stand on this subject? If the providers you eventually work for decide not to participate as a contracted provider, what chances will you have for reimbursement and at what percentage?

Materials Needed

2 different-colored highlighters
1 blue pen
1 AWP rule for your state found on the Web
1 FOC rule for your state found on the Web

Directions

1. Use your Web browser and search engine and type in phrases such as
   - any willing provider _____ (your state)
   - freedom of choice laws _____ (your state)
   - FOC
   - AWP
   - The insurance name of your choice along with FOC or AWP

2. Print the rules.

3. Use one color highlighter for generalized information, use the other for specified information the state has changed to fit the laws or regulations needed in that state. Highlight the following information (if stated) found in the rules:
   - How it defines any willing provider
   - How it defines freedom of choice
   - Any differences unique to the state or insurance company

4. Discuss the differences and similarities in the rules with your professor.

Professional Corner

Who in your office is responsible for handling claims of patients who do not participate in provider insurances? The following are some questions to consider if this is a part of your job description:

- *Does your office accept walk-in patients who do not participate with any insurances your provider contracts with?*
- *Does your office bill the patient's insurance as a courtesy?*
- *Is your provider willing to perform high-dollar-amount procedures knowing the patient's insurance is not one it contracts with?*
- *If the patient is referred to your provider as a consult but does not participate in the insurance, will your office bill the referring provider, the patient, or the patient's insurance expecting reciprocity or AWP to be considered?*
- *Does your office have procedures in place to handle payers who are obligated to pay yet use nonparticipation as an excuse not to pay?*
- *Is your office aware of appeals processes dictated by state insurance regulation?*

References

Texas Department of Insurance. (May 18, 2001). Prompt Payment of Physician and Provider Claims. "Commissioner's Bulletin No. B-0023-01". Austin, TX, Texas Department of Insurance.

Department of Health and Human Services. (4/25/07). Chapter 6, "Relationships with Providers." Medicare Managed Care Manual, (REV.82, 04, 27, 07). Washington, D.C, Centers for Medicare and Medicaid.

(February, 2006). "An Information Packet for Tenn-Care Providers." In Tenn-Care Provider and Independent Review. Nashville, TN, TennCare Oversight Division.

Blue Cross Blue Shield of Arizona. (6/21/07). "Non-Contracted Provider Request", BCBSAZ Network Management. Phoeniz, AZ BCBSAZ.

Aetna Health Inc. (4/17/08). "Provider Q and A." In Aetna Medicare Open Plan, page 5.

Glossary

The following are terms and their meanings found in this text.

A

á la carte billing   Instead of billing to the most comprehensive code, billing is done on an individual procedure(s) basis. This basis implies the procedures are all included in one comprehensive procedure.

AB 1455   Assembly Bill 1455, a California state law for payment and billing practices that relate to acknowledgement that the insurance company has received the claim within 15 working days.

Administrative Simplification Compliance Act (ASCA)   The Act requires claims to be submitted electronically to Medicare. The requirement date was October 16, 2003. The exception is small practices.

aggregate   The maximum amount that can be paid.

air grid   Out-of-area air miles from the point of the primary care office to the place of service used to calculate if a patient is in the catchment area or in the geographic area the plan agrees to pay for the service.

allegations   An allegation is something that allegedly happened but it has not been proven.

AMA   American Medical Association.

ambulatory surgi-centers   These can be freestanding or affiliated with a hospital. These are used for elective surgeries, and the patients usually go home on the same day. There are usually a small number of surgery rooms and recovery rooms. The center is specifically used for surgeries.

analyte   A type of chemical used in a lab test.

antitrust kickbacks   Antitrust laws break up monopolies that may form to fix the cost of something. A kickback is basically a bribe to get someone to steer a situation in the briber's favor.

any willing provider (AWP)   These laws do not let the health plan discriminate against providers who are willing to accept and meet the rules of participation in its plan. The AWP laws tell the networks they must let the providers participate.

audit of medical records   A verification of documents/records for correct information, whole information, requested information, and complete documentation. Audits sometimes look at exposure or risk.

average sales price (ASP)   From the Medicare drug list. This pertains to Medicare Part B drugs. Payments are allowed for drugs not included in the ASP Medicare file.

average wholesale price (AWP)   In drug pricing, it is the wholesale price, or the price that the drug is sold for to pharmacies, physicians, or hospitals, which are not the end users of the drugs. The cost to the patient, the actual end user, for the medications is not the same price.

B

balance billing   Charging or collecting an amount that is more than the reimbursement rate.

beneficiaries   People or entities who receive benefits.

Benefits Improvement and Protection Act (BIPA)   BIPA has to do with the appeals process of claims and a proposed cost to appeal those claims. Also, a fee for claims that cannot be processed would be paid by the provider of service per unprocessable claim. This is called a user fee proposal. For Medicare Part B claims, a provider has a time limit of 120 days to file an appeal after the initial claim has been filed.

C

capitation   A method of reimbursement by which providers are paid an agreed-upon, fixed amount per member per month (PMPM) for the delivery of management of specified services.

Carrier advisory committees (CAC)   Usually one committee is established per state to make recommendations about policy and educate peers on LMRPs. The committee reviews local medical review policy issues relevant to its state and can make recommendations to the state carrier medical directors regarding policy.

carve-out   A service not included in the capitation payment and that may be covered by a negotiated fee-for-service reimbursement. It can also apply expressly to services not covered under a particular contract.

CCI edit   Edits performed using CCI tables based on one patient and one provider on the same date of service.

Centers for Medicare and Medicaid (CMS)   An agency within the Health and Human Services Department of the federal government. Medicaid, Medicare, HIPAA and CLIA are all regulated through CMS.

CHEDDAR   An acronym that stands for chief complaint, history, examination, details, drug and dosage, assessments of observations, return.

claims for encounter data   Monies are paid on these claims through capitation. It benefits both the physician and the managed care plan to know the true cost of treating the patients in a plan.

clean claim   A claim that has all the information needed to pay it.

clinician   One who participates in a clinical practice.

closed networks   These networks usually have a closed group of physicians the patients must choose from. The network does not accept new physicians so the patients are limited to those who participate. Some networks have limited providers, while others have a larger variety for the patient to choose from.

Coder's Desk Reference   The book has basic guidelines, anesthesia crosswalks, surgery descriptions in layman's terms, etc... This guide is perfect for those who do not have a good command of medical language or maybe those billing for more than one medical specialty.

common working file (CWF)   A form of verifying eligibility of the patient for services. This verification is done before the claim(s) is paid.

compliance A mentoring system of rules and regulations; laws that must be adhered to. This ensures consistency and fulfillment of expectations of the entity, business, or practice.

comprehensive code A comprehensive code includes component codes that can be performed separately, but when performed together the one comprehensive code should be reported. The component codes are included in the comprehensive code because they are needed to complete the procedure.

Comprehensive Error Rate Testing Program (CERT) These are error rates based on a random sampling of paid claims broken into service type and provider type. A random sampling could mean every 10th claim the system has or a time period of claims in the database itself.

comprehensive medical care Complete medical care.

contracted rate The rate agreed upon by all parties through a contract.

co-payment (co-pay) An amount of money that a plan member pays directly to the physician at the time of the visit; co-pays are minimal office visit charges, typically between $5 and $25, to be collected by the physician's office in addition to any insurance plan payments for the visit.

Correct Coding Initiative, *CCI Manual*. A nationally used coding reimbursement manual based on current procedural terminology codes and published by the American Medical Association. It introduces concepts and terms needed to understand claims payment as well as the tools required for success. It also describes some of the exceptions that a coder may encounter in the coding process.

covered services These are services included in the plan and are mentioned in the booklet the patient gets from the insurance company. The patient is entitled to receive them if the patient is in need of them. The contract will identify all services covered by the capitation rate or contract and list all services not included but eligible for additional reimbursement.

current procedural terminology (CPT) Consists of service and procedure codes and their definitions most commonly reported on claim forms such as the CMS-1500 for professional medical procedures usually performed by a physician and ancillary staff.

D

deductible A set amount the patient must pay before her insurance pays anything for the calendar year. Usually, the full amount of the deductible needs to be met once a year, at the beginning of the calendar year.

division of financial responsibility (DOFR) In a managed care organization, a DOFR explains who is responsible for the procedure or care, the capitated provider group or the managed care organization itself. The information is usually written in a list, which clearly states specific procedures and which organization is responsible for them.

duplicate claim A claim submitted more than once.

durable medical equipment (DME) Appropriate medical equipment used for an illness, which is prescribed by a physician. The equipment is reusable.

durable medical equipment regional carrier (DMERC) A non-government entity, usually a private payer, that bids for a contract with Medicare to pay the claims for the durable medial equipment according to the rules and regulation Medicare has set forth.

E

encounter data Examines a pattern of use for a billable encounter.

enrollee A patient/spouse/dependent(s) enrolled in the plan. The enrollee is entitled to the services of the plan if he needs them. The enrollee may also be called *the patient*, *member*, or *enrollee*. However, the dependent of a dependent (for example, a grandchild) is covered unless express permission is given under the plan.

evidence of coverage This is a legal document that gives details about the plan. Usually this is a document given to the patient. It may describe the dates the patient enrolled, first date enrolled, and/or services he is entitled to under the plan. Also, it would state any deductibles, co-pays, and coinsurances.

exclusions Services paid outside of CCI edits based on specific contract language.

explanation of benefits (EOB) Describes services given to a patient, whether the services were covered by the plan, and how or if they were paid; physicians, hospitals, and sometimes patients receive these.

F

fee for service Fee is charged for each service delivered.

fee schedule A list of all services and procedures coded using the notation of CPT, HCPCS, or ICD-9-CM, and so on. Most fee schedules have a procedure code and an agreed-upon rate or fee for that specific procedure. Fee schedules are common for participating providers that contract with HMOs and PPOs.

freedom of choice (FOC) laws Allow patients to be reimbursed for services by a qualified provider that does not participate in their plan.

full-risk capitated plan Similar to the full-risk contract, only the capitated plan pays all the claims for all the patients, with the possible exception of out-of-area services.

full-risk claims The plan pays all the claims for all the patients; sometimes these claims must be in area.

full-risk contract A provider group responsible for two areas of risk: professional fund claims and hospital fund claims.

G

geographic area A specified land area.

good faith Working with a desire not to defraud.

group or payer reciprocity rates If a skilled nursing facility has contracted with both the health plan and a medical group, there must be a decision of which rates to use, the rates of the health plan or the medical group. The provider cannot pick and choose specific rates and procedures from both. This may also be called *piggybacking* of rates.

H

HCPC Health care provider codes.

Health Care Financing Administration (HCFA) Federal agency that administers Medicare and Medicaid Services (CMS).

Health Insurance Portability and Accounting Act (HIPAA) Enacted by Congress in 1996, HIPAA addresses such issues as confidentiality, security, and standards of how health care information needs to be handled. It also looks at patients applying for benefits from health care plans like limiting preexisting conditions clauses for the patients and protecting their rights to health care when they change jobs.

high dollar amount claims   A defined amount that can vary by group. An example could be anything over $2,500 from a physician, or a claim in excess of $10,000 by a facility.

HMO risk services   Those services paid in full by the HMO.

hold harmless clause   The physician and managed care organization (MCO) agree not to hold each other liable for corporate malfeasance or malpractice if either of the parties is found liable.

huffing addiction   Inhalant abuse, where mostly chemical vapors are inhaled to get high.

I

incentive   A motivator, could take the form of a reimbursement or something contributing to the success or an "extra." The incentive may provide extra value.

incidental procedures   When one procedure is part of another procedure.

independent practice association (IPA)   Independent physicians who together negotiate fees and rates with a plan or an HMO.

individual plan carve-outs   Durable medical equipment, home health, and mental health are common carve-outs of individual plans associated with patients with more serious health problems covered by a separate benefit and negotiated separately by the health plan. The health plan contracts with another health plan to cover the services.

in network   Providers who are within the network of approved physicians and/or hospitals to provide medical services to a patient who is assigned to the Physician's Medical Group, Independent Practice Association, Preferred Physician's Group and contracted with the health plan.

interval history   An interval history is usually taken on an established patient and looks at the history between visits. The physician may do a comparison of current and past history(s).

K

Knox-Keene Act   The Knox Keene Act regulates HMO plans in the state of California. Most states have similar laws regulating HMOs.

L

LMRP local medical review policies   These apply to claims directly made to the local carrier who pays the claims. The carrier looks at the LMRP to make sure the claims payment meets Medicare guidelines. The LMRP will state under what circumstance the service is covered, codes that are covered and not covered, and descriptions of services. A tool that helps to ensure coding meets the Medicare requirements set forth by regulations of payment and coding policies. LMRPs are developed for specific codes for various reasons. LMRPs can be different by area/region/state, and so on. In the state of California, LMRPs are separated by northern and southern regions. For a list of these categories log on to http://www.CMS.gov/medicare/mip/index-ar.htm.

local codes   HCPCS Level II codes.

local coverage determinations (LCD)   These specify how a service is covered and how it is coded correctly.

locum tenens   A floater doctor that has no practice of her own. She fills in for the physician when the physician is away.

M

medical director   Usually a physician who participates in the plan who is the agreed-upon liaison between the plan and the physician's group.

medical necessity   A treatment, standard, or medically accepted procedure that is recognized or furnished to treat a symptom, disease, or condition. How an insurance company defines what is needed or necessary can be decided by state laws, federal laws, by contract or by limits to the medical plan.

Medicare Advantage Plans (MA-PD)   These plans basically cover the patient from head to toe. Theoretically, the patient will not need any other plan. A patient who chooses these kinds of plans get Medicare Part A and Part B. There may be an additional charge to belong to this plan.

Medicare allowable   The Medicare fee schedule for participating or nonparticipating physician members.

Medicare Demonstration Project   This project looks at how traditional Medicare compares to Medicare Advantage Plans and will not begin until 2010.

Medicare fee schedule   A list of fees developed by CMS and used by Medicare.

Medicare Modernization Act (Public Law 108-173)   This act is to help bring more up to date services or modernize the service offered to Medicare patients.

Medi-Medi   These are patients who have both Medicare and Medicaid. The patients should not have any out-of-pocket expense/share of cost unless it is a monthly share cost stipulated by the plan.

member   Anyone enrolled in a managed care plan and entitled to receive benefits.

modifiers   Modifiers explain how a procedure was modified or changed in some way but not enough to choose a new code.

modulated   Adjusted or adapted.

Mohs surgery   Used for the removal of skin cancer. It is famous for only removing the cancerous tissue and leaving the healthy tissue.

mutually exclusive   Procedures that cannot be coded together; they must be coded individually. Mutually exclusive codes are codes that may not be coded for the same surgical session for a patient; it would be incorrect to code them together. The CCI manual states these.

N

necessary treatment alternative   A treatment not normally covered under the plan provisions.

nonclaim disputes   These are disputes that are not about claims. Physicians and HMOs participate in mediation, and work together in a nonconfrontational or cooperative manner to resolve a nonclaim dispute.

noncontracted providers   Physicians or facilities with which the insurer does not have contractual agreements.

nurse practitioners   Nurses doing some physician's work. They may diagnosis and treat minor illnesses. They usually have advanced degrees in nursing to be able to take patient histories, give prescription, and so on.

O

out-of-area air miles   From the point of the primary care office to the place of service, used to calculate if a patient is in the catchment area or in the geographic area in which the plan agrees to pay for the service.

out-of-area claims   Contractual language defining what coverage is available to subscribers beyond the service area of a medical group or hospital.

out-of-pocket maximum   Maximum dollar amount payable by the member based on the health plan contract. This can vary from one plan to another.

P

partial capitation   Partial capitation means some services a provider performs are not included in the per month per patient capitation payment. The provider may be paid for some of his services on a fee-for-service basis.

participating physician   A physician who participates in the plan usually by participating provider agreement. The physician will show current evidence of licensure, in the state he practices, to the plan before being considered to enter into such a plan. The physician may also get credentialed by the plan and/or the medical group, and then the medical group would submit the information to the HMO to let it know they are licensed physicians able to write prescriptions and have affiliations with certain hospitals in the area. Unless a physician is an independent physician, this part is done by the medical group.

participating provider   An entity or physician under a contractual agreement with the plan/HMO to provide services to its patients/members.

participating provider contract   A contract stating rules of participation agreed to by employers, physicians, group practices, and entities with insurance companies or government payers.

payee   The person or entity reimbursement/monies get sent to.

payer   The person or entity responsible for payment of claims.

payment schedule   A list or a graph stating when payment will be made; this can be based on government regulation or agreed upon by the parties involved.

per diem   Per day.

physician   A medical doctor licensed in the state in which he practices.

physician's assistants   Practice medicine under the supervision of a licensed physician, who is responsible for them. They usually have a master's degree in Physician Assistance Studies. PAs are usually listed as employees of the medical group and it is the group that contracts with the HMO on their behalf.

PIN   The personal identification number is used for billing purposes; this is how the provider receives payment.

point of service (POS)   Point-of-service plans work like PPOs and HMOs, but the patient does not decide how she wants to use her benefit until she receives services/treatment.

practitioner   A person who practices the art of healing and has a license in his area of expertise.

preferred provider   A preferred provider contracts with an insurer to provide its services of expertise for an agreed-upon payment type (percentage, capitation, flat fees, fee schedule, and so on). A preferred provider can be a physician, group, facility, or practitioner.

pricing criteria   The standard at which prices are based.

primary care physician (PCP)   This physician provides primary care service to plan members. He usually has a contract with an HMO plan. This physician can be a general practitioner, family practitioner, internist, and so on. Sometimes a patient can name a specialist as his primary care physician of the plan. The PCP is the first physician the patient sees for medical services. If the PCP deems specialty services necessary, he refers the patient out.

primary hospital   A contracted hospital in agreement to receive the patients of the plan, agreeing to admit and give inpatient/outpatient covered service under the plan.

primary procedure   First or main procedure.

Q

qualitative   Having to do with quality.

quantitative   Having to do with the amount.

R

RBRVS (Resource Based Relative Values System)   A payment computation that is dictated by CCI to make sure that payment meets uniform standards.

RBRVS fees   Charges are based on three key components of the Resource Based Relative Values Scale (RBRVS). It is a national value, and each procedure has value based on this system. It covers clinician's time, intensity, and technical skill required for the particular service provided. It also takes into account the practice's overhead expenses, including offices, rents, equipment, staff, supplies, and malpractice insurance.

rebundling   A grouping of several codes into the most comprehensive code.

reciprocity   Contractual agreement between insurance and providers regarding rates if a medical group or facility is paying a claim on behalf of its members.

referral   In an HMO, the participating provider directs care. The plan explains how the services are to be obtained that are covered under the plan. Division of **Financial Responsibility Matrix**. A referral would have to be authorized by the IPA. Or if the patient is out of network.

risk pool   A percentage of the capitation that is placed in a risk-sharing pool. If the cost of providing care (usually specialty and hospital services) exceeds an amount targeted by the plan, then all or a portion of the withhold is forfeited. If it is less than the targeted amount, the fees may be distributed back to the physicians.

risk stabilization fund   Money set aside from premiums to compensate physicians who have received an adverse patient selection.

S

self-insured companies   Companies with a large number of employees pay the medical claims of their employees and sometimes contract with reinsurers to pay catastrophic care claims. Sometimes self-insured plans are based on a distinctive factor of the population of the company.

self-refer   A patient self-referring out of network means the patient sees a provider that is not a participating provider and does not have an agreement with the insurance carrier for a specified rate.

services included in capitation   If the services are capitated, the biller is not billing the service for payment, but reporting the services performed based on real numbers. Physicians should be aware of their service percentages provided under the capitation.

shared risk   Providers share billing responsibilities. Hospital in-services and other treatment charges are the billing responsibility of the health plan. Professional claims are the billing responsibility of the medical group.

SNOCAMP   An acronym that stands for subjective, nature of illness, objective, counseling, assessment, medical decision making, plan.

SOAP   An acronym that stands for subjective, objective, assessment, plan.

split claims   Billing for more than one claim, per CPT codes, with the same date of service (for example, a surgical service, an office visit, or lab fees).

Stark Rules   When a provider refers a patient to a facility that they or their families have a financial interest in, this would be a violation. The Stark Act does not permit a provider to refer patients to a business they own or are financially involved in. This only applies to Medicare and Medicaid patients.

stop loss/catastrophic risk   An arrangement to limit physician's loss. This may be an agreement between a physician and a managed care organization whereby the MCO will assume responsibility for the cost of the patient's care when the cost rises beyond a specified level. Stop-loss insurance may be purchased on a monthly premium.

surcharge   An additional sum usually added for a specified reason.

T

termed   A patient who is no longer with the plan.

termination of contract   The circumstances and timing required for cancellation of the contract by each party.

the plan   The plan is the benefit program of the insurer (that is, the insurance company, HMO, maybe self-insured, preferred provider organization.) The plan lists all covered services the patient is entitled to. These also may be called *benefit services, evidence of coverage services,* or *provider services.* The evidence of coverage booklets are given to the patient at the original sign up and/or open enrollment times of the year. If there is any change in the plan, the patient would receive these in the evidence of coverage.

U

unauthorized services   These are services not authorized by the plan and/or the HMO. If the physician does not get authorization from the plan, the services usually will not be paid for.

unbundling   Billing all components of a code rather than using a comprehensive code.

Unique Provider Identifier Number (UPIN)   The number is used when the service requires a referring physician. The UPIN is not used for the provider billing number. CMS provides the UPIN number.

usual, customary, and reasonable (UCR)   Is a calculation of what a medical procedure is worth in a geographic area.

User Fee Proposal   User fees are charged when people use services that have a fee for public use. Here, the proposal fee may be set by federal or state government.

utilization rate   Number of times a service is rendered. Managed care organizations express utilization rates in annual units of service per thousand members.

utilization review   Committee of doctors and nurses that reviews requests for medical necessity (for example, for elective surgery procedures).

W

wet read   A wet read is when an ED physician reads the film(s) to examine the problem and embark on the right avenue of care for the patient during the time the patient is in the emergency room.

withhold   A set percentage of the monthly capitation payment that is withheld by the MCO. As an incentive for cost-effective care, all or part of the withhold may be returned to the physician when specified utilization requirements are met.

Index

A

acknowledgment of claims, 211
acknowledgment of disputes, 210–211
acknowledgment of receipt of the claim, 57
add-on codes, 198–199
administrative penalties, 54
Administrative Simplification Compliance Act (ASCA), 100
adopting national codes, 114
agreement correspondence address, 35
agreement terms, 42
ambulance providers and Medicare, 98
anesthesia, 186
    payment and reporting, 187
    position of a patient changes the base value, 187
    a surgeon who anesthetizes his own patient, 187
anesthesiologists and RVGs, 188
Antikickback Statute, 233
any willing provider (AWP), 169, 243
any willing provider laws and closed networks, 243
appeal process and annual audits, 210
audited claim payment, 57–58
audits
    practice considered for, 225–226
    of provider disputes, 210
average sales price (ASP), 97
average sales price list for Medicare Part B drugs
    about, 97
    drug infusions, 98
    drugs listed separately, 98
average wholesale price (AWP), 98

B

backing out overpayment from other claims, 212
balance billing
    and capitation contracts, 27–28
    contracted and noncontracted providers, 213–214
    rebundling based on claim check edit systems, 214
    regarding the write-off, 215
basic contract responsibilities between providers and HMOs
    eligibility of college students, 32
    HMO Payment Responsibilities, 32
    physician payment responsibilities, 32
    service responsibilities, 29–30
    specialty services, 30–32
basic identifying information needed for both the provider and payer, 205
basic Medicaid rates offering one fee for a series of codes, 117–118
beneficiaries, 69

Benefits Improvement and Protection Act, 99–100
billing for a component separately, 192
billing for services provided by others, 231
billing Medicare or Medicaid occasionally incorrectly, 229
billing the payer at the patient's request, 76
bundling, 5

C

capitation, 25–29
    balance billing and capitation contracts, 27–28
    carve-outs, 28
    claims for encounter data, 27
    payment schedules, 27
    referring a patient, 29
    risk pools, 28–29
    services included in capitation, 27
carrier advisory committees (CAC), 95, 96
carriers and fiscal intermediaries request for records, 230
carve-outs, 28
case studies
    add-on codes, 198–199
    anesthesiologists and RVGs, 188
    basic Medicaid rates offering one fee for a series of codes, 117–118
    billing for a component separately, 192
    catastrophically ill patients, 44–45
    chiropractic modalities not paid, 199
    claims coded incorrectly and correctly, 233
    code is covered on the fee schedule, 80
    code is not on the fee schedule, 79–80
    coding of multiple procedures – sinus, 250–251
    commercial HMO claim, 246
    consulting physician initiates care of a Medicare patient, 102–103
    correct coding, lab codes, 9–11
    correct coding based on impaction, 234
    dollar amounts in a coding series, 118
    e/m based on medical necessity of care, 182–183
    films not coded or billed separately for an e/m, 191–192
    how rates vary in Medicaid, 117–118
    immunization administration without bundling, 197–198
    incidental to primary procedures, 13–15
    incorrect coding, add-on codes, 9
    incorrect coding based on lavage method, 234
    incorrect e/m coding reporting, payers issues, 183–184
    interventional radiology, 194
    lab test billed separately because of coding ineligibility, 12

managed care fee-for-service rates vary in Medicaid contracts, 118
payment of a senior HMO claim, 245–246
preferred provider organization payment, 248–250
procedure denied due to a global allowance, 16
radiologist performing technical and professional components, 192
reported diagnosis justifies reported services, 168–169
services denied-not a covered benefit, 17–18
spider veins versus varicose veins, 79–80
sports billing scenario, 171–172
unbundled procedure stated as multiple procedures, 15–16
where the primary and secondary insurance rates are different, 214–215
CCI manual, 5, 19
centers for Medicare and Medicaid services (CMS), 86
change in the laws, 38
chief complaint, history, examination, details, drugs and dosage, assessment of observations, return (CHEDDAR), 182
chiropractic modalities not paid, 199
claim overpayment written notice, 217
claim produced from superbill without supporting documentation, 231
claims coded incorrectly and correctly, 233
claims for encounter data, 27
claims not meeting medical necessity, 248
claims processing policies
    final claims processing, 60–61
    notifying patients of provider nonparticipation, 58–59
    outcome of in network, 61
    outcome of out-of-network, 61–62
    patient finding a new physician, 59
    provider termination of the contract, 58
clean claim, 57
clearinghouse acceptance, 112
clinical labs, 101
closed networks, 243
code covered on the fee schedule, 80
code not covered on the fee schedule, 72, 79–80
    holistic medicine can be confusing, 73
    multiple fee schedules, 74
    noncovered services, 72
    the patient self-referred out of network– when might this be paid?, 72
    procedures not included in the fee schedule but eventually allowed into the plan, 73
    unlisted procedures, 73–74
Coder's Desk Reference, 9
code versions and effective dates, 3
coding guidelines, 55–56

coding of multiple procedures–sinus, 250–251

coding tools, 7

commercial HMO claim, 246

common working file (CWF), 92

compliance, defined, 223

compliance and audits, 222–235

the carriers and fiscal intermediaries are requesting records. can they do that?, 230

general policy guidelines most compliance plans address and their corresponding policy and procedures, 224–225

how might our practice be considered for an audit?, 225–226

if my provider is convicted of a misdemeanor, can the provider be forced not to participate or excluded from Medicare?, 232

introduction to compliance and audits, 223–224

my doctor wants me to bill for the services a nurse, not the doctor himself, furnished. is this fraud?, 231

my practice wants to do its own audit. what should i do?, 226–228

my provider has decided to come forward with the compliance problem, 232–233

my provider ignores compliance problems, 231

in order to make a billing quota, i billed services i knew would not be paid, 231–232

participation in Medicare and Medicaid, 228

postaudit findings, 228

the Stark Rules, 233

what if my employer retaliates for my being a whistleblower (qui tam)?, 232

compliance with laws, 37

comprehensive codes and component codes, 4–5

comprehensive error rate testing program, 96–97

comprehensive medical care, 110

confidentiality of information, 37

consideration for payment, 181

consulting physician initiates care of a Medicare patient, 102–103

continuity of care, 33

contract amendments, 37

contracted and noncontracted providers, 213–214

contracted rate, 71

contracting for unbundling, 7

conversion tables for changed icd-9-cm codes, 115–117

coordination of benefits, 40–41

correct coding, lab codes, 9–11

correct coding based on impaction, 234

correct coding initiative, 2

correct coding initiative (CCI)

effect of on the coding industry, 3–4

history of CCI, 2

organizations responsible for CCI contents, 2–3

correct coding initiative (CCI) changes

code versions and effective dates, 3

obtaining current updates from the internet, 3

correct coding initiative (CCI) coding

CPT modifiers, 7

HCPCS modifiers, 7

modifiers and mutually exclusive codes, 7

rebundling lab codes, 11

correct coding initiative (CCI) coding software used by payers, 4

correct coding initiative (CCI) for the coder

bundling, 5

CCI manual, 5

comprehensive codes and component codes, 4–5

method, initial, and subsequent services, 5

mutually exclusive codes, 5

other coding tools, 7

practices that lead to unbundling, 6

significant information for individual codes, 5

unbundling, 6

Correct Coding Initiative (CCI) Manual, 2

cosmopolitan/big-city scenario, 193

cost-effectiveness in billing, 216

covered service, 31

CPT conventions introduction, 179

credentialing process of physician and staff, 40

current procedural terminology (CPT), 2

current procedural terminology (CPT) conventions to be considered, 178–200

anesthesia, 186

evaluation and management, 179–180

introduction to CPT conventions, 179

medicine section, 196

pathology and laboratory, 195–196

radiology, 191

the six sections of the CPT, 179

surgery section, 189–190

current procedural terminology (CPT) modifiers, 7, 123–159

introduction to modifiers, 124

modifiers, scenarios of use, and their definitions, 124–157

customary, defined, 164

D

deceased patient, 102

deductible, 52

definition of -21, 125

denied claims sent to the patient, 247–248

disclosure of outside billing services, 112

distinct provisions to look for in a PPO contract

administrative penalties, 54

patient billed on discounted fees, 53

patient's right to treatment, 54

seeking payment from the patient, 54

service areas, 53

division of financial responsibility (DOFR), 27

documentation of the evaluation and management level of service, 96–97

dollar amounts in a coding series, 118

drug infusions, 98

drugs listed separately, 98

durable medical equipment (DME), 42

E

eligibility of college students, 32

e-mail addresses for modifiers, 158

e/m based on medical necessity of care, 182–183

emergency departments, 42

employer cost for health care, 42

employers may limit patient options, 242–243

EMTALA and billing charges, 247

encounter data, 27

equal opportunity, 41

evaluation and management, 179–186

consideration for payment, 181

second-opinion claims, 180–181

second-opinion issues not authorized, 181

standardizing physician notes in the medical record, 185–186

evidence of coverage, 42

F

fee schedule established by payer, 68–69

fee schedule established by payer type, 69

fee schedule established by provider, 69

fee schedules, 69–70

about, 68

examples of, 76

using the fee schedule, 69–70

fee schedule types, 68

insured patient fee for service, 74

introduction to fee schedules, 68

investigational procedures, 74

medical necessity, 75–76

negotiating the fee schedule, 69

reciprocity rates and fee schedules, 74

various types of fee schedules, 70

fee schedules, types of, 70

fee schedule established by payer, 68–69

fee schedule established by payer type, 69

fee schedule established by provider, 69

fee schedules for capitated providers reporting statistical claims, 71

when a code is not on the fee schedule, 72

when a referral becomes an issue, 71

fee schedules for capitated providers reporting statistical claims, 71

films not coded or billed separately for an e/m, 191–192

final claims processing, 60–61

financial records, 34

financial responsibilities, 33

forwarding the claim to another payer, 217

fraud, suspicion of, 230

freedom-of-choice (FOC) laws, 170, 243

freedom of choice and the price to the patient, 243

full-risk claims, 241

G

general policy guidelines, 224–225

geographic area, 166

good faith, 213

governing law, 37

government investigation

wants to ask me questions, 230

wants to search my office, 229–230

groupings of modifiers for CPT sections, 158

H

handling claims adjudication, 34
HCPCS codes for a state Medicaid program, 114
HCPCS modifiers, 7
Health Insurance Portability and Accounting Act (HIPAA), 112
HMO contracts introduction
    basic contract responsibilities between providers and HMOs, 29–32
    capitation, 25–29
    responsibility for payment of claims, 32–36
    subcap providers' claim types, 36–44
HMO Payment Responsibilities, 32
HMO Risk Services, 41
holistic medicine, 73
huffing addiction, 125

I

immunization administration without bundling, 197–198
implementation of codes, 97
incentive, 244
incentives for providers to participate in the plan, 243
incidental to primary procedures, 13–15
incorrect CCI coding, 7
incorrect coding, add-on codes, 9
incorrect coding based on lavage method, 234
incorrect e/m coding reporting, 183–184
independent practice association (IPA), 173
information the adjuster needs, 211
in-house audit for compliance, 224
in network, 51
    outcome of, 61
insured patient fee for service, 74
    nonparticipating providers – no fee schedules involved, 75
    participating providers, 75
intentional unbundling and the government, 7
interest on claims
    acknowledgement of claims, 211
    acknowledgment of disputes, 210–211
    audits of provider disputes, 210
    information the adjuster needs, 211
    is the appeal process included in annual audits of the health plan?, 210
internal tracking of disputes by the provider, 206–208
internet, obtaining current updates from, 3
interventional radiology, 194
investigational procedures, 74

K

Knox-Keene Act, 28

L

lab test billed separately because of coding ineligibility, 12
liability insurance, 40
local codes, 114
local coverage determinations (LCDs), 4, 96
local medical review policies (LMRP), 4, 94–96
    carrier advisory committees, 96
    local coverage determinations, 96

M

managed care fee-for-service rates vary in Medicaid contracts, 118
marketing physicians' services by the plan, 39
Medicaid, 104–119, 215–216
    adopting national codes, 114
    case study, 117–118
    clearinghouse acceptance, 112
    conversion tables for changed ICD-9-CM codes, 115–117
    cost-effectiveness in billing, 216
    disclosure of outside billing services, 112
    how rates vary in, 117–118
    introduction to, 86, 110
    introduction to Medicaid, 110
    Medicaid program funding process, 110–112
    the payer of last resort, 112–113
    pricing criteria, 115
    reimbursement, 216
    requesting New HCPCS codes for a state Medicaid program, 114
    timeliness issues are handled by each state, 112
Medicaid program funding process, 110–112
medical necessity, 75–76, 131
    billing the payer at the patient's request, 76
    examples of various types of fee schedules and what they tell us, 76
medical records, 36
Medicare, 85–104
    Administrative Simplification Compliance Act, 100
    ambulance providers and Medicare, 98
    average sales price list for Medicare Part B drugs, 97
    Benefits Improvement and Protection Act, 99–100
    clinical labs, 101
    deceased patient, 102
    implementation of codes, 97
    introduction to Medicare, 86
    local medical review policies, 94–96
    Medicare and other insurances, 91
    Medicare demonstration projects, 100
    Medicare's common working file, 92–93
    Medicare's future and information to access, 87–88
    misdemeanor impact on participation in, 232
    need for complete documentation of the evaluation and management level of service chosen by the physician or coder, 96–97
    patient deductibles, 92
    and the PPO, 249
    role of the social security administration, 87
    tracking of codes for utilization, 97
Medicare Advantage Plans, MA-PD, 90
Medicare demonstration projects, 100
Medicare fee schedule, 27, 68
    new procedure not on the Medicare fee schedule, 101
Medicare fee schedule example, 76
Medicare Modernization Act, 97

Medicare only, 249
Medicare's common working file, 92–93
Medicare's future and information to access, 87–88
    about, 87–90
    nonparticipating providers' limiting charge increases the patient level of responsibility, 91
    participating and nonparticipating providers, 90–91
medicine section, 196
Medi-Medi, 92
method, initial, and subsequent services, 5
miscellaneous reasons for a dispute, 209
modifier -21 or 09921, 125–126
modifier -22 or 09922, 126–127
modifier -23 or 09923, 127–128
modifier -24 or 09924, 128–129
modifier -25 or 09925, 129–130
modifier -26 professional component or 09926, 130
modifier -32 mandated services or 09932, 131–133
modifier -47 or 09947, 133
modifier -50 or 09950, 134
modifier -51 exempt, 135
modifier -51 or 09951, 135
modifier -52 or 09952, 136
modifier -53 or 09953, 137
modifier -54 or 09954, 136
modifier -55 or 09955, 139
modifier -56 or 09956, 140
modifier -57 or 09957, 141
modifier -58 or 09958, 142–143
modifier -59 or 09959, 143
modifier -62 or 09962, 144
modifier -63 or 09963, 145
modifier -66 or 09966, 146
modifier -76 or 09976, 147
modifier -77 or 09977, 148
modifier -78 or 09978, 149
modifier -79 or 09979, 150
modifier -80 or 09980, 151–152
modifier -81 or 09981, 152
modifier -82 or 09982, 153
modifier -90 or 09990, 154–155
modifier -91 or 09991, 155–156
modifier -99 or 09999, 156–157
modifiers, 124
modifiers, scenarios of use, and their definitions, 124–157
    definition of -21, 125
    e-mail addresses for modifiers, 158
    groupings of modifiers for CPT sections, 158
modifiers and mutually exclusive codes, 7
modifiers introduction, 124
Mohs surgery, 142
more than one provider on a claim, 9
multiple fee schedules, 74
mutually exclusive codes, 5

N

necessary treatment alternative, 31
negotiating the fee schedule, 69
nonclaim disputes, 40

nonclaim disputes resolution, 40

noncontracted providers, 216–217, 240–251

any willing provider laws and closed networks, 243

freedom of choice and the price to the patient, 243

incentives for providers to participate in the plan, 243

introduction to noncontracted providers, 240–243

providers who choose not to participate, 244

reciprocity and deciding not to participate, 244

noncontracted providers introduction, 240–243

employers may limit patient options, 242–243

the plan can terminate the provider contract at any time, 242

providers who are unable to participate, 241

some plans limit patient options, 242

noncovered services, 72

nonparticipating providers

limiting charge increases the patient level of responsibility, 91

no fee schedules involved, 75

notifying patients of provider nonparticipation, 58–59

nurse practitioners and physician's assistants and the modifier -80, 152

O

Office of the Inspector General work plan for the year, 228–229

organizations responsible for CCI contents, 2–3

out-of-network

deductibles, 52

outcome of, 61–62

out-of-pocket maximum, 52

P

participating and nonparticipating providers, 90–91

participating providers, 75

participation in Medicare and Medicaid

billing Medicare or Medicaid occasionally incorrectly, 229

the government investigator wants to ask me questions, 230

a government investigator wants to search my office, 229–230

office of the Inspector General work plan for the year, 228–229

pathologists work location, 196

pathology and laboratory, 195–196

patient billed on discounted fees, 53

patient deductibles, 92

patient finding a new physician, 59

patient grievance process, 40

patient options, plan limitations, 242

patient self-referred out of network – when might this be paid?, 72

patient's right to treatment, 54

payer of last resort, 112–113

paying claims, criteria for, 208–209

payment and reporting, 187

payment dates specified in the plan contract, 57

payment guidelines and fee schedules, 55

payment of a senior HMO claim, 245–246

payment schedules, 27

physician payment responsibilities, 32

point of service (POS), 169

position of a patient changes the base value, 187

postaudit findings, 228

practices that lead to unbundling, 6

preferred provider, 51

preferred provider organization and how it was paid, 248–250

preferred provider organizations (PPOs), 50–63

preferred provider organizations (PPOs) only, 249

preferred provider organizations introduction, 51

going out-of-network, 52

out-of-network deductibles, 52

self-referring within network, 51–52

staying in-network, 51

pricing criteria, 115

primary and secondary insurance rates difference, 214–215

primary care physicians (PCPs), 25

primary procedure, 135

procedure denied due to a global allowance, 16

procedures not included in the fee schedule but eventually allowed into the plan, 73

professional review and quality assurance, 39

provider compliance

my provider coming forward with, 232–233

provider ignores compliance problems, 231

steps to clean up noncompliance, 232–233

provider disputes and balance billing

balance billing, 213–215

claim overpayment written notice, 217

forwarding the claim to another payer, 217

how a payer is paying claims and the criteria, 208–209

interest on claims, 210

introduction to provider disputes and balance billing, 204–218

Medicaid, 215–216

miscellaneous reasons for a dispute, 209

noncontracted providers, 216–217

request for reimbursement of overpayment by the payer, 212

retention of files, 217

seeking resolution of a billing determination, 206

settling claims with noncontracted providers, 213

time limit on claim disputes, 209–210

tracking form, 206–208

when a payer backs out overpayment from other claims, 212

provider disputes and balance billing introduction, 204–218

basic identifying information needed for both the provider and payer, 205

single or multiple claims, 205–206

providers who are unable to participate, 241

providers who choose not to participate, 244

provider termination of the contract, 58

Q

quality of service expectations and timeliness, 38–39

R

radiologist performing technical and professional components, 192

radiology, 191

cosmopolitan/big-city scenario, 193

rural hospital scenario, 193

who reads the x-rays first, 193

range, 180–181

reasonable, defined, 164

rebundling based on claim check edit systems, 214

rebundling lab codes, 11

reciprocity and deciding not to participate, 244

reciprocity rates and fee schedules, 74

recoupment rights, 34–35

referral issue, 71

referring a patient, 29

regarding the write-off, 215

reimbursement, 216

request for records by carriers and fiscal intermediaries, 230

request for reimbursement of overpayment by the payer, 212

resource based relative values scale (RBRVS), 2

responsibility for payment of claims

about, 32

agreement correspondence address, 35

continuity of care, 33

financial records, 34

financial responsibilities, 33

handling claims adjudication, 34

recoupment rights, 34–35

subcap capitation, 35–36

retention of files, 217

review organizations, 4

risk pools, 28–29

role of the social security administration, 87

rural hospital scenario, 193

S

second-opinion claims, 180–181

second-opinion issues not authorized, 181

seeking payment from the patient, 54

seeking resolution of a billing determination, 206

self audit by practice, 226–228

self-referring within network, 51–52

senior HMO radiology/emergency scenario, 249–250

separate operating expenses, 40

service areas, 53

service responsibilities, 29–30

services denied (not a covered benefit), 17–18

services included in capitation, 27

settling claims with noncontracted providers, 213

significant information for individual codes, 5

single or multiple claims, 205–206

six sections of the CPT, 179

specialty services, 30–32

spider veins versus varicose veins, 79–80

standardizing physician notes in the medical record, 185–186

Stark Rules, 233

staying in-network, 51

steps to clean up noncompliance, 232–233

subcap capitation, 35–36

subcap providers' claim types, 36–44

agreement terms, 42

change in the laws, 38

compliance with laws, 37

confidentiality of information, 37

contract amendments, 37

coordination of benefits, 40–41

credentialing process of physician and staff, 40

emergency departments, 42

employer cost for health care, 42

equal opportunity, 41

evidence of coverage, 42

governing law, 37

HMO Risk Services, 41

liability insurance, 40

marketing physicians' services by the plan, 39

medical records, 36

nonclaim disputes resolution, 40

patient grievance process, 40

professional review and quality assurance, 39

quality of service expectations and timeliness, 38–39

separate operating expenses, 40

termed and ineligible patients, 43–44

termination of an agreement, 43

subjective, nature of illness, objective, counseling, assessment, medical decision making, plan (SNOCAMP), 182

subjective, objective, assessment, plan (SOAP), 182

surcharge, 32

surgeon who anesthetizes his own patient, 187

surgery section, 189–190

T

termed, 43

termed and ineligible patients, 43–44

termination of an agreement, 43

termination of the provider contract at any time by plan, 242

time limit on claim disputes, 209–210

timeliness issues are handled by each state, 112

tracking form, 206–208

tracking of codes for utilization, 97

U

unbundled procedure stated as multiple procedures, 15–16

unbundling, 6

contracting for unbundling, 7

intentional unbundling and the government, 7

practices that lead to unbundling, 6

unintentional unbundling, 6–7

unlisted procedures, 73–74

user fee proposal, 99

usual, customary, and reasonable rates (UCR), introduction

determining a geographic area, 166

developing a review system for procedures performed and reimbursed, 168

favorable reimbursement and fewer disputes with payers, 167

the importance of UCR rates by specialty for geographic area, 167

managing operation of the office and understanding what is expected, 167–168

the patient and UCR rates, 166–167

usual, customary, and reasonable (UCR)

any-willing-provider regulations from various states, 169–170

freedom-of-choice regulation, 170–171

introduction to usual, customary, and reasonable rates, 164–168

not all is fair, 171

the plan and the IPA, 173

point-of-service plans and UCR, 170

usual, defined, 164

utilization review

about, 54–55

acknowledgement of receipt of the claim, 57

audited claim payment, 57–58

coding guidelines, 55–56

payment dates specified in the plan contract, 57

payment guidelines and fee schedules, 55

W

Web sites, 20, 45, 63, 81, 104, 119, 159, 173–174, 200, 218, 235, 251

wet read, 193

whistleblower retaliation, 232

X

x-rays, 193